A0079679100l

D1762739

ART OF KATHERINE MANSFIELD

ROHRBERGER, MARY

PR9639.3.M258Z92 1977

SC

MONOGRAPH PUBLISHING ON DEMAND

SPONSOR SERIES

THE ART OF KATHERINE MANSFIELD

by

MARY H. ROHRBERGER

This work is published under the aegis of
Oklahoma State University Research Foundation
which deems it a significant contribution to scholarship

UNIVERSITY MICROFILMS
INTERNATIONAL
1977

Copyright © 1977
Mary Helen Rohrberger
All rights reserved

Produced and distributed *on demand* by
University Microfilms International
Ann Arbor, Michigan 48106

Library of Congress Cataloging in Publication Data

Rohrberger, Mary.
   The art of Katherine Mansfield.

   (Monograph publishing on demand : sponsor series)
   "Published under the aegis of Oklahoma State University
Research Foundation."
   Bibliography: p.
   Includes index.
   1. Mansfield, Katherine, 1888-1923–Criticism and
interpretation. I. Title.

PR6025.A57Z92   823'.9'12   77-70174
ISBN 0-8357-0195-6

CONTENTS

Chapter		Page
I.	Child of the Sun	1
II.	The Chekhov Standard	8
III.	The Achievement	23
IV.	Themes and Characters	35
V.	Point of View	73
VI.	Design	96
VII.	The Art	124
	Notes	145
	Bibliography	151
	Index	153

PREFACE

Existing studies of Katherine Mansfield have approached her work chronologically, in terms of developmental patterns. But as a craftsman, Mansfield's development was quick. Masterful short pieces occur at the beginning of her career as at the end, and lesser stories occur alongside better ones throughout her thirteen year writing period. I have chosen to approach her stories in terms of characteristic themes and techniques in an effort to evaluate her work as a whole. In so doing I have made an effort to discuss all of the completed pieces that are collected in Murry's edition of her stories, as well as some of the unfinished ones. Analysis of many of the better stories occurs throughout the book, whenever points to be made are appropriate to the discussion at hand. Believing, however, that "Prelude" and "At the Bay" stand as the most typical examples of her art, I have included separate and intensive analyses of these stories in the concluding chapter.

Chapter One

CHILD OF THE SUN

In her last _Journal_ entry, written three months before her death in 1923, Katherine Mansfield said that she wanted to be "a child of the sun." She hesitated over using the phrase, perhaps fearing that it sounded pretentious, a quality she abhorred, for she had just written that she desired to lose "all that is superficial and acquired in me and to become a conscious direct human being." But she could think of no other phrase, and, finally, she had to let it stand. "Let it be at that. A child of the sun."[1]

The obvious irony of the phrase and the paradox involved may be overlooked in an effort to understand her use of the words themselves, words that express in the metaphoric terms that she could not escape, a basis for a philosophy of life as well as a philosophy of art. The words define an identity in terms of a relationship. Plagued all of her adult life by sickness, and fearing an early death, she not only had to locate herself in a world of present time, but also to see present time in terms of the past and the future. The texture of immediate experience became for her a link with the past and the future. In her _Journal_, dated December 15, 1919, she titles an entry "Death," and writes:

> When I had gone to bed I realized what it was that had caused me to 'give way.' It was the effort of being up, with a heart that won't work. Not my lungs at all. My despair simply disappeared--yes, simply. The weather was lovely. Every morning the sun came in and drew more squares of golden light on the wall, I looked round my bed on to a sky like silk. The day opened slowly, slowly, like a flower, and it held the sun long, long before it slowly, slowly folded. Then my homesickness went. I not only didn't want to be in England, I began to love Italy, and the thought of it--the sun--even when it was too hot--always the sun--and a kind of wholeness which was good to bask in.

The experience of the moment hangs suspended. "It is timeless," she writes in her _Journal_ in 1920. "In that moment . . . the whole life of the soul is contained. One is flung up--out of life--one is 'held,' and then, -- down, bright, broken, glittering on to the rocks, tossed back, part of the ebb and flow."[2] This is the "glimpse of the relation of things," that which gives meaning to experience and to life.[3]

Her letters repeat the same thoughts. Expressing a changed view of life brought about through suffering, she writes to her husband, John Middleton Murry, in a letter dated October 18, 1920, "Even the appearance of the world is not the same--there is something added. Everything has its shadow."[4] To S. S. Koteliansky, a friend with whom she carried on an extensive correspondence, she wrote:

> Do you, too, feel an infinite delight and value in detail--not for the sake of detail but for the life in the life of it? I never can express myself (and you can laugh as much as you please.) But do you ever feel as the Lord threw you into Eternity--into the very

exact center of eternity, and even as you plunge you felt every ripple floating away and touching and drawing into its circle every slightest thing that it touched.[5]

In the ripple, floating and touching and drawing, in the ebb and flow, life touches death, and becomes life again. A letter to Dorothy Brett expresses the thought that life is a mystery. "We can never get over that. Is it a series of deaths and a series of killings? It is that too. But who shall say where death ends and <u>resurrection</u> begins. That's what one must do. Give it, the idea of <u>resurrection</u>, the power that death would like to have. Be born again and born again faster than we die . . . ."[6] A comment, dated 1920, with regard to Chekhov's The Cherry Orchard makes the same point. "The whole effect of dawn is produced by <u>blowing out the candle</u>."[7]

The philosophy of life is the basis for the philosophy of art. The true artist is also "a child of the sun." "Lord, make me crystal clear for thy light to shine through," she writes in her Journal in 1921.[8] The artist is not a scientist turning "life into a case." Yet, what he writes, if it is good, will be capable of being proved scientifically correct. But what inspires him to write is subconscious. He writes "he knows not what--he's <u>possessed</u>," she tells John Middleton Murry. "I don't mean, of course, always, but when he's <u>inspired</u>-- as a sort of divine flower to all his terrific hard gardening there comes this subconscious . . . wisdom."[9]

The artist must surrender himself to life, make an "act of faith," which is "like all great acts...pure risk." It takes humility and absolute belief in one's essential freedom. It is like "stepping into the blue," she writes, "And yet one's creative life depends on it and one <u>desires</u> to do nothing else."[10] The artist must accept life for what it is. "I don't believe a writer can ever do anything <u>worth</u> doing until he has--in the profoundest sense of the word--<u>accepted</u> life."[11]

> It is not the business of the artist to grind an axe, to try to impose his vision of life upon the existing world. Art is not an attempt of the artist to reconcile existence with his vision; it is an attempt to create his own world <u>in</u> this world. That which suggests the subject to the artist is the <u>unlikeness</u> to what we accept as <u>reality</u>. We single out--we bring into the light--we put up higher.[12]

"We are priests after all," she says in a letter to her brother-in-law, Richard Murry and continues to pursue the subject in letters to follow. "I think if artists were really thorough and honest," she says in one of them, "they would save the world. It's the lack of those things and the reverse of them that are putting a deadly blight on life. Good work takes upon itself a Life--bad work has death in it." Not only does great art constitute life, but like the ripple and the ebb and flow that mark the texture of a moment of experience, holding in itself life and death, so the "very feeling of inevitability that there is in a great work of art--is a proof--a profession of faith on the part of the artist that this life is not <u>all</u>."[13]

When the artist's act of surrender is complete, marked by total submission to the experience of the moment, it results in the creative act. She makes the point in a letter to Dorothy Brett:

> It seems to me so extraordinarily right that you should be painting Still Lifes just now. What can one do, faced with this wonderful tumble of round bright fruits, but gather them and play with them--and BECOME THEM, as it were. When I pass an apple stall I cannot help stopping and staring until I feel that I, myself, am changing into an apple, too, and that at any moment I can produce an apple, miraculously, out of my own being, like a conjuror produces the egg . . . . When you paint apples do you feel that your breasts and your knees become apples, too? Or do you think this is the greatest nonsense? I don't. I am sure it is not. When I write about ducks, I swear that I am a white duck with a round eye, floating on a pond fringed with yellow blobs and taking an occasional dart at the other duck with the round eye, which floats upside down beneath me . . . . In fact the whole process of becoming the duck (What Lawrence would perhaps call this consummation with the duck or the apple!) is so thrilling that I can hardly breathe, only to think about it. For although that is as far as most people can get, it is really only the 'prelude.' There follows the moment when you are _more_ duck, _more_ apple, or _more_ Natasha than any of these objects could ever possibly be, and so you _create_ them anew.[14]

This kind of total involvement in the experience of the moment is characteristic, and, for Mansfield, acts as a stimulus for creativity. But the involvement need not occur solely during waking hours:

> It often happens to me now that when I lie down to sleep at night, instead of getting drowsy, I feel more wakeful and, lying here in bed, I begin to _live_ over either scenes from real life or imaginary scenes. It's not too much to say that they are almost hallucinations: they are marvelously vivid. I lie on my right side and put my left hand up to my forehead as though I were praying. This seems to induce the state. Then, for instance, it is 10:30 p.m. on a big liner in mid ocean. People are beginning to leave the Ladies' Cabin. Father puts his head in and asks if "one of you would care for a walk before you turn in. It's glorious up on deck." That begins it. I am _there_. Details: Father rubbing his gloves, the cold air--the _night_ air, the pattern of everything . . . . All these things are far realer, more in detail, _richer_ than life. And I believe I could go on until . . . . There's _no_ _end_ to it.[15]

Sometimes the involvement occurs in dreams. A letter to Murry tells of one such time when in a dream the writer assumes the personality of a child: "I _dreamed_ a short story last night, even down to its name, which was _Sun_ _and_ _Moon_. It was very light. I dreamed it all--about children . . . . I didn't dream that I read it. No, I was in it, part of it, and it played round invisible me . . . . It was awfully queer--especially a plate of half-melted ice cream.[16] But when the artist does not attend to the experiences of the moment:

> Oh, I failed to-day; I turned back, looked over my shoulder, and immediately it happened, I felt as though I too were struck down. The day turned cold and dark on the instant. It seemed to belong to summer twilight in London, to the clang of the gates as they close the garden, to the deep light painting the high houses, to the smell of leaves and dust, to the lamplight, to that stirring of the senses, to the languor of twilight, the breath of it on one's cheek, to all those things which (I feel to-day) are gone from me for ever . . . . I feel today that I shall die soon and suddenly: but not of my lungs.[17]

In order for the writer to submit to the experience, a proper attitude toward life is necessary. _Journal_ entries of April 4, 6, 7, 1914, show a progression of the writer from estrangement to total involvement. On April 4 she writes, "Nothing that isn't satirical is really true for me to write just now. If I try to find things lovely, I'd turn pretty-pretty. And at the same time I am so frightened of writing mockery for satire that my pen hovers and won't settle." On April 6 she writes, "My mind is full of embroidery, but there isn't any material to hold it together or make it strong." But on April 7, "The heavens opened for the sunset to-night. When I had thought the day folded and sealed, came a burst of heavenly bright petals . . . . I sat behind the window, pricked with rain, and looked until that hard thing in my breast melted and broke into the smallest fountain, murmering as aforetime, and I drank the sky and the whisper. Now who is to decide between 'Let it be' and 'Force it'?"[18]

In a Journal entry dated October, 1921, Mansfield locates what she then feels is the source of most of her difficulty. "There seems to be some bad old pride in my heart;" she says. "This interferes very much with work." One needs, she continues, to be calm, clear, and good, so that one can forget oneself. "I can't tell the truth about Aunt Anne unless I am free to look into her life without self-consciousness." Failing, she cries out, "Oh God! I am divided still. I am bad. I fail in my personal life. I lapse into impatience, temper, vanity, and so I fail as thy priest . . . . I look at the mountains and I see nothing but mountains."[19]

Earlier, in a review, dated May 9, 1919, she attacked Maugham's Moon and Sixpence because of the character of the artist, Strickland.

> The one outstanding quality in Strickland's nature seems to have been his contempt for life and the ways of life. But contempt for life is not to be confused with liberty, nor can the man whose weapon it is fight a tragic battle or die a tragic death. If to be a great artist were to push over everything that comes in one's way, topple over the table, lunge out right and left like a drunken man in a cafe and send the pots flying, then Strickland was a great artist. But great artists are not drunken men; they are men who are divinely sober. They know that the moon can never be bought for sixpence, and that liberty is only a profound realization of the greatness of the dangers in their midst.[20]

Six months later she writes to her husband, "I am very glad you liked Miss Brill. I liked her, too. One writes (one reason why is) because one does care so passionately that one must show it--one must declare one's love."[21]

> I've two 'kick offs' in the writing game. One is joy--real joy-- the thing that made me write when we lived at Pauline, and that sort of writing I could only do in just that state of being in some perfectly blissful way at peace. Then something delicate and lovely seems to open before my eyes, like a flower without thought of a frost or a cold breath--knowing that all about it is warm and tender and 'ready.' And that I try, ever so humbly, to express.
>
> The other 'kick off' is my old original one, and (had I not known love) it would have been my all. Not hate or destruction (both are beneath contempt as real motives) but an extremely deep sense of hopelessness, of everything doomed to disaster, almost willfully, stupidly, like the almond tree and 'pas de nougat pour le noel.' There! As I took out a cigarette paper I got it exactly--a cry against corruption--that is absolutely the nail on the head. Not

a protest--a cry, and I mean corruption in the widest sense of the word, of course.[22]

A mere relation of surface impressions is not enough. A review dated June 20, 1919, of a novel by May Sinclair puts the relevant question:

> Can one think for one moment of the mystery of life when one is at the mercy of surface impressions? Can one think when one is not only taking part but being snatched at, pulled about, flung here and there, cuffed and kissed, and played with? Is it not the great abiding satisfaction of a work of art that the writer was master of the situation when he wrote it and at the mercy of nothing less mysterious than a greater work of art?[23]

The writer's habit of presenting things and people as separate, as distinct, as apart, becomes a treatment of trivia without meaning. It would be far better to link the soul with a larger whole. "Then, indeed," she states in another review, "as in the stories of Tchehov, we should become aware of the rain pattering on the roof all night long, of languid, feverish wind, of the moonlit orchard and the first snow, passionately realized, not indeed as analogous to a state of mind, but linking that mind to the larger whole."[24] In this way the writer can express "something more subtle, more complex, 'nearer' the truth," she writes in a review of a novel by Brett Young, dated October 24, 1919.[25] Another review of about the same date makes the point again.

> The citizens of Reality are 'tied to town' and very content to be so tied, very thankful to look out of window on to a good substantial wall, plastered over with useful facts and topped with a generous sprinkle of broken bottle glass. Nevertheless, they are for ever sighing to travel. Not that they are prepared for long and difficult journeys. On the contrary. What they cannot have enough of is the small excursion, the timid flight just halfway to somewhere, just so far that Reality and its wall is out of sight while they picnic in the unfamilar landscape, which distracts, but does not disturb.[26]

This kind of timidity sometimes afflicts her also. A Journal entry of July 5, 1918 states: "I must not forget my timidity before closed doors. My debate as to whether I shall ring too loud or not loud enough . . . . It's deep deep deep: in fact it is the 'explanation' of the failure of K. M. as a writer up to the present, and Oh! what a good anfang zu einem Geschichte!"[27]

Most of Mansfield's criticism not only of her own writing but also of that of her contemporaries is based on this kind of timidity before closed doors. Her Journal entry of August 21, 1917, takes E. M. Forster to task. "Putting my weakest books to the wall last night I came across a copy of 'Howard's End' and had a look into it. But it's not good enough. E. M. Forster never gets any further than warming the teapot. He's a rare fine hand at that. Feel this teapot. Is it not beautifully warm? Yes, but there ain't going to be no tea."[28] In a letter to John Middleton Murry, dated December 13, 1919, she comments on George Bernard Shaw, saying he is no artist. He is outside, not in, she says. He writes "at, not with."[29] In another letter dated December, a year later, she accuses D. H. Lawrence of "sinning against art." Lawrence denies his humanity, she say. "He denies Life--I mean human life." His people are animals, faceless, mindless. "All false. All a pack of lies!"[30]

Nor do her own stories escape her criticism. A *Journal* entry of 1918 states: "Whenever I have a conversation about Art which is more or less interesting I begin to wish to God I could destroy all that I have written and start again: it all seems like so many 'false starts!' Musically speaking, it is not--has not been--in the middle of the note--you know what I mean?"[31]

An exchange of letters with Murry in late 1919 and early 1920 reveals her feelings about her early stories collected in *In a German Pension*. He is seeking her permission to have the volume reprinted. On November 26, she writes that she doesn't want to: "If you read that book you would realize what I feel . . . . It's aristocatic (?) [sic] ignoring of all that is outside it's own little circle and its wonder, surprise, incredulity that other people have heard of William Shakespeare."[32] On February 4, she calls the stories in *Pension* a lie. Finally, on February 12, she agrees to the reprinting but only if the volume is provided with an introduction "saying it is early, early work."[33]

A set of *Journal* entries for July, 1921, are characteristic of dissatisfaction with completed stories:

> July. I finished Mr. and Mrs. Dove yesterday. I am not altogether pleased with it. It's a little bit made up. It's not inevitable. I mean to imply that those two may not be happy together--that that is the kind of reason for which a young girl marries. But have I done so? I don't think so. Besides, it's not strong enough. I want to be nearer--far, far nearer than that. I want to use all my force even when I am taking a fine line. And I have a sneaking notion that I have, at the end, used the Doves unwarrantably. Tu sais ce que je veux dire. I used them to round off something--didn't I? Is that quite my game? No, it's not. It's not quite the kind of truth I'm after. Now for Susannah. All must be deeply felt.
>
> . . . .
>
> July 23. Finished An Ideal Family yesterday. It seems to me better than The Doves, but still it's not good enough. I worked at it hard enough, God knows, and yet I didn't get the deepest truth out of the idea, even once. What is this feeling? I feel again that this kind of knowledge is too easy for me; it's even a kind of trickery. I know so much more. This looks and smells like a story, but I wouldn't buy it. I don't want to possess it--to live with it. NO. Once I have written two more, I shall tackle something different--a long story: At the Bay with more difficult relationships.
>
> . . . .
>
> July 25. All this! All that I write--all that I am--is on the border of the sea. It's a kind of playing. I want to put all my force behind it, but somehow, I cannot![34]

The act of surrender which results in a completed story is at once distressing and exhilarating. On February 28, 1918, Mansfield completed the story "Bliss" and sent it to Murry. A letter to him states in part, "Please try and like it, and I am now free to start another . . . . Once I start them they haunt me, pursue me and plague me until they are finished and as good as I can do."[35]

The completion of "The Man Without a Temperament" occasioned the following Journal entry, dated January 11, 1920: "Worked from 9:30 till a quarter after midnight only stopping to eat. Finished the story. Lay awake then until 5:30 too excited to sleep. In the sea drowned souls sang all night."[36]

"There is no feeling to be compared with the feeling of having written and finished a story," she writes on January 11, 1922, and continues, "I did not go to sleep, but nothing mattered. There it was, new and complete."[37]

Chapter Two

THE CHEKHOV STANDARD

In her book <u>Katherine</u> <u>Mansfield</u>, Saralyn R. Daly makes the point that no critical theory appeared to concern Mansfield; "she formulated none."[1] It is true that Mansfield never wrote a formal statement called, "my critical theory," or anything similar, but, as I have indicated in the last chapter, scattered throughout her letters, journal, scrapbook, and reviews is an abundance of comments on matters both generally philosophic and specifically aesthetic. Careful examination of these comments reveals that she had a coherent aesthetic and, moreover, a body of criticism based on that aesthetic.

Several elements of an aesthetic have already been touched on. The poet is a seer, communicating truth. Truth is the presentation of relationships having ultimately to do with life and death, seen Janus-like as manifestations of opposite sides of the same coin. Relationships derive from moments in time presented in such a way as to involve the reader in the texture of the experience and at the same time to indicate the relationships. The moments in time, then, can be said to expand to include all time--past, present, and future. A question arises as to whether particular kinds of experiences, forming the manifest content of her work, are more fruitful in terms of harboring the latent content?

Probably not. What appears to be a deeply felt fastidiousness sometimes causes Mansfield to make such comments as "who can believe in the suffering and potential greatness of little people whose distaste for life was typified 'in the recurring demands of the toilet'?"[2] But this kind of comment is usually in a context suggesting that a writer who emphasizes "the demands of the toilet" distorts the real world. The criticism, then is directed not so much at the subject matter itself as at a lack of credibility. This fastidiousness is likely the reason for her rejection of the writings of James Joyce, although it appears that she recognizes the cause and tries to account for her judgement on some rational basis. An incomplete and unposted letter dated simply 1922, makes such an attempt, but gets nowhere.

> I must reply about "Ulysses." I have been wondering what people are saying in England. It took me about a fortnight to wade through, but on the whole I'm dead <u>against</u> it. I suppose it was worth doing if everything is worth <u>doing</u> . . . but that is certainly not what I want from literature. Of course, there are amazingly fine things in it, but I prefer to go without them than to pay that price. Not because I am shocked (though I am fearfully shocked, but that's "personal"; I suppose it's unfair to judge the book by that) but because I simply don't believe . . . .[3]

Earlier, in a letter to Sidney Schiff with whom she exchanged several comments on Joyce, she wrote that she had reread <u>A</u> <u>Portrait</u> <u>of</u> <u>the</u> <u>Artist</u> <u>As</u> <u>A</u> <u>Young</u> <u>Man</u> and found it "on the whole awfully <u>good</u>." She acknowledges Joyce's importance, but says, "Sometime ago I found something so repellent in his work that it was difficult to read it. It shocks me to come upon words, expressions and so on that I'd shrink from in life." But, she goes on to admit that Joyce is seeking after "truth," and this is so important a quest that "one must conquer all minor aversions. They are unworthy."[4]

Schiff's answer must have questioned the apparent reversal of her feelings concerning Joyce's literary worth, for she writes him shortly afterwards, "Please do not think I am all for Joyce. I am not." She goes on to say that she feels that in the past she has been unfair and stupid and now is trying to be fairer than she really feels. Little of his writing, she says, is art. "It's a kind of stage on the way to being art. But the act of projection has not been made. Joyce remains intangled in it, in a bad sense, except at rare moments."[5] Her aversion to Joyce's novels, especially Ulysses is underscored further in a letter to Sidney Schiff's wife, Violet: "The further I am away from it [Ulysses]," Mansfield writes, "the less I think of it. As to reading it again, or even opening that great tome--never!"[6]

Not the particular experience itself,[7] but the repetition of the same experience in novel after novel causes Mansfield to comment in a letter to her husband, dated March 20, 1915:

> Yesterday I began reading and read on until past midnight. There are so many books of "the young men" here and I glanced through a number to get an impression. Heavens! what a set of lollipops! Really, I did not come across one that counted. Upon the same stage, with the same scenery, the same properties, to the same feeble little tune, one after one pipes his little pieces . . . . funny, if it weren't so damned ugly.[8]

Her objection in a review of March 19, 1920, to what she calls the "pastime novel" is based on the occurrence of the same kind of endless repetition. "By far the greater number of them [pastime novels] aim at nothing more positive than a kind of mental knitting--the mind of the reader is grown so familiar with the pattern that the least possible effort is demanded of it."[9] A review dated April 30, 1920 makes the comment, "We open novel after novel, we turn page after page, and there are the authors rummaging in dusty cupboards, turning over heaps of discarded garments to find something to fling at us."[10] These writers "take their readers for an excursion," she writes in a review of Joseph Conrad's The Arrow of Gold, "but always to put up at the same hotel, where they know the waiters' faces, and the way to the bathroom, and the shape of the biscuits that accompany the cheese."[11]

Not the experience, but the ineffective presentation of the experience accounts for her objection to the Oxford Book of English Verse. In a letter to Murry she writes that the poems contained in the collection are very poor, except for Shakespeare and Marvell "and just a handful of others." She continues: "It seems to me a mass of falsity. Musically speaking, hardly anyone seems to even understand what the middle of the note is--what that sound is like. It's not perhaps that

they are even 'sharp' or 'flat'--it's something very much more subtle--
they are not playing on the <u>very</u> <u>note</u> <u>itself</u>."[12]

<u>Detail</u> for the sake of <u>detail</u> is no good. A mere trivial happening leads nowhere, says nothing. "Why should writers exist any longer as a class apart if their task ends with a minute description of a big or a little thing?" she asks in a review of a May Sinclair novel. "If this be the be-all and the end-all of literature why should not every man, woman and child write an autobiography and so provide reading matter for the ages?" "It is not difficult," she says, becoming ironic:

> There is no gulf to be bridged, no risk to be taken. If you do not throw your Papa and your Mamma against the heavens before beginning to write about them, his whiskers and her funny little nose will be quite important enough to write about, quite enough, reinforced with the pattern of the drawing-room carpet . . . and the cook upstairs taking her hair out of pins, to make a whole great book. And as B's papa's whiskers and B's mamma's funny little nose are bound to be different again, and their effect upon B again different--why here is high entertainment forever!
>
> Entertainment. But the great writers of the past have not been 'entertainers.' They have been seekers, explorers, thinkers. It has been their aim to reveal a little of the mystery of life.[13]

The selection of appropriate details which constitute the texture of an experience is only a first step.

> Who can tell, watching the dragonfly, at what point in its swift angular flight it will suddenly pause and hover, quivering over this or that? The strange little jerk--the quivering moment of suspension--we might also fancy they were the signs of a minute inward shock of recognition felt by the dragonfly. 'There is something here; something here for me. What is it?' it seems to say. And then, at the same instant, it is gone. Away it darts, glancing over the deep pool until another floating flower or golden bud or tangle of shadowy weed attracts it, and again it is still, curious, hovering over . . . .
>
> But this behavior, enchanting though it may be in the dragonfly, is scarcely adequate when adopted by the writer of fiction. Nevertheless, there are certain modern authors who do not appear to recognize its limitations. For them the whole art of writing consists in the power with which they are able to register that faint inward shock of recognition. Glancing through life they make the discovery that there are certain experiences which are, as it were, peculiarly theirs. There is a quality in the familiarity of these experiences or in their strangeness which evokes an immediate, mysterious response--a desire for expression. But now, instead of going any further, instead of attempting to relate their 'experiences' to life or to see them against any kind of background, these writers are, as we see them, content to remain in the air, hovering over, as if the thrilling moment were enough and more than enough. Indeed, far from desiring to explore it, it is as though they would guard the secret for themselves as well as for us, so that when they do dart away all is as untouched, as unbroken as before.[14]

It is not a question of material or style or plot. One can lay down no rules. But there must be an illumination, what she calls a tragic knowledge born from facing death, "but through life," a recognition of "deserts of vast eternity," she writes in a letter to Murry, dated November 16, 1918. "But the difference between you and me is (perhaps I'm wrong) I couldn't tell anybody <u>bang</u> <u>out</u> about those deserts: they are my secret. I might write about a boy eating strawberries or a woman combing her hair on a windy morning, and that is the only way I can ever mention them. But they must be there. Nothing less will do."[15]

But how does one go about making the moment expand to the microscopic proportions latent within it? There is no doubt of the total relationship that is there to be expressed. A note in her Journal, dated June 21, 1919, comments:

> I had a sense of the larger breath, of the mysterious lives within lives, and the Egyptian parasite beginning its new cycle of being in a water-snail affected me like a great work of art. No, that's not what I mean. It made me feel how perfect the world is, with its worms and hooks and ova, how incredibly perfect. There is the sky and the sea and the shape of a lily, and there is all this other as well. The balance how perfect! (Salut, Tchehov!) I would not have the one without the other.[16]

But there are problems with getting the relationships expressed by means of the details. A Journal entry of 1918 sets down details of the scene, what will be a backdrop.

> On these summer evenings the sound of the steps along the street is quite different. They knock--knock--knock along, but lightly and easily, as though they belonged to people who are walking home at their ease, after a procession or a picnic or a day at the sea.
>
> The sky is pale and clear: the silly piano is overcome and reels out waltzes--old waltzs, spinning, drunk with sentiment---gorged with memory.
>
> This is the hour when the poor underfed dog appears, at a run, nosing the dry gutter. He is so thin that his body is like a cage on four wooden pegs . . . . His lean triangle of a head is down, his long straight tail is out, and up and down, up and down he goes, silent and fearfully eager. The street watches him from its creeper-covered balconies, from its open windows--but the fat lady on the ground floor who was no better than she should be comes out--down the steps to the gate, with a bone. His tail as he waits for her to give it to him, bangs against the gate post, like a broomhandle--and the street says she's a fool to go feeding strange dogs. Now she'll never be rid of him.

But the description stops and a parenthetical sentence follows, "(What I'd like to convey is that at this hour, with this half light and the pianos and the open, empty sounding houses, he is the spirit of the street--running up and down, poor dog, when he ought to have been done away with years ago.)"[17]

A Journal entry of 1922 sets down what is essentially the same problem.

> May 3. Paris. I must begin writing for Clement Shorter to-day 12 "spasms" of 2,000 words each. I thought of the Burnells, but no, I don't think so. Much better, the Sheridans, the three girls and the brother and the Father and Mother and so on, ending with a long description of Meg's wedding to Keith Fenwick. Well, there's the first flown out of the nest. The sister's Bead, who come to stay. The white sheet on the floor when the wedding dress is tried on. Yes, I've got the details all right. But the point is--Where shall I begin? One certainly wants the dash.
>
> Meg was playing. I don't think I ought to begin with that. It seems to me the mother's coming home ought to be the first chapter. The other can come later. And in that playing chapter what I want to stress chiefly is: Which is the real life--that or this?--late afternoon, these thoughts--the garden--the beauty--how all things pass--and how the end seems to come so soon.
>
> And then again there is the darling bird--I've always loved birds--

> Where is the little chap?. . . .
>
> What is it that stirs one so? What is the seeking--so joyful--ah, so gentle! And there seems to be a moment when all is to be discovered. Yes, that's the feeling . . . .
>
> The queer thing is I only remember how much I have forgotten when I hear that piano. The garden of the Casino, the blue pansies. But oh, how am I going to write this story?[18]

The same point is made in another comment, also dated 1922. She has written about five paragraphs of a story called "The Sheridans" and breaks to write:

> But this is not expanded enough, or rich enough. I think still a description of the hour and place should come first. And the light should fall on the figure of Mrs. S. on her way home. Really I can allow myself to write a good deal--to describe it all--the baths, the avenue, the people in the gardens, the Chinaman under the tree on May Street. But in that case she won't be conscious of these things. That's bad. They must be seen and felt by her as she wanders home. . . . That sense of flowing in and out of houses--going and returning--like the tide. To go and not to return. How terrible! The father in his dressing-room--the familiar talk. His using her hair brush--his passion for things that wear well. The children sitting around the table--the light outside, the silver. Her feeling as she sees them all gathered together--her longing for them always to be there. Yes, I'm getting nearer all this. I now remember S. W. and see that it must be written with love--real love. All the same, the difficulty is to get it all within focus---to introduce that young doctor and bring him continually nearer and nearer until finally he is part of the Sheridan family, until finally he has taken away Meg . . . that is by no means easy . . .[19]

Questions about technique are constantly put although there is no hesitation with regard to the end product for which the writer must strive. She quotes Chekhov, "What the writer does is not so much to solve the question but to put the question."[20] In a review of a novel by F. Brett Young, she asks the writer: "How do you write your novels?" This is a question she says that of all others authors dislike answering, but

> Never was there a moment when the question was more fascinating. How do you write your novels? Do you have a definite plan before you begin? Do you know exactly what is going to happen and would it be possible for anything else to happen instead? And do you think a plot is necessary? And do you really write all you know, or do you still hold back a little, just a little. . . and why?[21]

The necessity to write all that he knows is incumbent on the author. One must "go deep," speak "to the secret self we all have--to acknowledge that."[22] The novel that is not an attempt at truth "is doomed." "How are we to be expected to take seriously. . . any work which appears to have engaged less than the whole passionate attention of its author? To be fobbed off, at the last, with something which we feel to be less true than the author knew it to be, challenges the importance of the whole art of writing, and instead of enlarging the bounds of our experience, it leaves them where they are."[23] The successful story should quicken the reader's perception, increase his sense of the mystery of life, make him the richer for having partaken of the author's vision.[24] Not to achieve this is to fail "from the Tchekhov standpoint."

> The thing I prize, admire, and respect in his [Chekhov] stories is his knowledge. They are true. I trust him. This is becoming most awfully important to me--a writer must have knowledge---he must make one feel the ground is firm beneath his feet. The vapourings I read, the gush, wind,--give me a perfect Sehnsucht for something hard to bite on.[25]

And to achieve it:

> I have re-read The Steppe. What can one say? It is simply one of the great stories of the world--a kind of Illiad or Oddessey. I think I will learn this journey by heart. One says of things: they are immortal. One feels about this story not that it becomes immortal--it always was. It has no beginning or end. Tchekhov just touched one point with his pen (.------.) and then another point; enclosed something which had, as it were, been there for ever.[26]

The Chekhov standpoint is for Mansfield a constant standard for judgement. It involves both form and content, the one dependent on the other. The quest for the proper technique ends up being a quest for the proper form. "Delicate perception is not enough," she says in a letter to Sidney and Violet Schiff; "one must find the exact way in which to convey the delicate perception."[27] And in a letter to Richard Murry she writes, "You see I too have a passion for technique. I have a passion for making the thing into a whole if you know what I mean. Out of technique is born real style, I believe. There are no short-cuts."[28]

Form is organic:

> If a novel is to have a central idea we imagine that central idea as a lusty growing stem from which the branches spring clothed with leaves, and the buds become flowers and fruits. We imagine that the author chooses with infinite deliberation the very air in which that tree shall be nourished, and that he is profoundly aware that its coming perfection depends upon the strength with which the central idea supports its beautiful accumulations.[29]

The symbols used to illustrate the idea of organic form become the standard by which she judges Lawrence's Aaron's Rod. There are parts of the novel she does not like. "They are trivial, encrusted, they cling to it as snails to the underside of a leaf - no more, - and perhaps they leave a little silvery trail, a smear." "But," she continues, "apart from these things is the leaf, is the tree, firmly planted, deep-thrusting, outspread, growing grandly, alive in every twig. All the time I read this book I felt it was feeding me."[30]

Integration of form and theme is the basis for much of her criticism. Without form, she says, a novel is lost, for how is it possible to tell the relative importance of any one event over another? "Central points of significance" must be "transferred to the endeavors and emotions of the human beings portrayed."[31] There must be an orderly arrangement, a design; things can not be allowed simply to happen. There must be a central idea, about which the points of significance cluster in a pattern leading to a climax which reveals the central point significant to the action. The propaganda novel, the novel with the message, imposes the idea upon the action and is self-defeating. "Life," she says "cannot be made to 'fit' anybody, and the novelist who makes the attempt will find himself cutting something that gets smaller and smaller, finer and finer, until he must begin cutting his characters next to fit the thing he has made."[32] And again:

> The author who sets out deliberately to write a novel with a purpose must content himself with being a little less than an artist, a little more than a preacher. To accept life, and by thus accepting it to present us with the problem--that is not his chief concern. He is the brilliant lawyer who is bound to look at life from the point of view of his case--who cannot therefore afford to inquire into the evidence that would make the guilty less guilty, or, always with the success of his case in mind, to despise the ridiculous excess of painting the lily and throwing a perfume on the violet.[33]

New thoughts necessitate new expressions, new forms. In a letter to her husband, dated November 10, 1919, she speaks of a book she is reviewing, saying "It is a lie in the soul."

> The war never has been: that is what its message is. I don't want (G. forbid!) mobilization and the violation of Belgium, but the novel can't just leave the war out. There must have been a change of heart. It is really fearful to see the 'settling down' of human beings. I feel in the profoundest sense that nothing can ever be the same--that, as artists, we are traitors if we feel otherwise: we have to take it into account and find new expressions, new moulds for our new thoughts and feelings.[34]

A few days later in a review she writes:

> There is a title which the amateur novelist shares. . .with the true artist: it is that of experimentalist. However deep the knowledge a writer has of his characters, however finely he may convey that knowledge to us, it is only when he passes beyond it, when he begins to break new ground, to discover for himself, to experiment, that we are enthralled. The "false" writer begins as an experimentalist; the true artist ends as one.[35]

Her own struggle with technique is a search for the proper form. "Tchehov makes me feel that this longing to write stories of such uneven length is quite justified," she writes in her Journal in 1917,[36] and later in a review of several collections of short pieces she attempts to set down some thoughts about the form that concerns her.

> Suppose we put it in the form of a riddle: "I am neither a short story, nor a sketch, nor an impression, nor a tale. I am written in prose. I am a great deal shorter than a novel; I may be only one page long, but, on the other hand, there is no reason why I should not be thirty. I have a special quality--a something, a something which is immediately, perfectly recognizable. It belongs to me; it is of my essence. In fact I am often given away in the first sentence. I seem almost to stand or fall by it. It is to me what the first phrase of the song is to the singer. Those who know me feel: "Yes, that is it." And they are from that moment prepared for what is to follow. Here are, for instance, some examples of me: "A Trifle from Life," "About Love," "The Lady with the Dog." "What am I?"[37]

There is, it would appear, no name for the form that suits her, not "short story," nor "sketch," nor "impression," nor "tale." The examples she gives are Chekhov's pieces, commonly today called short stories. But his pieces are somehow different from other shorter pieces, she feels, as she wishes hers to be. That she sees the form as merging with the idea and involving all of the senses is clear. A letter to Dorothy Brett, dated October 11, 1917, talks about "At the Bay," "What form is it?" she asks. "How have I shaped it?" She answers "as far as I know it's more or less my own invention. This is about as much as I can say about it." But the explanation that follows presents a concrete image in which the senses merge:

> You know, if the truth were known I have a perfect passion for the island where I was born. Well, in the early morning there I always remember feeling that this little island has dipped back into the dark blue sea during the night only to rise again at gleam of day, all hung with bright spangles and glittering drops. (When you ran over the dewy grass you positively felt that your feet tasted salt.) I tried to catch that moment--with something of its sparkle and its flavour. And just as on those mornings white milky mists rise and uncover some beauty, then smother it again and then again disclose it, I tried to lift that mist from my people and let them be seen and then to hide them again. . . .[38]

Some two years earlier she had written in much the same way to Murry about a novel she was writing and later abandoned. She describes having walked along the Quai at dusk:

> The lights came out as I walked, and the boats danced by. Leaning over the bridge I suddenly discovered that one of those boats was exactly what I want my novel to be. Not big, almost 'grotesque' in shape--I mean perhaps _heavy_--with people rather dark and seen strangely as they move in the sharp light and shadow; and I want bright shivering lights in it, and the sound of water.[39]

The goal is to create a total inter-related world, recognizable both in its scale and context.

Plot should arise naturally from situation and characters. There should be a coherence and sharpness, a proper focus. The moment should unfold and open. Events should be seen rather than shown off and proceed until a climax is reached which has about it the aura of inevitability. The reader must share in the experience:

> Perhaps Dostoevski more than any other writer set up this mysterious relationship with the reader, the sense of _sharing_. We are never conscious that he is writing at us or for us. While we read, we are like children to whom one tells a tale; we seem in some strange way to half-know what is coming and yet we do not know; to have heard it all before and yet our amazement is none the less, and when it is over, it has become ours.[40]

But situation, plot, and character are only parts of the whole. Something else is needed--what she refers to as a "covering atmosphere." A letter to Murry makes the point. She is complaining that she can't do what she calls "real creative work." "It's the atmosphere," she continues, "the . . . tone which is hard to get. And without it nothing is worth doing." It is that "atmosphere" that gives the story "continuity."[41]

This "covering atmosphere" is likely the same factor that she has in mind when she writes in a review:

> It is strange how content most writers are to ignore the influence of the weather upon the feelings and the emotions of their characters, or, if they do not ignore it, to treat it, except in its most obvious manifestations--"she felt happy because the sun was shining"--"the dull day served but to heighten his depression"--as something of very little importance, something quite separate and apart. But by 'the weather' we do not mean a kind of ocean at our feet, with broad effects of light and shadow, into which we can plunge or not plunge, at will; we mean an external atmosphere which is in harmony or discordinate with a state of soul; poet's weather, per-

haps we might call it. But why not prose--writer's weather, too? Why indeed! Are not your poet and your writer of prose faced with exactly the same problem?

The incorporation of what she calls "poet's weather" links the moment expressed with a larger whole; it expands the moment, gives it greater depth and significance: "Then, indeed, as in the stories of Tchehov, we should become aware of the rain pattering on the roof all night long, of the languid, feverish wind, of the moonlit orchard and the first snow, passionately realized, not indeed as analogous to a state of mind, but as linking that mind to the larger whole."[42]

Language, too, is an important factor in the expression of the total created world. A letter to Richard Murry, dated January 17, 1921 makes the point:

> It's a very queer thing how craft comes into writing. I mean down to details. Par example. In Miss Brill I chose not only the length of every sentence, but even the sound of every sentence. I chose the rise and fall of every paragraph to fit her, and to fit her on that day at that very moment. After I'd written it I read it aloud--numbers of times--just as one would play over a musical composition--trying to get it nearer and nearer to the expression of Miss Brill--until it fitted her.
>
> Don't think I'm vain about the little sketch. It's only the method I wanted to explain. I often wonder whether other writers do the same--If a thing has really come off it seems to me there mustn't be one single word out of place, or one word that could be taken out. That's how I AIM at writing. It will take some time to get anywhere near there.[43]

Even punctuation plays a part. A letter to Murry, dated March 14, 1921, explains her intention in "Bliss."

> You're of course, absolutely right about 'Wangle'. He shall be resprinkled mit leichtern Fingern, and I'm with you about the commas. What I meant (I hope it don't sound high falutin') was Bertha [in "Bliss"] not being an artist, was yet artist manquée enough to realize that those words and expressions were not and couldn't be hers. They were, as it were, quoted by her, borrowed with . . . an eyebrow . . . yet she'd none of her own. But this, I agree, is not permissible. I can't grant all that in my dear reader. It's very exquisite of you to understand so nearly.[44]

And a letter to him, dated November 28, 1920, attempts to explain her punctuation in "The Stranger."

> About the punctuation in The Stranger. Thank-you, Bogey. No, my dash isn't quite a feminine dash. (Certainly when I was young it was.) But it was intentional in that story. I was trying to do away with the three dots much tho' I need them. The truth is-- punctuation is infernally difficult.[45]

Mansfield's reviews collected in the volume Novels and Novelists by John Middleton Murry were written for The Athenaeum, which he edited, and are dated from April, 1919 to December, 1920. Murry says that they form "a body of criticism unique in its kind."[46] He goes on to say that it is regrettable that she was not called upon to give her opinion of the novels of some of the more important novelists of the time, such as H. G. Wells, Arnold Bennett, and D. H. Lawrence. It is noteworthy that of the three writers he mentions only Lawrence is considered today to be of the first rank of novelists and although, as has been noted, there was much in Lawrence's writing that Mansfield deplored, she was able to look at each work separately, both to criticize and praise. It is noteworthy, also, that there are a group of writers considered eminent by today's standards whom Murry does not mention who did publish during the interim period April, 1919 to December, 1920, and whose works Mansfield did review for The Athenaeum. There are reviews of Maugham's Moon and Sixpence and Conrad's Arrow of Gold as have already been mentioned. Further, there are reviews of two novels, Interim and The Tunnel by Dorothy Richardson, In Chancery by John Galsworthy, Night and Day by Virginia Woolf, Age of Innocence by Edith Wharton, Three Lives by Gertrude Stein and a review of Esther Waters by George Moore, which had been printed in a new edition. The majority of critics today would likely agree with the judgement expressed by Mansfield in her review of these works.

Dorothy Richardson has a place in literary history not so much for the novels in themselves, but because she was in the forefront of the movement toward the stream-of-consciousness novel. Mansfield's judgement of Richardson's novels can be expressed simply, in a series of phrases: no plan, no structure, no depth. The review of The Tunnel says that the book has no plot, no beginning, middle or end. "Things just 'happen' one after another with incredible rapidity and breakneck speed."[47] The review of Interim is the occasion for an essay comparing certain writers to dragonflys who hover and quiver and dart away, but remain forever in the air.[48]

The review of the Galsworthy novel notes that it is a continuation of others included in The Forsyte Saga. She found the novel to be admirably composed, closely packed, and firmly related to the whole background. It is not, she says, a great novel, but she assures her readers that it is a fascinating, brilliant book.

The review of Night and Day by Virginia Woolf is a lengthy one, and it is clear that Mansfield is well aware of Woolf's stature and achievement. She begins the review by saying that the fate of the novel as genre has been the subject of much critical controversy. She goes on to say that in all the division and confusion there is general critical agreement that this period is an age of experiment in the novel. "If the novel dies it will be to give way to some new form of expression; if it lives it must accept the fact of a new world." Night and Day is strange, Mansfield says. It is aloof, showing no signs of any experimentation. On it there is absence of any scar. It is much like the writing of Jane Austen, but Jane Austen brought up to date.

> It is extremely cultivated, distinguished and brilliant, but above all-deliberate. There is not a chapter where one is unconscious of the writer, of her personality, her point of view, and her control of the situation. We feel that nothing has been imposed on her: she has chosen her world, selected her principle characters with the nicest care, and having traced a circle round them so that they exist and are free within its confines, she has proceeded, with rare appreciativeness, to register her observation.

But there is something different. Whereas the spell created by Austen's novels continues after the novel is finished, "Mrs. Woolf's looses some of its potency. What is it that carries us away? With Miss Austen, it is first her feeling for life, and then her feeling for writing; but with Mrs. Woolf these feelings are continually giving way the one to the other so that the urgency of either is impaired." While one is reading, the characters seem to live, Mansfield continues, however, "once the author's pen is removed from them they have neither speech nor motion." She continues: "Were they shadowy or vague this would be less apparent, but they are held within the circle of steady light in which the author bathes her world, and in their case the light seems to shine at them, but not through them"[50]

The review of Age of Innocence by Edith Wharton begins with compliments. "The time and the scene together suit Mrs. Wharton's talent to a nicety. To evoke the seventies is to evoke irony and romance at once, and to keep these two balanced by all manner of delicate adjustments is so much a matter for her skillful hand that it seems more like play than work." But the reviewer wants more than irony and romance. She accuses Wharton of creating characters that are not human beings. Is it, she cries out, vulgar to ask for more? "To ask that the feeling shall be greater than the cause that excites it, to beg to be allowed to share the moment of exposition (is not that the very moment that all our writing leads to?), to entreat a little wildness, a dark place or two in the soul?"[51]

Gertrude Stein's position in literary history is mainly due to the stature of the writers who visited her living room in Paris in the Twenties and who were greatly influenced by her--Ernest Hemingway, Scott Fitzgerald, Sherwood Anderson, to name a few. Mansfield's review of Three Lives is heavy with irony.

> Miss Gertrude Stein has discovered a new way of writing stories. It is just to keep right on writing them. Don't mind how often you go back to the beginning, don't hesitate to say the same thing over and over again--people are always repeating themselves--don't be put off if the words sound funny at times: just keep right on and by the time you've done writing you'll have produced your effect.

But an effect is produced, and it would appear that it is the effect that Mansfield does not like. By the time she got to the last story, the reviewer notes, she found herself reading in syncopated time. The page, she says, began to rock. Melanctha is characterized by Mansfield as negro music with "all its maddening monotony done in prose." One would think that Mansfield would have appreciated the skill and handling of language that produced the effect, but she does not appear to. Perhaps she simply did not like the music. "It is writing in real rag time. Heaven forbid Miss Stein should become a fashion!"[52]

George Moore's place in the development of the English novel rests not so much, most critics would agree, on his novels, Esther Waters among the best, but on the fact that he was one (and perhaps the best) of the very few British novelists writing in the naturalistic mode.

Mansfield's judgement, often quoted, represents a majority opinion.

> Having read it [Esther Waters] carefully and slowly--we defy anyone to race along or skip--from cover to cover, we are left feeling that there is not a page, paragraph, sentence, word, that is not right, the only possible page, paragraph, sentence, word. The more we look into it, the more minute our examination, the deeper grows our amazement at the amount of sheer labour that has gone to its excution....And yet we would say without hesitation that Esther Waters is not a great novel, and never could be a great novel, because it has not, from first to last, the faintest stirring of the breath of life. It is as dry as the remainder biscuit after a voyage. In a word it has no emotion.[53]

The majority of the reviews in Novels and Novelists are based on the writings of authors who quickly passed into oblivion. Mansfield found little to praise. But the reviews did serve as a means by which she expressed her views about what constitutes great art and how it is to be achieved.

There are, of course, many comments about other writers, great ones, scattered through her journal and letters, and collected in the clean-up volume that Murry titles Scrapbook. The names of Chekhov and Shakespeare appear more often than any others, but she comments also on Chaucer, Marlow, Tolstoi, Dostoevsky, Stendhal, Bunin, Maupassant, Dickens, Eliot, Joyce, Proust, and Lawrence. Bunin, Maupassant, Joyce, and Proust, in her opinion miss greatness. Her opinions of Lawrence and Joyce have already been discussed, although, perhaps, one more comment on Lawrence is in order. A letter to Koteliansky asks:

> Have you read Lawrence's new book? I should like to very much. He is the only writer living whom I really profoundly care for. It seems to me whatever he writes, no matter how much one may 'disagree,' is important. And after all even what one objects to is a sign of life in him. He is a living man. There has been published lately an extremely bad collection of short stories-- Georgian Short Stories. And The Shadow In The Rose Garden by Lawrence is among them. This story is perhaps one of the weakest he ever wrote. But it is so utterly different from all the rest that one reads it with Joy. When he mentions gooseberries these are real, red, ripe gooseberries that the gardener is rolling on a tray. When he bites into an apple it is a sharp, sweet, fresh apple from the growing tree.[54]

About Bunin she writes, again to Koteliansky:

> Bunin has an immense talent. That is certain. All the same-- there's a limitation in this story "The Gentleman From San Francisco" so it seems to me. There is something hard, inflexible, separate in him which he exalts in. But he ought not to exalt in it. It is a pity it is there. He just stops short of being a great writer because of it. Tenderness is a dangerous word to use, but I dare use it to you. He lacks tenderness--and in spite of everything, tenderness there must be.[55]

A letter to Murry dated December 1, 1920, expresses her opinion of Maupassant and Proust. Her letter was in answer to one of his which suggested that Maupassant is a better writer than the Russians and Proust the greatest living writer. Her answer is decided: "I would give every single word de Maupassant and Tumpany [sic] ever wrote for one short story by Anton Tchekhov. As to Proust...let him tinkle away."[56] This is so forceful a statement that one might feel she was over responding and thus over stating her views. Other comments with regard to Maupassant, however, repeat the same judgment. In 1918, for example, while in France and terribly disenchanted with it, she wrote to Murry: "There are two submarines in the bay and a black steamer with a big white cross on her bows. The officers take their meals here. Their talk and grouping, etc., is pure Maupassant--not Tchekov at all, not deep enough or good enough. No; Maupassant is for France."[57]

Her opinion of Proust is somewhat surprising, particularly when one considers that the letter to Murry was written in 1920. Sylvia Berkman in her book Katherine Mansfield, says that Mansfield did not come to read Proust until 1921, at the urging of Sidney Schiff. Berkman says that at that time Proust "aroused her warmest sympathy, though one would have thought that his nostalgic melancholy, his fine dissections of human experience, would have evoked more excitable enthusiasm than she expressed."[58] Perhaps Mansfield had read some of Proust earlier but was unable to judge the total achievement since Remembrance of Things Past was then only about halfway in print. Or again, perhaps husbands should not write to wives who themselves inspire to greatness that another living writer is the greatest.

Mansfield says little about Dickens except to note that he at times touches greatness:

> There are moments when Dickens is possessed by this power of writing: he is carried away. That is bliss. It certainly is not shared by writers to-day. The death of Cheedle: dawn falling upon the edge of night. One realizes exactly the mood of the writer and how he wrote, as it were, for himself, but it was not his will. He was the falling dawn, and he was the physician going to Bar.[59]

About Eliot, she writes to Violet Schiff in a letter dated August 21, 1922: "I see Eliot's new magazine is advertized to appear shortly. It looks very full of rich plums. I think Prufrock by far and away the most interesting and the best modern poem. It stays in the memory as a work of art--so different in that to Ulysses."[60]

A comment about Stendhal appears in an early letter to Murry. She has been talking about skimming through a group of modern novels:

> Afterwards I began to read Stendhal's Le Rouge et le Noir. You can imagine how severe and noble it seemed and does still by morning seem to me. But what I feel most deeply is--how tragic a great work of art appears. All these young 'nez--au--venticistes' have their place and their meaning in this world, but I seemed to see Stendhal with his ugly face and pot belly and little pig's legs confined within a solitary tower, writing his book and gazing through the window chink at a few lovely stars.[61]

She reads much in Dostoevsky and often comments about him, sometimes taking exception, as in the Journal entry of 1916, when she comments that a re-reading of The Idiot confirms an earlier feeling about Nastasya Filipovna: "She is really not well done. She is badly done. And there grows up as one reads on a kind of irritation, a balked fascination, which almost succeeds finally in blotting out those first and really marvelous 'impressions' of her. What was Dostoevsky really aiming at?" But a few lines later she praises the characterization of

Shatov in The Possessed:

> There is something awfully significant about the attitude of Shatov to his wife, and it is amazing how, when Dostoevsky at last turns a soft but penetrating and full light upon him, how we have managed to gather a great deal of knowledge of his character from the former vague side-lights and shadowy impressions. He is just what we thought him; he behaves just as we would expect him to do.[62]

Tolstoi is mentioned often, usually with praise. A comment in the Scrapbook is pointedly expressive: she is talking about War and Peace. "This is great art--this book. This is the real thing. It is a whole created world."[63]

She reads Shakespeare critically and takes abundant notes. A 1921 Journal entry compiles a number of them. Examples of a few will show her critical judgment at work:

> All's Well That Ends Well: The First Lord is worth attending to. One could have thought that his speeches and those of the Second Lord would have been interchangable; but he is a very definite quick-cut character.
>
> Romeo and Juliet: When the old nurse cackles of leaning against the dove-house wall it's just as though a beam of sunlight struck through the curtains and discovered her sitting there in the warmth with a tiny staggerer. One positively feels the warmth of the sunny wall . . . .
>
> Antony and Cleopatra: A creature like Cleopatra always expects to be paid for things.[64]

Chaucer, Shakespeare, Marlow, and Tolstoi nourish her.

> About the old masters. What I feel about them (all of them--writers too, of course) is the more one lives with them the better it is for one's work. It's almost a case of living into one's ideal world--the world that one desires to express. Do you know what I mean? For this reason I find that if I stick to men like Chaucer and Shakespeare and Marlowe and even Tolstoi, I keep much nearer what I want to do than if I confuse things with reading a lot of lesser men. I'd like to make the old masters my daily bread--in the sense in which it's used in the Lord's Prayer, really--to make them a kind of essential nourishment. All the rest is--well--it comes after.[65]

The frequency with which the name Chekhov appears in Mansfield's writings (indeed, in this chapter) expresses better than more words can Mansfield's opinion of the writer she took as mentor. Greatly influenced by him, she expressed her debt in numbers of ways and perhaps even as early as 1910 with the writing of "The Child--Who--Was--Tired," the first of her stories published in The New Age. There has been much critical controversy with regard to this story. Most major critics of Mansfield have discussed the question of whether it was plagiarized: Alpers, in his biography Katherine Mansfield, Berkman in her critical biography, Daly in her critical study. And there have been articles written on it. Alpers calls it a free adaptation of the Chekhov story, "Stap Khocetsia." He says there is no doubt that Mansfield knew the Chekhov story since incidents in both stories are clearly alike. But, he says, "The Tiredness of Rosabel," her first published story, already had exhibited "every essential feature by which a characteristic Katherine Mansfield story can be recognized," and, he concludes, coming after "The Tiredness of Rosabel," "The Child--Who--

Was--Tired" "is in the nature of an exercise, an a la maniere de Chekhov by an artist who had already hit upon her metier unaided."[66] Berkman believes that the story was a conscious adaptation.[67] Elizabeth Schneider, in an article called "Katherine Mansfield and Chekhov," suggests that unconscious memory on Mansfield's part was responsible.[68] Ronald Sutherland, in an article, "Katherine Mansfield: Plagiarist, Disciple, or Ardent Admirer?" takes the position that she did not learn from Chekhov. Similarities in the two stories are the results, he believes, of similarities in the storehouse of existing literature known to both writers.[69] Daly appears to agree with Sutherland.[70]

It seems to me impossible to believe that there was any conscious plagiarism involved, particularly in view of the following excerpt from a letter written to Arnold Gibbons on July 13, 1922. The letter is in answer to one written by Gibbons to her:

> I am appalled that I expressed myself so clumsily as to make it possible for you to use the word "plagiarism." I beg you to forgive me; it was far from my meaning. It was absorbed I meant. Perhaps you will agree that we all, as writers, to a certain extent, absorb each other when we love. (I am presuming that you love Tchekhov.) Anatole France would say we eat each other, but perhaps nourish is the better word. For instance, Tchekhov's talent was nourished by Tolstoi's Death of Ivan Ilyitch. It is very possible that he never would have written as he did if he had not read that story. There is a deep division between the work he did before he did it and after. . . All I felt about your stories was that you had not yet made the "gift" you had received from Tchekhov your own. You had not yet, finally, made free with it and turned it to your own account. My dear colleague, I reproach myself for not having made this plainer . . . .[71]

Perhaps when she wrote "The Child--Who--Was--Tired" she had not altogether "absorbed" Chekhov. But the question is not really important. There are obvious similarities between the two stories and even more obvious differences. And anyone familiar with Chekhov and Mansfield stories would immediately recognize that "Stap Khocetsia" is a Chekhov story and "The Child--Who--Was--Tired," a Mansfield one. It is reasonable to let the controversy end.

Chapter Three

THE ACHIEVEMENT

In his introduction to the Journal, John Middleton Murry wrote:
Her affinities are rather with the English poets than the English prose-writers. There is no English prose-writer to whom she can be related. The revolution which she made in the art of short story in England was altogether personal. Many writers have attempted to carry on her work; not one has come within a measurable distance of success. Her secret died with her. And of the many critics who have tried to define the quality in her work which makes it so inimitable, every one has been compelled to give up the attempt in despair.[1]

The statement is, for the most part, true, although surely each critic attempting the task anew feels he can at least give it a good try. One problem arises from the necessity to use discursive prose in the process of analysis. Another from the fact that no analysis, the critic is always aware, can ever stand for or even come close to the original work. It is basically the old problem of trying to use the intellect to describe a sensual experience. Poets have always known that the process is altogether unsatisfactory. How to describe in discursive prose the complex and altogether sensual experience of seeing, holding, biting into and tasting an apple? Impossible. The poets know it, and critics, too. But the intellect will not be idle. Men have always found it necessary to inquire, to analyze--what? how? why?-- and the more difficult the task, the more fascinating it is, the more compelling it becomes, the more seductive.

There is surely a "special prose," which Murry says in his introduction to her collected Poems, "was the peculiar achievement of her genius." He quotes a statement from her Journal, dated January 22, 1916: "I feel always trembling on the brink of poetry."[2] Three years later she comments in a letter to Lady Ottoline Morrell, "I _do_ believe that the time has come for a 'new word' but I imagine the new word will not be spoken easily. People have never explored the lovely medium of prose. It is hidden still--I feel that so profoundly."[3] But words, even "new words" do not function by themselves. They operate within a form, as Mansfield well knew, and the particular achievement of her "special prose" lies in this: the language suits the form. It is in this that her "affinities are rather with the English poets than the English prose-writers." She did write poems; few are distinguished.[4] Mansfield, however, knew the poet's secret: metaphor and imagery combined with appropriate sound and syntax to create the texture of experience. But most of her poems lack metaphor; the language is discursive; the sound and structure unrelated to the meaning. When, occasionally, form and meaning come together, the poem seems derivative as in the early "Sea Song."[5]

I will think no more of the sea!
Of the big green waves

And the hollowed shore,
Of the brown rock caves
No more, no more
Of the swell and the weed
And the bubbling foam.
Memory dwells in my far away home,
She has nothing to do with me.

She is old and bent
With a pack
On her back.
Her tears are spent,
Her voice, just a crack.
With an old thorn stick
She hobbles along,
And a crazy song
Now slow, now quick,
Wheeks in her throat.

And every day
While there's light on the shore
She searches for something;
Her withered claw
Tumbles the seaweed;
She pokes in each shell
Groping and mumbling
Until the night
Deepens and darkens,
And covers her quite,
And bids her be silent,
And bids her be still.

The ghostly feet
Of the whispery waves
Tiptoe beside her.
They follow, follow
To the rocky caves
In the white beach hollow...
She hugs her hands,
She sobs, she shrills,
And the echoes shriek
In the ricky hills.
She moans: "It is lost!
Let it be! Let it be!
I am old. I'm too cold.
I am frightened...the sea
Is too loud...it is lost,
It is gone..." Memory
Wails in my far away home.

Murry is right when he says:

It seems to me that nothing like <u>Prelude</u> or <u>At The Bay</u> or <u>The Voyage</u> or <u>The Dove's Nest</u> had ever been written before. English prose was turned to a new and magical use, made crystal clear and filled with rainbow-beauties that are indefinable. What might, in another writer of genius, have become poetry, Katherine Mansfield put into her stories.[6]

Nothing like "Prelude," or "At the Bay," or "The Voyage," or "The Dove's Nest" had ever been written before, but English prose writers had already found appropriate language to suit their own particular forms. Jane Austen's language is completely suited to her subject matter and adds a dimension of meaning to her novels. Emily Bronte in <u>Wuthering Heights</u> found a language to express the stark outlines of her particular vision. Charles Dickens in such a novel as <u>Great Expectations</u> uses the poet's language in scene after scene to suggest meaning underlying the action, and Joseph Conrad had announced in 1897 his famous credo in the essay "The Condition of Art," published as a preface to The Nigger of the Narcissus: "My task which I am trying to achieve is, by the power of the written word to make you hear, to make you feel--it is, before all, to make you see. That--and no more, and it is everything." The artists task, he continued is to present vibration, color, form, "and through its movement, its form, and its colour, reveal the substance of its truth--disclose its inspiring secret: the stress and passion within the core of each convincing moment."[7]

If Mansfield's language is different, it is because her vision is different and the form that it took. The revolution in the short story that Mansfield effected was not so much the creation of a functional language but rather a more consistent reliance upon it in a story concentrating on a single moment in time, eliminating a strongly plotted action line and using imagery and metaphor to expand the moment and give it significance beyond itself.

In 1908, with the publication of "The Tiredness of Rosable," she announced theme and technique. Although flawed in places, the story exhibits most of the essential features of a characteristic Mansfield story. Alpers describes many of them:

> ...the focus on a single moment, isolating one cry from the heart to make it represent the whole of a human problem; the use of the faculty of impersonation, making everything the characters say or think reveal some further aspect of their nature; the using of a daydream to assist this process; the dextrous control of three time levels simultaneously; and the inimitable sense of concreteness; and of course the central theme--a fastidious feminine recoil from the arrogant male, conflicting with a romantic idealism and resulting in disillusionment.[8]

"The Tiredness of Rosabel" was Mansfield's first published story. The plot line is slight. After a tiring day working in a millinery shop, Rosabel takes a bus home. Thinking of a good dinner for which she feels she would sacrifice her soul, she sits down next to a girl who is reading a sentimental novel. The warm and humid bus with its garish advertisements contrasts with the streets outside which under reflected lights appear magical. Later, in her own room which is marked by signs of poverty, Rosabel recalls an incident that took place in the shop earlier in the day when two well-dressed young people, a man and a woman, came in to buy a hat for the young lady. They had been hard to please until Rosabel remembered a hat that entranced them, as it had Rosabel. A subtle tense shift about here from past perfect to past brings the incident from past to present time in Rosabel's memory. The young woman asks Rosabel to model the hat, and then, pleased with the result, buys it. The couple then leave the shop, but not before the young man speaks familiarly to Rosabel and with a touch of insolence in his voice. But Rosabel pays no attention, and for the rest of the day she thinks about the handsome young man. Now, in her room, she imagines that she is the young woman and creates a fantasy of love presumably not dissimilar from the novel the girl on the bus was intently reading. But the white and silver frock of Rosabel's dream merges with her real coarse and calico nightdress, and her dream merges with the cold fingers of dawn.

The story is built upon a series of juxtaposed contrasts which form a repetitive pattern. Rosabel's essentially romantic nature is fixed in the first sentence of the story: "At the corner of Oxford Circus Rosabel bought a bunch of violets, and that was practically the reason why she had so little tea--for a scone and a boiled egg and a cup of cocoa at Lyons are not ample sufficiency after a hard day's work in a millinery establishment." She dreams of a good dinner "roast duck and green peas, chestnut stuffing, pudding with brandy sauce--something hot and strong and filling." Although the bus is crowded and uncomfortable, her feet wet, and her skirts coated with mud, Rosabel sees out of the window, streets of opal and silver and shops like fairy palaces.

The girl on the bus is Rosabel's age. The novel she reads is tear-spattered in the rain. The girl is completely engrossed in her reading. Later, in her room, Rosabel is the girl engrossed in a fantasy. What Rosabel reads over the girl's shoulder "something about a hot voluptuous night, a band playing, and a girl with lovely white shoulders" forms a part of Rosabel's dream, "Yes, it was a voluptuous night, a band playing, and _her_ lovely white shoulders." The girl on the bus mouths her words and licks her finger and thumb each time she turns a page in a way that Rosabel detests, but the figure of the girl on the bus merges with the figure of Rosabel and comments on Rosabel and on the whole row of people opposite her who "resolve into one fatuous, staring face." When Rosabel gets up to leave the bus she accidentally bumps into the girl and apologizes, but the girl does not look up from her book. At the end of the story Rosabel is not aware of her coarse nightdress. She cuddles the blankets and grimy quilts around her neck and sleeps and dreams and smiles in her sleep. In the morning, still half asleep, she smiles again; only a "little nervous tremor around her mouth" reveals her awareness of the nature of the real world, a world made explicit for the reader by the structure of the story.

Rosabel's walk to her room through Westbourne Grove which she imagines to be like Venice, "dark and mysterious," "the hansoms like gondolas, the flickering lights," "magic fish swimming in the Grand Canal," is corrected by her apprehension about the four flights of stairs she must climb to get to her room, and at the first landing by the stuffed albatross head glimmering ghostlike which causes her to want to cry. But she is not a pitiful figure. Her responses are true. She is aware of her weariness and of her plight, and if climbing up the stairs is "very like bicycling up a steep hill, but there was not satisfaction of flying down the other side," she has a recourse. Kneeling on the floor, pillowing her arms on the window sill, she peers through the pane, and the "one little sheet of glass between her and the great wet world outside" becomes her means of entry into the fantasy. But she is first on the inside looking out and her memory is her world.

The recalled scene with the couple in the shop is graphic, revealing Rosabel's position and showing how the incident is the immediate basis for the fantasy to follow. The hat exists first in Rosabel's memory. It is in the big "untouched" box upstairs. Something the young man says, his demand for the "impossible," releases the memory, and Rosabel goes running breathlessly to cut the cords on the box and to scatter tissue everywhere. It is, in reality, her hat and when she tries it on it becomes her, in both senses of the word. "'It suits you beautifully,'" the girl says, and Rosabel feels suddenly, ridiculously angry. She resents the girl who will get the hat from the hands of the handsome young man.

The fantasy takes up from the point that the young couple drive away. Rosabel becomes the girl in the brougham and she imagines going home to put on the hat, her hat, before they drive away together. From this point more parallelisms emerge. The story had opened with Rosabel buying violets for herself. In her dream the young man buys her great sprays of violets and still there is money for a lavish lunch of the kind she had dreamed of earlier, but more elaborate, more suited to her new position: "Soup and oysters, and pigeons, and creamed potatoes, and champagne, of course, and afterwards coffee and cigarettes." The afternoon is spent not trying to sell hats to unwilling customers but answering myriad invitations and dressing for the evening's ball. But the ball tires her as her days' work had done, and the young man brings her home to clasp her in his arms.

Her real weariness hastens the end of the fantasy and the story. In two short paragraphs an engagement is announced and a wedding and wedding journey take place. Then the fantasy joins the real world. In her dream "She was tired after the journey and went upstairs to bed. . .quite early. . . ." In the real world she rises from the floor and undresses slowly.

The pattern of images emerging from the stories is consistent, paralleling the theme. The bunch of violets in the opening sentence of the story announces a symbolic motif to run throughout. Rosabel is as violets delicate of taste and sensitive, charming and innocent. The color of the flowers associated with royalty suggests the role Rosabel would like to play. The bunch of violets bought for herself become later in the story "great sprays" as purchased by the young man and, still later, the presence of violets drenches the air. Rosabel's own room is dull and lifeless, but the room she imagines is decorated in pink and white with roses everywhere "in dull silver vases." Her imaginary clothes are silver, too--dress, shoes, scarf, fan. This fantasy of wish-fulfillment is never complicated by the crudely physical.

At the climax of her fantasy the young man folds her in his arms while the firelight shines on her hair and he repeats her name, chanting "Rosabel, Rosabel, Rosabel," but the consummation of their marriage never takes place. She goes to bed alone.

In this merging of fantasy and reality, Mansfield's youthful touch is remarkably sure. There are only three lapses. Twice she inserts into the narrative parenthetical expressions intended to keep the reader aware of Rosabel's actual position in the real world. These sentences break the narrative at awkward places and are really not necessary. The facts that Rosabel's knees are getting stiff and that she is so taken by her fantasy that she laughs aloud are interesting details, but not vital ones and not important enough to justify the intrusions. Nor is the last sentence in keeping with the tone and focus of the story. It is a violation of point of view even more glaring than the two previously mentioned. It destroys the tone of the story and makes the point directly that the whole story has been carefully designed to reflect.

The story is told by an omniscient narrator focused through Rosabel who is the viewpoint character. Except for lapses mentioned, point of view is consistent and functional. The narrator's comments, cast in the syntax and vocabulary used by Rosabel merge with Rosabel's thoughts and create a total atmosphere that decreases the distance between reader and story, drawing him into the created world and keeping him there. The position that the narrator assumes, hovering just outside of Rosabel's consciousness allows easy access to interior and exterior views, both necessary in the presentation of character and situation in a story that moves rapidly between action in the real world, action in the world of memory, and action in a fantasy world.

Since the language employed by the narrator is the same as Rosabel's, the style is hardly distinguishable from point of view. Careful analysis, however, reveals the deft hand of the author creating sentence structure to control tone and selecting concrete details to present the texture of the experience. The first paragraph of the story continuing for thirty-two lines contains twelve sentences, the earlier ones averaging from four to five lines in length. The weight of the sentences provides a certain heaviness in line with Rosabel's tiredness and weariness. The sentences pull down almost like Rosabel's wet feet and her skirts heavy with mud. The tone established here is contrasted with, but not relieved by, the memory and day dream passages, many of which move rapidly because of the dialogue and an accumulation of short sentences. The details selected to render the experience call into play every one of the five sentences. The street is blurred and misty; her feet are horribly wet; there is a sickening smell of warm humanity; the girl licks her fingers and mouths her words; Rosabel feels stifled.

The expansion of the moment into a significant statement is accomplished by means of repetitive patterns. Parallel scenes and events, juxtaposed one with the other, create metaphors that move to symbolic levels, causing an identification to be made between the three girls and revealing Rosabel's desires and frustrations, fears and anxieties, dreams and defeat. The structure creates the metaphor; the metaphor holds the meaning. This is the form. And this is what was revolutionary in short British fiction in 1908. Not short fiction, but short British fiction. We must be careful to make the distinction and to remember that the short story in England at the time that Mansfield began to write had no status as an art form, that few English writers of any stature had seriously explored its possibilities or considered its structure as being different from the novel's, and that it was primarily thought of, as Alpers points out, as a beginner's medium, or an occasional medium, or as merely entertaining.[9] Mansfield discovered the short story by herself, grappled with its form, justified its being. But it had already been discovered, in America and on the Continent.

The short story, as distinguished from the story that is merely short, had its beginnings in the Romantic movement in literature. The earliest practitioners of the form--Washington Irving, Nathaniel Hawthorne, Edgar Allan Poe in America and Nikolai Gogol in Russia--have each at one time or another been called "the father" of the genre. Grounded in myth and legend and fairy tales of the kind written by Hans Christian Anderson, the brothers Grimm, and E. T. A. Hoffman, the earliest stories exhibited a strain of the supernatural presented as though it were real. The influence is easily seen in "Rip Van Winkle" and "The Legend of Sleepy Hollow," in the stories collected in "Evenings on a Farm Near Dikenka," and in "The Nose," and "The Overcoat." It is not as readily apparent in Hawthorne's stories as in Poe's, whose Romantic origins are clearly displayed in the Gothic trappings of such stories as "Berenice," "The Fall of the House of Usher," and "The Masque of the Red Death."

But it is actually to Hawthorne that we must look to find the first example of the short story as it was later recognized and named. Irving's stories are diffuse; they are rambling and leisurely, more like the earlier fairy tale in form, interest lying clearly on the plot line. Although it might be argued that "The Nose" and "The Overcoat" are true short stories, none of the pieces in Evenings on a Farm Near Dikenka exhibits the unity and freedom from excrescence derived, for the most part, from a skillful use of metaphor and symbol that marked the first short stories. Poe's efforts in this direction are antedated by Hawthorne who published in 1832 a story called "My Kinsman, Major Molineux," which may be the first true short story. The dream structure of the narrative provides the appropriate metaphor accounting for the total unity of the piece. Symbols operate on several levels to provide multivalence within the context of the dream structure. Hawthorne's avowed purpose as expressed in many of his later writings was to get beyond the surface level of impressions, beyond ephemeral facts, to something lasting, eternal. His artistic credo is announced in the famous definition of The Romance, which he set down in the preface to The House of the Seven Gables: Unlike the novel which aims at "minute fidelity, not merely to the possible, but to the probable and ordinary course of man's experience," the romance, Hawthorne wrote, "has fairly a right to present that truth under circumstances, to a great extent, of the writer's own choosing or creation," so long as it presents "the truth of the human heart."[10] The necessity that Hawthorne felt to get beyond the facts, to penetrate them, so to speak, in an effort to locate "the truth of the human heart" is the philosophic basis for the structure his successful pieces took. There is always a surface level, what might be called a manifest content, which embodies symbols that must be understood before the meaning of the story is revealed. Everything in the story functions to guide the reader to an understanding of the latent content, the realm of truth.

Edgar Allan Poe might not have understood the purpose, but it is clear that he appreciated the achievement. In his well-known review of Hawthorne's Twice-Told Tales, he set down what many readers feel is the first definition of the short story.

> A skilful literary artist has constructed a tale. If wise, he has not fashioned his thoughts to accomodate his incidents; but having conceived, with deliberate care, a certain unique or single _effect_ to be wrought out, he then invents such incidents--he then combines such events as may best aid him in establishing this preconceived effect. If his very initial sentence tend not to the outbringing of this effect, then he has failed in his first step. In the whole composition there should be no word written, of which the tendency, direct or indirect, is not to the one pre-established design. And by such means, with such skill and care, a picture is at length painted which leaves in the mind of him who contemplates it with a kindred art, a sense of the fullest satisfaction.[11]

But Poe speaks only of unity, of the artistic and harmonious relationship of the parts to the whole. In essence he did nothing more than proclaim the artistic integrity of Hawthorne's stories. That is, he separated the kind of story Hawthorne was writing from the kind of story Irving, for example, wrote, what is today commonly called the tale. But unity can be achieved and is achieved not only in other literary genres but in all successful art works. The majority of Poe's own stories are unified, but not all of them exhibit the characteristic structure that Hawthorne's stories take. "The Fall of the House of Usher," "The Masque of the Red Death," "The Cask of Amontillado," among others, do exhibit the structure, and it is perhaps because of their structure that they are so often anthologized as examples of the short story form.

About forty years after Poe's famous review, another American, Brander Matthews, proclaimed the birth of the new genre. It is not that there had never been pieces of short prose fiction written before. Obviously the short narrative is as old as prose fiction itself. But this was a different kind of short prose narrative, Matthews insisted, the short story (with the hyphen) as differentiated from the short story, the story merely short. It is unfortunate that we did not continue to spell with the hyphen in order to make the distinction, because short stories (stories merely short) continued to be written and alongside of them, short stories of the new kind. And we call them all short stories, a nomenclature that causes many difficulties. Another cause of difficulty is that Matthews, too, like Poe, although recognizing something different, did not locate the real difference, but rather, like Poe again, insisted that the difference lay in the area of unity. The short story, he maintained, has a unity of impression which the sketch or tale does not have and which the novel cannot have.[12] This, of course, is nonsense. Different genres achieve unity in different ways. The novel one way, the story that is merely short another way, and the short story another. The difference lies not in the idea of unity but rather in the formal structure of each.[13]

Some students of the short story believe that it it peculiarly American in origins and development. This is not entirely true, although a list of the most notable practitioners of the short story beginning with Hawthorne and Poe, might tend to support the view. Following Hawthorne and Poe came Herman Melville, Stephen Crane, Henry James, Sherwood Anderson, William Faulkner, Ernest Hemingway, Eudora Welty. English writers, besides Mansfield, who must be added to the list are Joseph Conrad, D. H. Lawrence, and James Joyce. Europeans include, besides Gogol, Chekhov, Bunin, Babel, deMaupassant[14] Kafka, Mann. Almost half are American.

Broadly speaking there are two essential differences between the stories written in the nineteenth century and those written in the twentieth century. One is the difference in the surface content of the stories; the other, the difference in plot line. Neither is a difference basic to the formal structure of the genre. In the nineteenth century, surface content tended to be unrealistic and/or spectacular, in some way out of the ordinary--Young Goodman Brown takes a midnight journey to a Black Mass, Giovanni discovers a modern Garden of Eden created by a God-like scientist, Rappacini. Robin searches for his kinsman, Major Molineux, and finally finds him, the object of hoots of derision, in tarred and feathered splendor; the Red Death stalks and finally overtakes Prince Prospero and his guests; the House of Usher cracks in two and falls into a ghostlike tarn; Bartelby prefers not to involve himself in the affairs of living and finally dies of starvation in a prison cell; Benito Cereno's ship is overrun by black mutineers in an atmosphere of unspeakable horror; four men struggle for survival in an open boat; a white man travels to a stagnant lagoon and hears a Malayan tell a story while his wife dies. Strange religious ceremonies, deadly plagues, strange psychoses, fearful mutinies, shipwrecks, are extraordinary occurrences, not usually experienced by people living an ordinary mudane existence. These experiences were incorporated into stories developed by a plot line in which the something that happened

happened at a climactic point and afterwards a resolution was effected. Rising action proceeded to a climax; falling action to the denoument.

Although, of course, stories of this kind continued to be written into and during the twentieth century, the most significant development in the short story turned it away from the extraordinary and spectacular to the ordinary and everyday, from a reliance upon a strongly plotted action line to a story where plot almost literally disappeared. On the Continent with Chekhov, in England with Katherine Mansfield, in the United States with Sherwood Anderson, the short story became a means for the presentation of moments of everyday experience involving ordinary people in predictable settings. This is not to say that the "old" stories were merely "plot" stories or that the extraordinary experiences did not have particular significances; nor is it to say that the "new" stories lacked form or that the everyday experiences they presented were without universal significances; nor is it to say that there were not an abundance of "plot" stories whose significances were derived from the simply ironic. It was in rejection of the last named that the change was instituted--a revolt against "plotty" stories as Katherine Mansfield named them with derision or "poison plot" stories as Sherwood Anderson referred to them.

What happened in the United States where the short story had its longest history and the most practitioners may shed some light on the revolution that occurred. The emphasis on unity of effect and on the notion of the "pre-established design," the increase in the middle class reading public together with the multiplication of journals publishing short fiction, resulted in a proliferation of stories written by minor authors whose products tended more and more to become formulistic. Another phenomenon of the period was the appearance of a host of "how to write short stories" books which emphasized the formulas and provided step by step instruction in plot building and description writing. The result was that the short story in America almost died.

Writing for the *Atlantic Monthly* in July, 1915, Henry Seidel Canby says:

> What impresses me most in the contemporary short story as I find it in American magazines, is its curious sophistication. Its bloom is gone. I have read through dozens of periodicals without finding one with fresh feeling and the easy touch of the writer who writes because his story urges him....The good short stories that I meet with in my reading are the trivial ones....As they mount toward literature they seem to increase in artificiality and constraint; when they purport to interpret life they become machines and nothing more, for the discharge of sensation, sentiment, or romance.[15]

"Made to order" stories, Canby calls them, constructed by means of a formula derived from the nearest textbook on "Selling the Short Story."[16] "The story must begin," Canby continues, "with action or with dialogue ....Once started the narrative must move, move, move furiously, each action and every speech pointing directly toward the unknown climax.... Then the climax, which must neatly, quickly, and definitely end the action for all time...."[17]

In the May 3, 1917 issue of the *Dial*, Herbert Ellsworth Cory makes essentially the same point. The short story, he says, "is on its last legs." "Its technique has grown more and more self-conscious. And self-consciousness is the mortal foe of true originality."[18]

But a form so vital as it had been in the hands of such master craftsmen as Hawthorne, Poe, Melville, and Crane did not die. It lay dormant waiting for someone of equal or near equal stature to revive it. And the publication of *Winesberg, Ohio* in 1919 did just that. Sherwood Anderson's reflections upon the short story form are remarkably similar to Katherine Mansfield's, although there is no apparent connection between the two. His search was, like Mansfield's, a search for a form and a language. There are no "plot stories" in life, he said in his autobiographical *A Story Teller's Story*.[19] But the magazines were filled with plot stories. "'The Poison Plot,' I called it in conversation with my friends as the plot notion did seem to me to poison all story-telling."[20] "What was wanted," he continued, "was form, not plot, an altogether more elusive and difficult thing to come at."[21] A plot is formulistic, mechanical, and does violence to the imaginative world. But how to avoid the spoiling of tales in the telling of them? How to "get them into form, to clothe them, find just the words and the arrangement of words that would clothe them"?[22]

> How significant words had become to me! At about this time an American woman, living in Paris, Miss Gertrude Stein, had published a book called "Tender Buttons" and it had come into my hands. How it had excited me! Here was something purely experimental and dealing in words separated from sense--an approach I was sure the poets must often be compelled to make. Was it an approach that would help me? I decided to try it.[23]

A year or two earlier Anderson had had a similar exciting experience with paintings that he related to the same problem.

> Suddenly there had flashed into my consciousness, for perhaps the first time in my life, the secret inner world of painters. Before that time I had wondered often enough why certain paintings, done by the old masters, and hung in our Chicago Art Institute, had so strange an effect upon me. Now I thought I knew. The true painter revealed all of himself in every stroke of his brush.[24]

Words, Anderson decided then, "were as the colors used by the painter," but his palette of colors, he feared, was small. In his *Memoirs* he wrote, "I had no Latin and no Greek, no French. When I wanted to arrive at anything like delicate shades of meaning in my writing I had to do it with my own very limited vocabulary."[25] He knew from books more words than he could pronounce, but he realized that he had to work with the words he knew intimately, words that were a part of his own everyday speech and thought, and he knew further that these words were also the words that would express what he had to say, if he were to say it truly. "'You will have to stay where you have put yourself,'" he said, and continued: "There was the language of the streets, of American towns and cities, the language of the factories and warehouses where I had worked, of laborers' rooming houses, the saloons, the farms." It was his language, he decided and, limited as it was, he would need to learn to work with it: "There was a kind of poetry I was seeking in my prose, word to be laid against word in just a certain way, a kind of word color, a match of words and sentences, the color to be squeezed out of simple words, simple sentence construction."[26]

His ultimate success in merging content, form and language is attested by the revolution he affected in the art of story-telling in America, in turning it back from the mechanical to the organic, from the bloodless and formulistic to the vital art form it remains.

The revolution that Mansfield effected grew out of similar circumstances and took a similar direction. As Saralyn Daly points out, "if Mansfield was familiar with the writings of her contemporaries, she found in them traditional form." "The older style of writing, from which Miss Mansfield departed immediately, relied heavily on a plot in which 'something happened'" a significant change in the situation, with stress on a climax and a conclusion."[27] The form that Mansfield sought and found moved the short story away from the formulistic in England and established it as an art form to take its place beside the other and older literary genres.

What Mansfield recognized in Chekhov's stories and valued highly was organic form, although the form that her stories take grew not out of imitation but rather, as has been pointed out, from her own philosophy of life and art. The resemblances to Chekhov, the use of a functional language in a story concentrating on the single moment and eliminating a strong plot line, the use of imagery and metaphor to expand this moment, are similar to Anderson as well as other modern short story writers; and the differences between Mansfield and Chekhov are as striking as the differences between any author's work and another's. The Mansfield created world is not the Chekhov created world any more than it is Anderson's or Faulkner's or Kafka's or Welty's.

In a special sense, then, Murry's statement is true. The revolution Mansfield effected was "altogether personal." No writer has (or could) carry on her work or come within a "measurable distance" of it. It is inimitable and peculiarly hers, and in this sense, "her secret died with her." But it is possible to analyze her created world; it is possible to discover her characteristic themes and techniques and to understand how and why the stories are successful; it is possible, the critic wagers, and then can do nothing else but make the attempt.

Chapter Four

THEMES AND CHARACTERS

She was seldom satisfied with anything she did. Sometimes at the moment of completion of a story she felt exhilaration, but usually after a lapse of time she questioned her achievement and often waited with anticipation for her husband's response to a story she had sent him. Up to the time of her death she was seeking new ways to embody her vision and to purify it. But despite her own lack of complete confidence and her continuing search for appropriate forms and despite the comparative few years she had in which to write, the body of her work is impressive. The scope is wide and varied and the depth surprising.

It is only slightly helpful to list her recurrent themes. Professor Berkman makes such a list. The total pattern, she says, "emerges as a dichotomy--the irreconcilable cleavage between the rich potentialities of life and the inescapable brutalities of human experience which must evoke despair." Subsidiary themes include 1) loneliness and frustration; 2) sexual maladjustment; 3) purposeless suffering; 4) the falseness, ostentation and sterility of modern life; 5) the denial of emotional fulfillment.[1] Professor Daly makes a list of recurrent subjects: isolated women, overbearing businessmen fathers, adolescents. Her summary of Mansfield's overall theme is that man finds himself finally "isolated, with hope of neither human understanding nor supernatural help or pity. Though Mansfield affirmed beauty to the end, Daly continues, "the casual destructive forces always lurked nearby, and in any joy sadness waited."[2] "Death seen beneath transparent life, death seen 'in a flower that is fresh unfolded,' as she expressed it herself," Alpers says, "this is the theme that consistently drew forth Katherine Mansfield's finest work...."[3] The statements made by Berkman, Daly, and Alpers obviously belie the earlier charge made by H. E. Bates that Mansfield's stories are monotonous, all having been written in a delicate and rippling style and having a sameness of characters and situations.[4] The fact that there is a persistent theme running throughout her work is not surprising. A persistent theme runs throughout any given author's work and pervades it. Mansfield writes of childhood joys and fears, of adolescent pleasures and pains, of adult aspirations and failures, and of the memories and final knowledge of the aged.

But statements of theme are abstractions existing in a realm outside of the concrete, in a vacuum of unreality. The reality is the individual living in the reader's mind, put there by a feeling caught and transmitted in such a way that the reader knows him as real, living, but always mortal. From the early "How Pearl Button Was Kidnapped" to the later "The Wrong House" the child exists in life knowing, whether consciously or unconsciously, violence and death, and the aged face death, holding on to life.

"How Pearl Button Was Kidnapped," written in 1910, is a virtuoso achievement, a fantasy of wish fulfillment, an embodiment of the desire to escape the constrictions of life symbolized by the house of boxes. Pearl Button is a child dressed in a clean pinafore with a frill. As the story opens she is swinging on the front gate, singing a little song in the sunshine of early afternoon. Behind her looms the house in which she lives. As she swings on the gate, loose but still tied to the house, outside because, it must be assumed, her mother has sent her out to play while she does the "ironing-because-its-Tuesday," she is like a pearl button on a frock that her mother might be ironing. But with the entry of the two strange women there begins a pattern of events: the loose button pops off and rolls free and is lost. This, perhaps the major metaphor in the story, is never stated but it is implicit. The fantasy is that of a child who imagines herself to be such a button. It is a fantasy filled with color and movement but with an absense of normal sounds which gives it its peculiar air of unreality. Over and over again in places where there is a description of a scene, sounds of the ordinary world are lacking. Pearl swings on the gate and the wind is blowing, but the sounds of rushing and rustlings made by the wind are absent. In silence the two strange women approach. Big and fat, dark, dressed like gypsies, they are seen vividly, with their baskets of ferns, their bright clothes of red, green, yellow, the pink kerchiefs over their heads. They approach and the magic begins with their motion, bare feet upon the road, the slow measured tread and sway of their fat bodies. They smile and they talk but it is a language strange and incomprehensible. Then Pearl laughs out loud, a sound of delight, played against the unearthly silence of the dreamscape. The laugh acts as a signal for them to approach and to speak words that the child understands, words that are in their essence the creation of the child's mind, like conversations that children create, the dialogue of a dreamer. "'You coming with us, Pearl Button? We got beautiful things to show you,'" whispers one of the women. At this point the Erlkonig theme is strong, legends of children lured to death by strange people, elves, fairies, gypsies, by promises of the beautiful, the joyous, the free. Without answering Pearl gets down from the gate, slips out into the windy road and walks with little running steps. Again there is a strong sense of motion, but motion without sound, progression without movement. They walk for a long way and, when Pearl gets tired, one of the women carries her. She is, Pearl thinks, softer than a bed and she has a nice smell "that made you bury your head and breathe and breathe it." The place where they bring her is a log room full of people. There is a feeling of great vitality, a freedom, a joyousness in the room. One of the women releases Pearl's hair ribbon and her hair shakes loose. They kiss her on the back of her little white neck. The people laugh, but the laughter does not have enough character or quality to be heard. In the same silence a man across the room rolls a peach toward the child. Pearl's words, "Please, may I eat it," stand out and lend a touch of the bizarre to a scene that is already strange and magical. Again they laugh and clap their hands, but the sounds are not heard, although a strong sense of motion is present. Pearl lifts her skirts and sits down, juice runs from the peach through her hands and on to her dress, and for the first time the child is frightened. "'Oh!'" she says. "'I've spilt all the juice.'" But it doesn't matter at all. They seem not in the least concerned whether she dirties her clothes.

The journey to the sea that they take in carts is again motion without progress. They do not move into the country; the country comes to them. During the journey Pearl is cuddled in the arms of one of the women and experiences the greatest sense of happiness she has ever known. But her happiness ends abruptly. They stop on a hilltop. Down below there is a great big piece of blue water "creeping over the land." "'What is it?'" she screams "'Will it hurt us--is it coming?'" The woman's answer is a part of the fantasy of the child. "'No, it stays in its place.'"

The caravan begins again and finally comes to a stop at some little houses close to the sea. The houses have wooden fences around them and gardens inside, and the sight of them comforts Pearl. Later Pearl sits on the floor and eats and thinks what a funny place. "Haven't you got any Houses of Boxes?" she asks. "Don't you all live in a row. Don't the men go to offices? Aren't there any nasty things?"

Later Pearl is led to the beach by the two women. She is afraid of the wet sand but is coaxed by the women and gradually she is led into the water. "Lovely, Lovely," she cries and she paddles and plays and hugs and kisses the woman close to her. But suddenly she screams with a knowledge born of intimation. She slips in the sand and looks toward the land. Then she sees the "little men in blue coats." They are running toward her with shouts and whistlings--a crowd of little blue men to carry her back to the House of Boxes." The story ends before she is rescued by the forces of law and order, of life that is like the house that is a rigid structure of boxes in a rigid construction of time into hours, days, years.

The symbolic journey to the sea taken in the arms of the earth mother is a movement toward both life and death. The sea symbolizes natural order and movements in life at the same time that it connotes a dark oblivion, a return to a deep sleep, the security born of the subconscious knowledge of darkness.

"The Wrong House," written nine years later when Mansfield is at the height of her power, is about an aged woman, but is almost a companion piece to the earlier story about a child. Where "Pearl Button" is flooded in light and color, "The Wrong House" is a study in darkness. Pearl Button swinging on a gate is paralleled by Mrs. Bean sitting at her window, knitting. Her murmer "Two purl--two plain--

woolinfrontoftheneedle--and knit two together," provides a recurring motif throughout the story. It is like an old song "that she had sung so often that only to breathe was to sing it." The rhythm provided by the motion of the knitting is an extension of the ticking of the clocks in the house and later of the sound of the horses' hooves, "clockety-clock-clock. Cluk! Cluk! Clockety-clock-cluk!" The patterns of Mrs. Bean's life are fixed, like the knitting. She sits in "her seat by the window" knitting constantly, one vest after another, for the "mission parcel." The house is darkened. It is a cold autumn day. Dusk comes floating into the room even though it is only three o'clock. Heavy powdery dust settles on the furniture, films over the mirror.

From down below comes a faint noise, the sound of horses' hooves. Mrs. Bean leans out the window to see the street below. "Good gracious! It was a funeral." She looks to the houses to see which have the blinds down. Then she notices with growing apprehension and fear that they are coming up her garden path. For an instant, it is real, a knowledge of her own death. "No!" she groans, twice. She gasps, a cold shiver runs through her. Somehow she gets to the door, opens it, manages to gasp out, "The wrong house." Later she leans against the door, whimpering, "go away, go away." The reader knows it is almost the right time and almost the right house and Mrs. Bean knows it too, with a knowledge, deep and abiding but non-verbalized. "She thought of nothing; she did not even think of what had happened. It was as if she had fallen into a cave whose walls were darkness. . . ."

Later when her aged servant gets home, Mrs. Bean calls for a lamp, even though it is only four o'clock, and, when she picks up her knitting again, she begins to unwind what she has done. But habit takes over; she picks up again the pattern of her life. "Don't forget the mace," she says to Dollicas, the servant, thinking of the night's supper. "It's a lovely young bird," Dollicas answers, before she pulls down the blind at Mrs. Bean's window.

"How Pearl Button Was Kidnapped" and "The Wrong House" represent the extremes in the pattern of life which makes up the texture of Katherine Mansfield's stories. In between there are many other children and old people and between them adolescents and adults, ranged over a broad spectrum balanced as a fulcrum, somewhat like a see-saw. Indeed, Mansfield must have been consciously aware of this fulcrum, because whe wrote a story called "See-Saw," in which she balances children and old people by means of a structure which juxtaposes two children playing house with two old people weary of "house" already played. It is springtime in a park. The sweet smell of the grass pervades the atmosphere; the trees are in full leaf; a light wind blows; tiny white clouds cluster in the blue sky. People wander around, "the old ones inclined to puff and waddle after their long winter snooze; the young ones suddenly linking hands and making for that screen of trees in the hollow. . . ." The plank of the see-saw is in balance.

Now the "teeter" movement begins. The scene shifts to a hollow beneath a tree where two little people have set up house "with a minute pickaxe, an empty match box, a blunted nail and a shovel for furniture." The age of the children is not given but their appearance and conversation suggest that they are five or six. The girl sends the boy for sticks to make a fire and he comes back with a make-believe armful which she gathers together in her skirt. Then they go through the business of making a make-believe fire before they sit down to create a make-believe pie.

The "totter" begins: the scene shifts to the top of the hollow by the tree where two "fat old babies" plump themselves down on a bench. Again age is not given but their appearance and conversation suggest that they are in their late seventies or so. They talk about someone named Nellie who cut her finger at dinner, but not very badly. Then a bird flies over them with a "great jet of song." The man stands up and waves his hat in the direction of the tree. "Don't want bird muck falling on us," he says.

Again the scene shifts as the see-saw moves. The children's fire is hot and they are delighted with it, but soon they get into an argument over whether dogs have kittens. It frustrates both of them. He shouts and waves his shovel; she throws her dress over her head. Suddenly he lifts his pinafore and makes water. She is appalled. "You've put out my fire." "Never mind," he says, and they move to another cave to make another fire.

The see-saw moves and the story ends with a single sentence: "The old babies began to rumble, and obedient to the sign they got up without a word and waddled away."

The title of this story provides the major metaphor with the structure reinforcing it; the pattern is of reciprocating motion. Out of the alternating pattern the meaning emerges. The children play house, anticipating the experience, alternating roles (she is wife and mother, he, husband and son) experiencing joy and anger; the old people are spent by life, there is no longer a joy in it, although they continue to participate in it. Bird muck bothers them; make-believe food won't sustain them. But it is clear that the old people are a natural outgrowth; they occupy a rightful place on the plank that is the see-saw of life.

Juxtaposition of a child with old people is again the subject of the story "The Voyage." In this one, a child, Fenella, is being brought by her grandmother to her grandmother's home after the death of her mother. The bulk of the story is taken up with an account of the journey told from the child's point of view. The apparent pathos of the situation is underlined as the reader is made keenly aware of the situation which has not yet become a reality for the child. But the story ends on a surprising note. The grandmother's house has a fairy-tale like quality and the old grandfather lying in bed looks somewhat like a Santa Claus as he looks at Fenella "so merrily that she almost thought he winked at her."

Another story which juxtaposes children with adults but in a somewhat different way is "Sun and Moon." The children appear to be about the same age as their counterparts in "See Saw" and "The Voyage," but they are more carefully drawn and in the course of the story, the boy, Sun, experiences a fall from innocence, while the parents in their insensitivity remain kinds of perennial innocents.

In this story, as in "See Saw," a clear differentiation between the sexes is made. The children's names, of course, indicate the roles they play. Sun is male, stocky, aggressive, shy, serious; Moon is female, dainty, seductive, outgoing, flighty. Sun is the protagonist; the conflict is his, and it involves a crisis in his male identity. Always overshadowed by the pretty little girl, always second in the affections of people, never understood but more sensitive, often a thing in the way and being sent stumping off to the nursery, he becomes emotionally involved with a confection house with a nut for a door handle which is to be part of the decorations for the table at a party held by his parents.

As the story opens it is clear that the whole house is involved in preparing for the party. Decorators have arrived, the dining room is being cleared, food is being prepared, Nurse is helping the mother alter her dress. Everywhere there is a frenzy of activity. Nothing is normal. Even Cook is nicer than usual, red in the face and laughing (there is a man helping her in the kitchen). Once she takes the children by their hands and shows them the confection house which is being kept in the refrigerator. The multipersonal point of view records the children's response. "Oh! Oh! Oh! It was a little house. It was a little pink house with white snow on the roof and green windows and a brown door and stuck in the door was a nut for a handle." Sun is particularly taken by the nut. When he sees it he feels tired and has to lean his head against Cook. Moon responds differently. She wants to touch the house, to put her finger on the roof. Later Sun asks whether people are going to eat the food. Cook laughs when she answers and Moon laughs, too, but Sun "didn't want to laugh. Round and round he walked with his hands behind his back." Later, when the children are dressed and brought down to the party to be introduced, Sun finds only one man whom he really likes, a little grey man who walks around by himself. Afterwards when Sun falls asleep on the stair landing he sees all the guests walking round and around the table with their hands behind their backs. But the little grey man likes the house best. Sun dreams that when the old man sees the nut for a handle he rolls his eyes and says to Sun, "Seen the nut?"

After all the guests have left, their parents find Sun and Moon on the stairs and bring them down to the dining room. The parents are behaving differently, Sun notices. The father is more jolly, the mother playful and seductive in her behavior with her husband. In the dining room again the multipersonal view records the children's responses. "But--oh! oh! what had happened?" Everything is a mess. And the little pink house is "broken--broken--half melted away in the center of the table." Again the children's responses are different. Moon squeaks and shrieks and then noticing that the little nut handle is intact, reaches over and picks it out of the door and scrunches it up, "biting hard." But Sun has not moved from the doorway. And when his father calls to him he puts up his head and gives a loud wail. "I think it's horrid--horrid--horrid!" he sobs, and once again Sun is banished from the room and sent stumping off to the nursery by parents who are unable to understand his needs or his anxieties. The confection house had come to represent an ideal for Sun, the nut for a door handle, his male ego. When Moon grabs it and eats it up, that ego is again assailed and when his parents banish him to the nursery, his male dignity is again assaulted.

A child's needs, symbolized by a condition of hunger, is the basic theme of another story, "A Suburban Fairy Tale," which in its fantasy structure is more like "How Pearl Button Was Kidnapped" than like "Sun and Moon." The characters in "A Suburban Fairy Tale" are Mr. and Mrs. B and their son, Little B, who is most unlike his parents. Indeed Mr. and Mrs. B share a common fantasy concerning food. At the breakfast table, visions of entire meals pass between them like words, but the visions do not include Little B who is "starving" in the midst of plenty, and although he tries to interrupt their shared fantasy they pay him no mind. Once he interrupts by calling his father's attention to a flock of sparrows on the front lawn, insisting that they are hungry, begging that they be fed. But the parents go on eating their breakfast and exchanging their own dreams of food. Finally Little B creeps to the window and watches as the sparrows turn into little boys, squeaking, "Want something to eat, want something to eat." Little B tries once more to gain the attention of his parents. But, the narrator says, "Nobody noticed his nonsense." Instead his father goes on with his conversation. "All this talk about famine," he cries, "all a Fake, All a Blind," while the little sparrows-turned-into-boys dance on the lawn squeaking, "Want something to eat--want something to eat."

The upshot of all of this is that Little B joins the little boys on the lawn and then they all, including Little B, turn back into sparrows and fly away.

Not much characterization is provided for Little B, but what is provided helps to make credible, or at least acceptable, the fantasy end. He is a misfit in the family, undersized, looking like a tiny animal, "with legs like macaroni, tiny claws, soft, soft hair that felt like mouse fur, and big wide-open eyes." He sits "perched" between his parents, "swathed" in a napkin, and "tapping" his soft boiled egg. Little B's conversation before he notices the sparrows is all about eggs. The bird motif extends even to Mrs. B, who looks like a pigeon "preening" herself, and, of course, to the name itself, "B." Although it is apparent that the cry of the sparrows is Little B's cry for affection and understanding, it is also apparent that his parents are cruel only in so far as they are insensitive to anyone's needs but their own.

More cruel and insensitive are the Carsfields, particularly Henry, in "New Dresses," who have a total lack of understanding of their daughter, Helen. The Carsfield's difficulties with their daughter arise from her feelings of hostility which are caused by the insecurity she feels within the family structure. Only the grandmother understands the child, and she is powerless to act.

"New Dresses" is an early New Zealand story featuring the Carsfield family, Anne and Henry, the parents, her mother, two girls, Rose and Helen, and a baby, called Boy. The family is a prototype of the later Burnells who appear in "Prelude," "At the Bay," and "The Doll's House." In "New Dresses," the youthful Katherine Mansfield presents some presumably complex people in an intricate family relationship, but the story itself lacks focus and appears contrived. It opens on a scene between Anne Carsfield and her mother, who are sewing new dresses for the two girls. Conversation and interior monologue reveal that the new dresses satisfy Anne's ego. She had "set her heart" on seeing the two girls in the new dresses at church the following morning. There is some sewing litter about, a situation made possible by the fact that Henry is at a political meeting and thus not around to object to the litter. Anne is tired, worried that the thread will give out, and annoyed by her mother's constant references to a flickering gas jet. She ignores what her mother is saying, possibly because the flickering gas jet represents a problem she does not want to face. Instead she speaks of the two dresses and her remarks begin to introduce her feelings for the two girls. Rose has gotten leggy lately and Helen is constantly rubbing her hands on grubby things. These, of course, are problems, too. The mother reflects that Anne has "such a down on Helen--Henry was just the same. They seemed to want to hurt Helen's feelings." Anne continues to complain about Helen. Her clothes are black from head to foot as compared with Rose's, and she stutters, an affectation, Anne believes. The mother remains calm, speaking of the fact that Anne herself as a child, stuttered, "You did just the same when you were her age, she's highly strung."

As the conversation continues it is revealed that Anne does have a problem with Helen, but it is also subtly suggested that the problem has perhaps been created by Anne. Although she insists that "[Helen] is treated exactly like Rose," Helen's hostility toward the baby is perhaps caused by her feelings of insecurity. This conclusion is supported by the thoughts of the grandmother who is unable to correct the situation. Her impotence is mirrored in the incessant ticking of the dining room clock and her statement, "How loudly the clock ticks," is perhaps an unconscious identification of the ticking clock with Anne's continual complaints.

Anne's hostility seems also to include her mother who, from the external evidence in the story, is really very handy about the house. But she, too, is a constant irritation for Anne.

Henry's arrival presents further problems. He has been drinking and is jovial and happy. When he asks to see the bills, Anne tries to put him off, knowing that an argument will follow, as it always does. By the next morning, however, Henry and Anne are reconciled. Henry is proudly watching his son while Anne readies herself for church. Finally the girls in their new dresses come in, ushered by the grandmother. Helen is fidgety, revealing her nervousness about the new dress she wears, but Anne is thrilled because they look "so superior." Later, on the way to church, she squeezes Henry's hand, thinking, "It was for your sake I made the dresses; of course you can't understand that, but <u>really</u>, Henry." The omniscient author comments, "And she fully believed it."

On their way home they meet Doctor Malcolm, the family physician, who asks about Boy and thus puts the proud Henry in such a good humor that he invites the doctor for dinner. After Anne compliments Rose, "Her complexion is so much more vivid than Helen's," the doctor thinks, "Give me Helen every time." Later, while Helen is showing Doctor Malcolm around the garden she is seen more fully in her own right. He asks if she likes the new dress. Mansfield's skill in characterizing young girls with their antithetical feelings is clearly revealed here. Yes, Helen likes the dress. "I'd like to be born and die in it." Then later she declares, "Oh, booh! It's just a dirty old cashmere." When she says things are hellish, she is laughing and dancing over the lawn. Later, when she tears the new dress, she feels "neither frightened nor sorry." But she hides it and lies about where she hid it.

The lost dress causes an uproar. Helen continues to lie and even invents the fantastic tale that a "funny-looking man in a white cap" has been staring in at the windows. Anne's response is significant: "I <u>know</u> you are telling lies." "She turned to the old woman, in her voice something of pride." But, although Helen wants to shout at them, "I tore it, I tore it," she remains silent even when her father promises her a whipping the next day.

Henry Carsfield is pictured without sympathy. He is seen entirely from the outside. The omniscient narrator never enters his mind. It is as though he has no inner being but is a hollow exterior, unthinking, unfeeling. After chastizing Helen he returns to his room putting his booted feet on the clean starched bolster. Later he wakes his wife in the middle of the night to tell her he thinks Doctor Malcolm is "at the bottom" of the lost dress.

The next day Dr. Malcolm comes to the house to find only the grandmother at home. He brings the lost dress with him. Helen has given it away to the daughter of one of his patients. He had the tear fixed and brought it over. "I knew what would be happening at this end of the line--and I knew you'd see Helen through for the sake of getting one in at Henry," he tells the grandmother. But he is annoyed with the reception he receives. The old woman is calm, even regretful, that the dress has turned up so soon. "But of course Helen would have forgotten the whipping by tomorrow morning, and I'd promised her a new doll," she tells the doctor.

The story would better have ended here without the doctor's last remark, for it adds nothing to the story. His character and the situation have already been sufficiently revealed. There is some question as to his real need in the story, as to the role he plays. He functions to help the plot move along, but he seems to serve no other real purpose. It might be argued that he provides an outsider's view to reinforce the reader's notion that Helen is being discriminated against, but this is not necessary either.

Although the members of the family, especially Helen, emerge as vital characters, the focus of the story wavers. Anne, her mother, and Helen provide something of a focal point but the neat parallelisms that Mansfield later employs are not present here. Helen is not so much her mother's daughter as Anne is her daughter's mother. And although the reader gets the idea that Anne's mother had problems with Anne, and Anne has problems with her mother, the complex relationships involved are passed over lightly without sufficient pointing or developing.

More skillfully done, and therefore more satisfying is the controversial "The Child-Who-Was-Tired," which recounts the effect on a child of brutalizing treatment. This is one of the few Mansfield stories where feelings of hostility are expressed through overt criminal behavior. The child's murder of the baby that is in her care is made entirely credible by the skillful movement in and out of dreams, by the merging of the real world and the dream world, and by the reversal of the orders of reality. The real world emerges as a nightmare, grotesque and one-dimensional. It is in this world that the murder takes place, and the murder is at once a waking out of the nightmare that is the child's life, since she accomplishes symbolically her own destruction, finishing up the destruction of herself that her mother had started, and a waking to the infinitely better world of her dreams. Another motif that is skillfully presented in the story and serves to explain motivation is the pattern of pregnancy images which gradually overpowers the child and drives her to complete despair. The bruised sky seems to "bulge heavily" over the dull land; the clothes, hanging on the line "bulges" out; the man and woman "swell to an immense size"; the movements of the woman are heavy. Then as the child's tension heightens, as she becomes more weary, as her point of view becomes increasingly distorted, the pregnancy motif shifts into birth imagery.

The child feels a "fluttering feeling just at the back of her waistband"; her shadow looks "like a grown up person with a grown up baby." Finally the breakdown of rationality which results in the murder is described in terms of a distorted and grotesque birth scene. The child presses down "with all her might; the baby struggles and wriggles to free itself; and afterwards the child feels exhausted relief and heaves a long sigh before she falls back.

Another kind of brutalizing of girl children is found in the early "Frau Brechenmacher Attends A Wedding." Rosa Brechenmacher is a minor character, but she plays an important symbolic role. She is being prepared (although unconsciously) by her mother to be offered for the sacrifice on an altar of carnality. At the age of nine she becomes a substitute mother, is allowed to wear her mother's shawl and feels competent to take her mother's place. She is even called upon by her mother to help feed her father's ego. She is pressed by her mother to help her father dress and then when that feat is accomplished to offer compliments. "Rose, come and look at your father."

The wedding ceremony that the Brechenmacher's attended has the characteristics of an orgy; the holy wedding becomes a kind of Black Mass the culmination of which will be the sacrifice of the bride in the consummation of the marriage. At the celebration Frau Brechenmacher relives her own wedding which had the same kind of culmination and then goes home to await her husband in bed, once again expecting to be hurt.

Children are brutalized not only by adults but also by other children who imitate adult behavior. The Kelveys in "The Doll's House" suffer continual humiliation. Forced to remain separated from the other children because of their social position, they remain on-lookers, pathetic in their separateness. But they understand each other and they stay close to one another for support. Everywhere Lil goes, our Else follows and when our Else wants anything she gives Lil's skirt a twitch and Lil stops to help. At the end of the story our Else wants to see the doll's house, and, although Lil thinks better of it, she gives in for our Else, and the children are once again humiliated, but our Else doesn't mind because she has finally seen the little lamp which is the story's central symbol.

"The Doll's House" is one of the New Zealand stories, featuring the Burnell children, who are in their roundness the most complete of the children Mansfield created. In "The Doll's House" Kezia Burnell is the one who invites the Kelveys to look at the little house, although she knows her action would bring disapproval.[5] The other Burnell children are Isabel and Lottie and closely associated with them, their cousin's, Rags and Pip Trout. It is through these children most especially in "Prelude" and "At the Bay" that Mansfield's world of childhood is most vividly evoked. There are games of make-believe, of playing ladies or mother and father; the adventures of playing at the beach and digging into the sand for buried treasure; the kinds of imaginings that convert a piece of green glass into an emerald as big as a star and far more beautiful. There is the sense of freedom that comes from playing safe from the eyes and ears of the adults in an old unused wash shed, where it is possible to shout and talk as loudly as possible. There are mysterious projects and schemes with all the attendant dangers that children thrill to and are captured in; and the delights of the kitchen when cakes are being prepared and licking the spoon and scraping out the mixing bowl. The bowl is for Pip, who is older, and the spoon and beater for Rags. There is the quality of discovery and wonder as Kezia explores the garden of their new home and the pleasures of creating small presents and surprises for her grandmother from match boxes, shells, and flowers. There is Isabel's satisfaction at being able to direct and control others, even if they are only younger sisters or cousins. Overall is the fluidity of play that imagination allows to incorporate any circumstance or event into a make-believe world.

But hand in hand with pleasure and delight is fear. Fear and anxiety, and guilt shape in subtle ways the course of play or erupt suddenly and terribly in fantasy. Fear of death, of being deserted, fear of the dark, fear of the power of parental authority and control, all are part of the merging of reality and fantasy, so that it is at times impossible to determine the actual from the pretended. In "At the Bay," for example, when the children see Jonathan at the window and start screaming, "A face at the window!" their panic and terror is no less real than it would have been had they not already conditioned themselves by their fantasies. But real or imagined, their need to explore the regions of danger, the dimensions of life, death, and violence, are inescapable. In varying degrees this concern is explored in each child as it is related to or characteristic of his age, sex, or relationship. This exploration is juxtaposed with the same kind of exploration of the adult characters, thus creating a developmental pattern, so that it is possible at any point to view the adult characters as they were as children and the children as they will be as adults.

Lottie, the youngest of the girls, is quite content with being in the company of the other children, with being allowed to participate in their games. But being younger and lacking the skills of the others, she is always crying, "Wait for me!" At the beach she is afraid to go into the water and at the stile she in unable to take the step that will bring her over.

Kezia, on the other hand, is not afraid of playing alone and encountering her fears, but she is afraid of the dark. Her fantasies, innocent enough in the beginning, often end in terror. Her questions to her grandmother bring the child face to face with the idea of death, a notion that she is unable to cope with except by translating it into a nonsensical game. She dreams of animals that rush at her, and withdraws, instinctively it would seem, even from Pip's dog, Snooker, who customarily goes about with his tail between his legs. Her view of the stars in the heavens leads her to the question whether they ever blow out. Her exploration of the garden, in which we see, scaled down as it were, the beauty of the flowers and the leaves and where she discovers secret little places hidden from casual view, is juxtaposed with the other side of the path where the trees are high and the strange bushes thick.

Isabel, the oldest of the group is taken up with her role and exerts herself in controlling her sisters. Dominating and demanding, she encounters little resistance from Lottie and scarcely more from Kezia. Caught up in these patterns of authority, her fears are related naturally enough, to the parental authorities who control her. They must not only be obeyed, but pleased. Her efforts in this direction lead her to tattle on the younger children. "Isabel is more grown up than all of us," Linda Burnell says of her daughter. But it is Isabel who hesitates when the hired man, Pat, is going to take the children to the pond. And it is Isabel who cries, "Oh, why don't they come and call us?" when the children are playing cards in the wash shed and have failed to notice that it is getting dark, and when their imaginations have created strange noises as they become aware of the encroaching darkness.

Pip, the older of the boys, has some of the same characteristic concerns as Isabel. He demands and receives obedience from Rags. His insistence that Snooker is a hunting dog of fierce strength magnifies his mastery over him. He likes to play with the girls because it is so easy to fox them. But he is the first to panic in the wash shed, and he is the first to leave after having witnessed the decapitated duck running around spurting out a stream of blood from its neck.

Rags, on the other hand, overcomes his fear enough to timidly touch the head of the duck with a finger and ask, "Do you think it would keep alive if I gave it something to drink?" Although Rags gives Pip the obedience due an older brother, he, like Kezia, maintains a certain integrity, and he, like Kezia, trustingly takes Pat's hand to go along with him to the creek, while Pip hangs back and Isabel makes excuses.

Most of the adolescents whom Mansfield presents are girls, and the points of view used most consistently are the multipersonal with the major focus through the protagonist who is the adolescent, or the third person with the adolescent protagonist used as the point of view character. This focus through the protagonist allows for the use of a language that creates the particular air of expectancy that characterizes the Mansfield adolescent. An exception to this use of point of view occurs in "The Young Girl," where the story is told in the first person by a narrator whose sex is never clearly revealed.[6] Nor is it ever revealed what the function of the narrator is within the family structure. The narrator seems to be an outsider, perhaps a tutor for the twelve year old brother, Hennie, perhaps a young friend of the mother, Mrs. Raddick. In any case, the narrator looks upon both Hennie and "the young girl" with a great deal of sympathy and understanding, which is the view that the reader takes. However, since this point of view is used the reader never gets the same knowledge of "the young girl" as he does of the other adolescents. In other words, "the young girl" is seen from the outside and not from the inside. It is, however, an interesting story and, if the narrator is seen as a woman, perhaps a good story. "The young girl" is seventeen and going through the throngs of growing up, experiencing the pleasures and the pains, playing roles, over-dramatizing. She wants to be adult and sophisticated and she rejects childish things on the one hand, and on the other, the childish things give her greatest pleasure and the adult cause her the greatest pain.

The story opens on the steps of a gambling casino where the family and the narrator have just been delivered by cab. Mrs. Raddick, who appears to be a compulsive gambler, wants to take her daughter into the casino to introduce her to its pleasures. The narrator is to take Hennie off for an hour while mother and daughter are in the casino. After the mother and daughter leave, the narrator and Hennie linger for a while on the steps of the casino watching the people. Hennie points out a bulldog and then points to the figure of an old woman, an ancient withered creature, who is described somewhat like a witch. She wears a green satin dress and a black velvet coat and a white hat with purple feathers. She is jerking herself up the steps, staring, laughing, nodding, cackling. Her fingers are described as claws that clutch her handbag. "Is she a gambler?" Hennie asks. But the narrator doesn't get a chance to answer, because just at that moment Mrs. Raddick and "the young girl" appear again with another lady in the background. The authorities will not allow the girl to enter even though Mrs. Raddick has sworn she is twenty-one. The woman standing in the background is a friend with whom Mrs. Raddick wants to reenter the casino because the friend has had a run of luck. The problem is what to do with "the young girl," who is standing by, furious that she has been made the center of attention in such a distasteful manner. The narrator invites the young girl to join them (the narrator and Hennie) for tea.

The episode in the restaurant is very skillfully done. "The young girl" abhors the situation and tries to act in a grown up manner but finds herself accepting chocolate and pastries and ices, complaining the whole while about everything that happens, especially about the behavior of her twelve year old brother.

When the refreshments are over they hurry back to the casino, but Mrs. Raddick is not there. The narrator hesitates to leave the young girl alone on the steps, but the girl insists, almost on the point of tears. "I love waiting," she says, "I'm always waiting." The story ends with a description of the child-woman. "Her dark coat fell open, and her white throat--all her soft young body in the blue dress-was like a flower that is just emerging from its dark bud."

If the narrator is accepted as being a young woman, understanding because she has only recently passed through the same stage, then the story presents a carefully controlled picture of four stages of women: "The young girl," the narrator, Mrs. Raddick, and the ancient withered creature. The integrating symbol, then, might be the gold powder box which the young girl carries and in whose mirror the young girl sees herself. Perhaps the other women are reflections of what she might become in succeeding stages of development. It is not a pretty picture, if the ancient withered creature is the end product and if the casino is a microcosm of life. Such a reading of the story hardly seems improbable in veiw of the fact that most of the stories concerning adolescents project some kind of image into the future.

In "Her First Ball" for example, the adolescent, Leila, is seen juxtaposed against the row of aged women "in nice black velvet" beating time with their fans; and the fat man who has been attending dances for thirty years makes the point quite clearly, "Before long you'll be sitting up there on the stage....And your heart will ache, ache." And in "The Garden Party," Laura dressed for a party and recently come from one faces death in the figure of the young man killed accidently. Often anthologized, both these stories present adolescents in moments of extreme happiness then plunged into deep despair before their natural vitality renews their faith. But the reader knows that those things which caused the despair are real and ultimately must be reckoned with, and the gentle ironic tone which pervades the stories underlines the reader's knowledge of the necessity for the final confrontations.

The adolescent's penchant for role playing and indulging in fantasy is the subject of the lesser known but excellent story, "Taking the Veil." Again, it is spring and a beautiful morning. Everything is in movement, light and swift. Trees flutter, street boys whistle, a dog barks, but Edna, aged eighteen, in a French blue frock and a new spring hat trimmed in cornflowers, is trying her best to look tragic, for on the evening before "an awful thing had happened." She and her "fiance," Jimmy, had been to the theater and "without a moment's warning--in fact she had just finished a chocolate almond and passed the box to him again--she had fallen in love with an actor. But--fallen--in--love. . . ." The play, a melodrama, had held her intensely involved, and, Jimmy, who had not cried as she had but instead had passed her chocolates, was a poor substitute, for the heroic actor on the stage. Life, Edna knew, could never be the same and she had shut the chocolate box for ever.

On this morning she knows that she can never marry Jimmy and also that he will never get over it. "His life was wrecked, was ruined.... But he was young....In forty years...he might be able to think of her calmly." But, she continues to think, "what did the future hold for her?"

She has stopped her walk at a place overlooking some convent gardens and she can hear the voice of Sister Agnes giving a singing lesson. Mournful tones sound and echo, "Ah-me." Then dialogue comes to her as she begins to write her own fantasy play and to act it out in her imagination. She will go into a convent and take the name of Sister Angela. "Snip! Snip! All her lovely hair is cut off." She will wear a blue gown and a white head-band. Visitors will be told of her youth and her beauty and her "tragic, tragic love."

Then in her fantasy play the scene shifts and it is winter. She is in her icy cell and she hears an animal cry, "a kitten or a lamb or--well, whatever little animal might be there." And white and shivering, but fearless, she gets up and brings it in. Then she takes fever and dies. "Rest in Peace, Sister Angela. . . ." The scene shifts again. Mourners are present, her aged parents, and Jimmy with snow-white hair and tears streaming down his face. He is crying now, but it is "too late, too late." The wind shakes "the leafless trees," and Jimmy gives "one awful bitter cry."

This last cry does it; she drops her book, jumps up, her heart beating. "My darling! No, it's not too late. It's all been a mistake, a terrible dream. Oh, that white hair!" Everything is still possible. The trees are in bloom, pigeons are flying, and now she really knows what it is to be in love, "but-in-love!"

In "The Wind Blows" the protagonist, Mathilde is also trying to accommodate herself to an image of womanhood. For her, it is a picture called "Solitude" of "a dark tragic woman draped in white, sitting on a rock, her knees crossed, her chin on her hands." Her adolescent fears and trepidations are embodied in the language and movement of the story. The blowing wind, which is the major metaphor, is the concrete embodiment of her anxieties. From the beginning of the story which is cast in the present tense to the end the wind never stops blowing. Her anxieties, however, are not allowed to remain entirely undifferentiated. The picture of the woman, her relationship with her music teacher, Mr. Bullen, the trembling of her fingers and the beating of her heart when she sits close to him, identified by "It's the wind," her comment, "Life is dreadful," and his answer, "something about 'waiting' and 'marking time' and 'that rare thing, a women,'" focus her anxieties on changes within her which cannot be stopped, any more than the wind.

Identity crises involving sexual roles are the subjects also of "Carnation," "Something Childish But Very Natural," and "At Lehmann's." The latter, one of the earliest stories and included in the Pension group, is the most obvious in its statement. Its protagonist, Sabina, is a young innocent, pretty, warm serving girl. Her youth and innocence is contrasted immediately with the older servant, Anna, who is fat and tired, and with Frau Lehmann, spent and swollen with child. Upstairs lies the pregnant woman, waiting to be delivered, while downstairs Sabina flies around, cheerfully doing the extra work, happy, exuding a magical child air.

Once while Sabina is wondering where exactly babies come from and how they get delivered a Young Man enters the cafe and calls for a glass of port wine. The "magical child" tone previously attached to Sabina now shifts. She is obviously attracted to him and the whole scene takes on sensual tones: The words "hot" and "languid" are used and then repeated in an inverse pattern.

> Very languid felt Sabina in the hot room, and the Young Man's voice was strong and deep. She thought she had never seen anybody who looked so strong--as though he could take up the table in one hand-- and his restless gaze wandering over her face and figure gave her a curious thrill deep in her body, half pleasure, half pain....She wanted to stand there close beside him, while he drank his wine.

But she goes back to a corner seat and listens to the sound of leaves and the loud ticking of the clock. Upstairs she hears the heavy dragging footsteps of Frau Lehmann and thinks how dreadful it would be someday to be like that. But, at the same time, she acknowledges it would be sweet to have a little baby. The unconscious smile that comes to her lips is noticed by the young man and when he asks about it she blushes. Not unexpectedly, since her behavior has been, although unknowingly, completely seductive, he calls her over to look at a colored sketch of a naked girl. She responds to his advances with the kind of complete innocence that one might take to be impossible and thus affected. The young man says he will come again.

The next day, Sabina wakes, tired. She feels there is something heavy pressing on her heart. This skillful juxtaposition of Sabina's feelings with those of the pregnant woman marks the time of delivery. The house is in a frenzy. Sabina rejects the whole situation. She complains about the load of work and says "I would like to go away--I hate this talk." But suddenly the young man comes in and she springs to her feet, laughing, all her troubles forgotten. His coat is wet and she allows him to accompany her to the cloak room, laughing and beckoning. Inside it is warm and close. When they touch a strange tremor thrills her. Suddenly his confused feelings tumble out, and he asks roughly, "Are you a child or are you playing at being one?" She is frightened. He kisses her and touches her breasts. The room swims around her. Suddenly, from above, there comes a frightful "tearing shriek," and then the "thin wailing" of a baby, and Sabina breaks away and shrieking herself rushes from the room.

"Carnation" is a much more subtle story. Images of heat, light, odors, sound, the red carnation itself, create a pervasive sensuality until at the end of the story all images fall together in a brilliant climax. A schoolgirl, Katie, is the protagonist in this one; Eve, a seductrous, like her namesake, is the antagonist. The setting is a schoolroom, the occasion a French lesson. It is hot, sultry. Eve, "curious Eve," she is called, has brought a flower to class, as she always does, we are told, on hot days. Her usual practice is to sniff it, and twirl it in her fingers, hold it to her cheek and to her lips, tickle Katie's neck with it, and finally end by pulling it to pieces and eating it, "petal by petal." Today she has brought a deep red carnation which looks as though it has "been dipped in wine and left in the dark to dry." To Katie, Eve appears thin and cruel with "a long sharp beak and claws and two bead eyes." "Isn't it a darling?" Eve says to Katie. The teacher, M. Hugo, calls for silence and the girls in the class settle down, each in her separate way. They wear pale blouses and have ribbons in their hair and all loll and gape in the hot room, where no breath of air stirs, although the windows are half open and the blinds half up.

Eve is fingering the carnation while Mr. Hugo reads poetry, in his peculiar manner.

> He would begin, softly and calmly, and then gradually his voice would swell and vibrate and gather itself together, then it would be pleading and imploring and entreating, and then rising, rising triumphant, until it burst into light, as it were, and then--gradually again, it ebbed, it grew soft and warm and calm and died down into nothingness.

When M. Hugo read poetry the girls felt uncomfortable, funny. As he reads Eve kisses the "languid" carnation and cups it in her hands, capturing its odor, but part of the scent escapes to float across to Katie. But the heat, and the sound of the poetry and the scent are too much for Katie and she turns away "to the dazzling light outside the window."

Although she cannot see it from where she sits she knows what is down below: "a cobbled courtyard with stable buildings round it." They smell faintly of ammonia, sharp and vivid and biting. Now she can hear a man clatter over the cobbles and the sound of a great gush of water. She imagines that he is flinging the water over the wheels of a carriage and in her mind she can see them, spinning around, scarlet and black. Over all she can hear the man's "high bold whistling." He goes away and then comes back leading a horse. She can hear the water again and in her imagination see him swooping water over the horse and brushing. He is dressed in a faded shirt, open at the chest, and his sleeves are rolled up. He is whistling as he swoops and bends. Now the man's movements coincide with M. Hugo's voice which begins to "warm, to deepen, to gather together, to swing, to rise" and move with the scent of the red carnation until they become "one great rushing, rising, triumphant thing, bursting into light." And suddenly, "The whole room broke into pieces." The careful plotting of the movement of this story to suggest the sex act together with the sounds and odors that pervade it, the gathering of the images in the climax and then the sudden release, are punctuated. Mr. Hugo dismisses the class and Eve pops the red carnation "down the front of Katie's blouse." The seduction is complete.

"Something Childish But Very Natural" is told through the viewpoint of the male adolescent, Henry, but it is as much Edna's story as it is his. She is "over sixteen" and he is "nearly eighteen," and they accomplish their fall from innocence because Edna withdraws, leaving Henry in another kind of darkness. Henry is aggressive, given to matter of factness, sensitive, a symbolic Adam, and a god, confused about his feelings and his needs; Edna is innocent, apprehensive, seductive, a hesitant Eve, fearful. They meet and are drawn together and fall in love. But the world that they inhabit is a child's world, a toy world, a dream world. Their dreams are dreams on top of dreams, and Henry's dream at the end represents the nightmare waking into a reality they feared and thus never allowed themselves to know. Introduced at the beginning of the story the dream pattern is the most important integrating structural device that Mansfield uses. The patterns of images, those associated with light (birds, butterflies, flowers, springtime) and those associated with darkness (the shadows, the moth, the tunnel, the snake, the night) together with the symbolic movement of each episode, from light to dark, from hope to frustration, from pleasure to pain, set the total structure of the story so that the break to the end is credible and acceptable.

Henry is one of the few male adolescents whom Mansfield creates. Others are the twelve year old Hennie of "The Young Girl" who is still more child than adolescent; Mathilde's brother Bogie in "The Wind Blows," a somewhat insubstantial figure, and Laura's brother, Laurie, who comes to meet her at the end of "The Garden Party." Both Mathilde and Laura make strong identifications with their brothers, but the boys are seen fleetingly and through the eyes of the girls.

There are two incomplete stories introducing female adolescents, "Father and the Girls" and "The Dove's Nest." The structure of both these stories indicates that Mansfield's plan was to place these adolescents in juxtaposition with older women and so get the spectrum that enlarged the moment and gave it additional significance. Ernestine, the young woman on whom "Father and the Girls" opens is seen only briefly, but the imagery suggests that some kind of sexual theme was to be developed. The train that she sees in the opening paragraph is described in phallic terms. It comes "tearing" its way through a valley, "plunging" between the mountains. The engine is a "dark flat breast," bare and powerful, and when it comes hurling toward Ernestine, she feels a "weakness," so strong that she "could have sunk to the earth." The next section of the story begins to develop the characters of Emily and Edith, middle-aged spinsters, still girlish but weary, who are traveling with their aged father. The story breaks off, however, before any particular significance emerges from the juxtaposition.

Milly, in "The Dove's Nest," is developed by means of bird imagery, as indeed, is her widowed mother. The part of the story that is completed suggests that some kind of revelation concerning the relationship between mother and daughter is desired. The whole female household, mother, daughter, female companion, and female servants, is set out of kilter by the visit of a gentleman, old enough to be a proper mate for the mother, but young enough to set jumbled feelings stirring in Milly. As is a usual practice, Mansfield makes the setting a concrete objectification of internal feelings. Just before the story breaks off, as mother, daughter, and gentleman caller are sitting on the balcony a descriptive passage sets the anticipatory mood:

> Beyond the balcony, the garden, the palms and the sea lay bathed in quivering brightness. Not a leaf moved; the oranges were little worlds of burning light. There was the sound of grasshoppers ringing their tiny tambourines, and the hum of bees as they hovered, as though to taste their joy in advance, before burrowing close into the warm wide-open stocks and roses. The sound of the sea was like a breath, was like a sigh.

Milly, it appears, is as receptive as the wide-open stocks and roses, and she stretches out her hand to the sun.

As it is hard to make a clear-cut distinction between adolescents and young adults, adolescents sometimes behaving like adults and adults sometimes behaving like children, so some of the young women in Mansfield stories exhibit adolescent feelings, and there are many whose responses indicate they are in a state of arrested development and will never grow up. The protagonist, Viola, in "The Swing of the Pendulum," has feelings that are in essence very similar to those of the eighteen year old Edna in "Taking the Veil." Viola, too, is very adept at role-playing and creating wish fulfillment fantasies. Viola is a proud young woman writer, taking a chance on life, but behind in her rent, and being pressed by her landlady to pay immediately or else leave. She is alternately ashamed of her position and fearful to face the landlady and "immensely calm and indifferent" about money matters. When she is alone she sometimes paces up and down and then confronts "a tragic reflection" in her mirror, saying, "Money, money, money!" Then her poverty is like "a huge dream-mountain." But when it comes time for action, "with no time for imaginings," her poverty becomes a "hold-your-nose affair, to be passed by as quickly as possible, with anger and a strong sense of superiority." She has received a letter from her lover, Casimir, saying he will be with her on this afternoon. Her first response is anger that he would expect her to wait for him, but she knows her rage is "only half sincere."

It is a grey day, and her room, lit by sudden flashes of sunlight, looks tumbled and grimy. The jar of hyacinths on the table exude a sickly perfume. She goes over to the washstand and sponges her face and neck, and, role-playing, wonders how it would be to drown in a bucket, when she hears a knock at the door. Thinking it is Casimir, she runs to the door, still wet from her ablutions and disarrayed, to find a strange man who stands smiling at her. His smile is infectious and she wants to smile, too, feeling "fresh and rosy." It is clear that the man has knocked at the wrong door, but Viola holds him there while she runs back for a towel, wondering all the while why she has caused him to wait. After a further exchange he leaves and Viola thinks of what a "fascinating interlude" the exchange has been. The gentleman is everything she isn't, happy, well-dressed, carefully groomed, jolly, well-fed, sane and solid. His visit causes her to think of Casimir and again she feels rage and impotence. She rationalizes "I certainly was in love with Casimir," and then pulling herself out of her role, says to herself, "Oh, be sincere for once....I was not in love. I wanted somebody to look after me--and keep me until my work began to sell--and he kept bothers with other men away." Casimir was the only solution, she had thought, and besides she thought he would be successful. "I wasn't born for poverty." Then the image of the strange man rises before her and she thinks he would be the one for her. She wants to be taken care of; she wants ease and luxury. "There is only one thing I'm fitted for and that is to be a great courtesan. But she did not know how to go about it." But she thinks about it and how she would behave; she feels warm and soft and practices voluptuous glances. Then she gets more and more involved in the fantasy. Perhaps he is still outside. She buttons on a long white gown and thinks she is playing "a delicious game--this strange man and she." The game becomes real; she opens the door to find him still there and she invites him in. When they get back into her room it has undergone a change. A miracle has happened. It is full of "sweet sunlight and the scent of hyacinth."

She behaves in a seductive manner, burying her face in the flowers, and the man responds, but she cannot cope with it. Then the dream game that she is playing turns into a nightmare. When he tries to force her to kiss him, she demands that he get out and finding another role to play she "thrills at her own angry voice," and bites his hand. Then, still role-playing, she rolls her eyes and threatens to bite him again. When he leaves, she laughs and dances around the room, delighted by her victory. She looks at her arms which are reddened from the struggle and thinks that her ribs will be black and blue. Then quickly she passes into another role. Of course she loves Casimir; nothing is his fault; and in her mind she imagines his arrival when she will run toward him and throw her arms around his neck.

The young woman in "The Little Governess" finds herself in much the same kind of situation. Remarkably naive and completely inexperienced in sexual matters she allows herself to be picked up by an old man whom she thinks of as a grandfather and thus safe to be with. But her innocent interlude turns into a nightmare when he presses her against a wall, trying to kiss her, and she runs away, in panic.

Linda Burnell's sister, Beryl, has adolescent sex fantasies, as she dreams about a lover in "At the Bay." At the end of the day she moves stealthily about her room, kisses herself in the mirror, imagines a man is with her, holding her. One fantasy leads to another; she

imagines a lover outside calling her. But then the fantasy becomes
real. A real man, Harry Kimber, does come to her window and call her
to come out. And she steps out of her dream into a real garden to
find herself terrified by his approaches.

Sometimes the women are married but have not come to terms with
their sexual roles. The first person narrator in the Pension stories
is one such young woman as are the protagonists of "Bliss," "A Cup of
Tea," and "Blaze." The narrator of the Pension stories emerges as a
real character of considerable more interest than any single character
in other of the related Pension stories. Of the 13 stories collected
in In A German Pension seven are told by a narrator who is the protagonist in conflict with one or a set of the Germans, and in the seven
stories where the narrator is protagonist the character of the narrator
is consistently developed. In this way the Pension stories concerning
the first person narrator are more similar to Anderson's Winesberg
stories or Joyce's Dubliners; that is, the stories taken together, as
a group, reveal more, state an overall theme, different from any single
story.[7]

The narrator in the Pension stories is a young Englishwoman, married, but childless, who appears to have rejected what is usually taken
to be the female role. She can't cook and is not interested in food.
She is fastidious and recoils from talk about health and babies.
Although she rejects German coarseness and vulgarity and snobbishness,
she tries to be a part of the group and is herself taken in by apparent royalty. At the same time that she rejects the physical, she is
immensely romantic. In "The Sister of the Baroness," for example, she
is caught up in the ferver of the developing romance between the al-
leged sister of the baroness and the young student. She is disturbed
that the Frau Docktor feels that English women are unromantic and so
she takes to reading Morike lyrics and even tries her hand at writing
poetry. But she finds it impossible to involve herself in such a relationship. In "Frau Fisher," the narrator recoils from the German
woman's marked curiosity concerning her sexual life and withdraws into
a fantasy world where she is either the virgin shepherd child she is
reading about in Miracle of Lourdes ("Not even the white roses upon
the feet of the Virgin could flourish in that atmosphere.") or to a
situation where she is a kind of pseudo virgin with a husband "a sea-
captain on a long and perilous voyage." In "The Modern Soul," she
finds herself terribly annoyed by Fraulein Sonia's behavior with the
Herr Professor, an annoyance which indicates her jealousy. In "The
Luft Bad." she recoils from banal female conversation about husbands
and babies and tries to escape by means of a swing:

> I got up and climbed on to the swing. The air was sweet and cool,
> rushing past my body. Above, white clouds trailed delicately
> through the blue sky. From the pine forest streamed a wild per-
> fume, the branches swayed together, rhythmically, sonorously. I
> felt so light and free and happy--so childish! I wanted to poke
> my tongue out at the circle on the grass, who drawing close to-

gether, were whispering meaningly.

But there is no escape. The women tell her that to swing is upsetting to the stomach, and all she can do is retreat to the bath shelter for a shower and, in succeeding trips to the bath, hide behind her husband's umbrella. All the people in the Pension stories are sick, taking a cure of some kind, and the narrator is no exception.

The thirty-year old protagonist of "Bliss," Bertha Young has never made a satisfactory ego identity, and she is alienated from life because of it. She functions in various roles of household manager, mother, wife, hostess and friend, none of which she fills adequately. She must be admitted into her own home, like a guest; she does not dare question the nurse's treatment of her own baby, having to ask permission to hold it and finish feeding it; although she loves her husband, she is sexually frigid: "They'd discussed it so often. It had worried her dreadfully at first to find that she was so cold, but after a time, it had not seemed to matter. They were so frank with each other--such good pals." And she chooses her friends in much the same way and for the same reasons that she chooses decorative fruit for her table, purple grapes to tone in with the new dining room carpet. Her identification with the pear tree in the garden is for the reader a painfully ironic one. The tall, slender pear tree in full bloom does not have a single bud or a faded petal. It is perfect, but becalmed against the jade-green sky. Bertha, however, sees the wide open blossoms of the pear tree as a symbol of her own life and then in her mind recounts all she has. But her account of her full life, when seen juxtaposed against the reality of that life, makes ironic comment:

> Really-really--she had everything. She was young. Harry and she were as much in love as ever, and they got on together splendidly and were really good pals. She had an adorable baby. They didn't have to worry about money. They had this absolutely satisfactory house and garden. And friends--modern, thrilling friends, writers and painters and poets or people keen on social questions--just the kind of friends they wanted. And then there were books, and there was music, and she had found a wonderful little dressmaker, and they were going abroad in the summer, and their new cook made the most superb omelettes. . . .

But the baby belongs more to Nurse than to her, and Harry goes through the motions of a faithful husband and family man; he calls before he starts for home; he presides at his table with proper authority; he says precisely the right things; but he is having an affair on the side and there is a suggestion that it is not the first. The friends are the Norman Knights and Eddie Warren, a charlatan; the table conversation is inconsequential and banal. And Pearl Fulton, bathed in a womanly "mystique," is having an affair with Harry.

"A Cut of Tea" is a kind of a morality piece and a less effective story because of it. Rosemary Fell is not exactly beautiful, we are told by a narrator whose voice is present throughout the story, but she has everything. She is young, brilliant, modern, well-dressed, well-read, married two years to an adoring husband, the mother of "a duck of a boy." But she must be insecure because she picks up an impoverished girl to bring her home to tea. "She was going to prove to this girl that--wonderful things did happen in life, that fairy godmothers were real, that--rich people had hearts, and that women <u>were</u> sisters." But when she gets the girl home her husband comments on how pretty she is, and Rosemary Fell decides not to invite the girl to dine with them. At the end of the story she goes to her husband for reassurance, "'Phillip,' she whispered, and she pressed his head against her bosom, 'am I <u>pretty</u>?'"

"Blaze," a much earlier story is more successful, but just as slight. This one is told by an omniscient author who is completely objective and is structured by means of a tripartite arrangement. The first episode introduces two men, Max and Victor. It is apparent that Max is under some great tension, while Victor is completely relaxed. The second episode concerns Max's visit to Victor's wife, Elsa. It is apparent that Elsa has been flirting with Max, but when he presses the issue, she withdraws completely. Max says, "Even a prostitute has a greater sense of generosity." The third episode concerns Victor's return home to Elsa, showing, ironically, his complete satisfaction with her. "What a woman you are," he exclaims at the end of the story.

Man-woman or husband-wife relationships are the subjects of many Mansfield stories. "Psychology," "This Flower," "A Dill Pickle," "Revelations," "Poison," "Je Ne Parle Pas Francais," and "An Indiscreet Journey" are about couples, who for one reason or another do not marry. In "Psychology," the problem between the man and woman is that they are determined to keep their relationship platonic and avoid the physical. In "This Flower," on the other hand, they have allowed the physical, but the woman refuses to marry the man, even knowing that she is pregnant. The woman's desire to exist on a completely equal basis with the man is the crux of the problem existing in both situations. The sexual attitude and position which makes the male the aggressor and the woman submissive and the romantic notion which puts the woman on a pedestal and the man at her feet contain the areas of uncertainty giving rise to the identity crises. In "Psychology," the couple attempts to maintain a relationship where their minds, not their bodies, lie completely open to each other. "And it wasn't as if he rode into hers like a conqueror, armed to the eyebrows and seeing nothing but a gay silken flutter--nor did she enter his like a queen walking soft on petals. No, they were eager, serious travelers, absorbed in understanding what was to be seen and discovering what was hidden." But this relationship cannot sustain them and they reach a time when the old answers, attitudes, and postures will not work. "Well. Why didn't they just give way to it--yield--and see what will happen then? But no. Vague and troubled though they were, they knew enough to know their precious friendship was in danger. She was the one who would be destroyed--not they--and they'd be no party to that." In the end, he flees, and she sits to write him a note in another attempt to maintain the old relationship. In "This Flower" the woman refuses to marry her paramour, indeed refuses to let him know that she is pregnant for fear that he will insist upon marrying her, because he feels it a responsibility, and she cannot allow herself to be placed in that position. The name of the man repeats the theme in a subtle manner, Roy King, and in the end, she refuses to be his queen. That her behavior results from a knowledge of him and of the real situation is made clear at the end of the story. At her insistence he has been told by the doctor to whom he has brought her that she is only a bit run down and there is nothing else wrong. He has gone out with the doctor to settle the fee. The story concludes:

> She heard the front door close and then--rapid, rapid steps along the passage. This time he simply burst into her room, and she was in his arms, crushed up small while he kissed her with warm quick kisses, murmuring between them, "My darling, my beauty, my delight. You're mine, you're safe." And then three soft groans. "Oh! Oh! Oh! the relief!" Still keeping his arms round her he leant his head against her shoulder as though exhausted. "If you knew how frightened I've been," he murmured. "I thought we were in for it this time. I really did. And it would have been so--fatal--so fatal!"

In "A Dill Pickle," a couple meet again, after they have not seen each other for six years, and as the episode develops, the reasons for their separation become clear as well as the knowledge that marriage between them could not work. She is the first to recognize him as she approaches him in the restaurant, and she feels that it is incredible that he does not know her. Later, when they are seated together they recall certain incidents from their past relationship, but their memories are different; when his are of pleasant details of the scene, hers are of his behavior that had annoyed her and still does; and when hers are pleasant, his are of unpleasant things, like the cost of caviar. But as they talk she begins to think that his pleasant memories are perhaps the truer and that she had been wrong to throw away her happiness as she had. She is just about to succumb again when he suddenly shatters the mood and by his manner, although unknowingly, dismisses her. She turns and leaves; he sits thunderstruck. The title of the story refers to a story he recounts of an experience he had had in Russia. He tells about a picnic he was having with friends when the coachman came up and offered them a dill pickle that he wanted to share. As he is telling the story she is imagining the scene as she thinks it occurred, and although she does not know what a dill pickle is, when she thinks about how it must taste, she draws in her cheeks: "The dill pickle was terribly sour." The obvious comparison is to be made. He is the dill pickle.

In its use of wind as a central motif, "Revelations," shares a certain likeness with "The Wind Blows." But, since the protagonists in each story are different, the character of the blowing wind is also different. Where Matilda is an adolescent, having normal feelings of turmoil, Monica Tyrell is a grown woman behaving in an abnormal adolescent manner. The opening paragraph of the story immediately reveals the situation, defining the protagonist. "From eight o'clock in the morning until half-past eleven Monica Tyrell suffered from her nerves, and suffered so terribly that these hours were--agonizing, simply. It was not as though she could control them." These words, cast in the idiom and syntax peculiar to the protagonist leave no doubt in the reader's mind that Monica Tyrell is play-acting, and as the story continues it becomes increasingly clear that Monica has cast herself in a role that she continues to play until another more satisfying one comes along. She is thirty-three, and much concerned with her age, constantly calling her lover, Ralph's, attention to it, and constantly seeking reassurance. But he will not play her game, and she is annoyed with him. When she tells him of her terrible problem with being disturbed in the morning, he answers, matter-of-factly, "Why don't you get Marie to sit outside your door and absolutely forbid anybody to come near your room until you ring your bell?" But, Monica points out, the problem is not so simply solved. What would she do about the post? Who could wait until eleven for his letters?

On the morning that the events of this story take place, everything goes wrong for Monica Tyrell. She is awakened by a slamming door; when the servant comes in, the blinds fly up, and the curtains flap and jerk; the tassel of the blind knocks against the window. As Marie is trying to fix the curtains, the telephone rings; its noise sounds: "ring-ting-a-ping-ping, ring-ting-a-ping-ping." It is Ralph, inviting her to lunch at Prince's. This is the last straw. She has just told him how agonizing her nerves are in the morning. She decides it is all over with Ralph; it is the end. And now another role emerges for her to play. She asks Marie for two handsful of carnations and sits at her mirror, pale. It is a "wild, white morning," and there is a "tearing, rocking wind." The maid combs her dark hair back off her face, and she notices that her face looks like a mask. Her tragic appearance against the background of the morning and the wind pleases her by its appropriateness and she feels excited. "I'm free. I'm free. I'm free as the wind." This "vibrating, trembling, exciting, flying world" is hers, her kingdom. She belongs to "nobody but life." Quickly she calls for her hat and coat and rushes out, her movements attuned to the rhythm of the wind. In a taxi, she wishes the cabman would drive faster and faster. She is going to her hairdresser's because they more than anyone else really understand her there and at this moment she needs her "real" self to be discovered and understood. But, at the hairdresser's everything is different. The shop is abnormally quiet; she is left waiting; when her hairdresser, George, comes out he is unshaven and inattentive. Only the wind continues to blow, hooting, mournful now. Creating another role for herself, she thinks:

"We whirl along like leaves, and nobody knows--nobody cares where we fall, in what black river we float away." As she is leaving, George tells her that his small daughter has died. She leaves the shop crying and enters a cab, telling the driver to take her to Prince's. On the way she sees a flower shop full of white flowers and thinks she will send some to the dead child. "From an unknown friend. . . .From one who understands. . . .For a Little Girl. . . ."She sees, herself, of course, in another role as the dead little girl, and the flowers commemorate her passing youth. She leans forward to tap on the glass, but it is too late; they are already at Prince's. The turmoil within Monica Tyrell, which is reflected in the blowing wind, is by this time close to hysteria and one wonders whether she will release her tensions by means of an emotional tirade or continue them through some other role.

"Poison" and "Je Ne Parle Pas Francais" are among the few stories told from a male viewpoint. In "Poison" a man recounts an earlier experience he had while he was young, innocent, and terribly in love with a woman already twice married. The poison is the shaping metaphor. He believes their love idyllic and throughout the whole episode is completely taken by her charm and beauty, while she, it is made clear, is waiting for the postman, for a letter that will call her away from their paradise. But no letters come, which prompts her to remark, "The world forgetting, by the world forgot." He is shaken for a moment and goes to smoke a cigarette and then trying to recapture his original feelings he goes over to where she has been reading a newspaper. But she tosses it aside saying there is nothing in it except a story about some murder trial, where "either some man did or didn't murder his wife." The young man wants to forget the newspaper, but she continues to talk:

> The man in the dock may be innocent enough, but the people in court are nearly all of them poisoners. Haven't you ever thought ...of the amount of poisoning that goes on? It's the exception to find married people who don't poison each other....Oh,...the number of cups of tea, glasses of wine, cups of coffee that are just tainted. The number I've had myself....Both my husbands poisoned me.

But the narrator objects, telling her that he hasn't tried to poison her and she is incapable of poisoning anyone. She isn't listening. "I was wondering," she interrupts, "whether after lunch you'd go down to the postoffice and ask for the afternoon letters." This does it. The young man lifts his glass and drinks and fancies that what he drinks tastes "chill, bitter, queer."

If the woman is the villain in "Poison," the narrator, Raoul Duquette, in "Je Ne Parle Pas Francais" outdoes her in villainry. The story is told in the first person by the protagonist who reveals everything about himself through his dialogue with other characters, responses to situations, and interior monologues. Most of what the narrator reveals about himself, he knows. He is constantly aware of his appearance and constantly analyzing his actions. He assumes the role of a kind of director on the stage of life, and at the end when he tries to cast himself in a real role opposite to a real woman, he withdraws from the situation, unable to fill the demands of the role. Like many others of Mansfield's male pseudo-artist types, he is vain, mannered, egotistical, parasitic, sensual, seductive, effeminate, both prostitute and pimp, but he is all of this to an extreme, the type par excellence, cast off and captured in one portrait that stands as an embodiment of the type, all the other "literary artists" being variations upon it -- the singing teacher in "Mr. Reginald Peacock's Day," the assemblage of "artists" in "Marriage a la Mode," Eddie Warren in "Bliss," the "literary gentleman" in "Life of Ma Parker," the absurd young painter in "Feuille d'Album," and perhaps, even, the pallid figure of the little corporal in "An Indiscreet Journey."

The latter story is a strange one, operating on a level somewhere between the real and unreal worlds. On the surface level it appears to recount the adventures of a young woman, the protagonist, who takes a journey into wartime France to meet a man. The purpose of the journey is never made very clear. The use of the word indiscreet in the title of the story may refer to the fact that this kind of travel was forbidden to civilians, or it may, on another level, suggest that the assignation itself without reference to the situation was indiscreet because in some way immoral. In fact, the guilt feelings of the narrator, together with the maze pattern that she runs, and the images used suggest that the whole story might operate on a dream level, embodying the sexual fears and fantasies of a young woman, prior to a first sexual experience. The story opens on a note of hysteria; the tone and pace is frantic; images are juxtaposed in absurd ways. The narrator asks directions and doesn't hear the answers; she doesn't know the time; people take on grotesque proportions. Indeed, at times, the story cries out its resemblance to Kafka tales: "But what could I have done? I could not arrive at X with two fishes hanging on a straw; and I am sure it is a penal offence in France to throw fish out of railway-carriage windows...." The invented aunt and uncle are unreal, but "more real, more solid than any relations I had ever known." The little corporal is almost a shadow figure, having no real proportions or substance; and he takes her to a white house and a white room. Later, she is unable to find a cafe even though they have been there to lunch and dinner every day. "But now in the dusk and alone I could not find it....I could not even remember what it looked like, or if there was a name painted on the outside, or any bottle or tables showing at the window." There are abrupt and jarring shifts in narrative and tonal patterns, and images suggesting religious connotations. The concierge is like St. Anne (the mother of the Virgin), playing a mother role; there is an old man carrying a basket of fish who appears as in a holy picture, but the narrator refuses to buy any, and feeling guilty, submits to God I and God II. The family in the last scene appear like a scene from the last supper, but the narrator stands outside, unable to participate.

The young couple in "Mr. and Mrs. Dove" are going to be married, but nothing in their relationship presages that their marriage will be a happy one. Indeed, the relationship between the male and female doves stands as a fore-shadowing of the relationship that has developed between the young man and woman and will continue to be maintained. The story is told through the viewpoint of the young man, Reggie, who is naive and innocent, a little foolish, but likeable. He is in England at his mother's home recovering from an illness contacted in Rhodesia where he works. The figure of his mother and his relationship with her helps to set his symbolic role. His mother is tall and stout, an imposing figure, aggressive. In a short episode she is seen in the garden with a scissors snapping the heads from dead plants. The scene is revealing:

"You are not going out, Reginald?" she asked, seeing that he was.
"I'll be back for tea, mater," said Reggie weakly, plunging his hands into his jacket pockets.
Snip. Off came a head. Reggie almost jumped.

He is on his way to visit a young woman, Anne, with whom he has fallen in love. Although he does not think that there is much chance that she could love him, he feels compelled to ask. The young woman, greets him with laughter, a habit. "For some strange reason that Reggie wished to God he understood, Anne had [always] laughed at him. The laughter acts as a harbinger to the coos of the doves which are heard before the doves are seen. "Coo-roo-coo-coo-coo.....Roo-coo-coo-coo." "To and fro, to and fro over the fine red sand on the floor of the dove house, walked the two doves. One was always in front of the other. One ran forward, uttering a little cry, and the other followed, solemnly bowing and bowing." Anne explains that the one in front is Mrs. Dove and the one following is Mr. Dove. But Reggie is not paying her any attention since he is gathering his courage to ask if she could love him. Finally he blurts it out and she answers that she could never marry a man she laughs at. Reggie accepts her statement conjuring in his mind a vision of the kind of tall, handsome, aggressive man she should marry. And: "He bowed to his vision." Anne admits that she has never been so happy with anyone as she has with Reggie, but she adds "we'd be like . . . like Mr. and Mrs. Dove." But when he turns to leave she is unhappy and calls him back to the accompaniment of the coo of the doves. "Come back, Mr. Dove," said Anne, And Reginald came slowly across the lawn."

The young couple in "Honeymoon" are, of course, already married, but the prognosis for their continued happiness is about as good as for the young couple in "Mr. and Mrs. Dove." With her usual skill, Mansfield fixes the situation in the opening lines of the story:

And when they came out of the lace shop there was their own driver and the cab they called their own cab waiting for them under a plane tree. What luck! Wasn't it luck? Fanny pressed her husband's arm. These things seemed always to be happening to them ever since they--came abroad. Didn't he think so too? But George stood on the pavement edge, lifted his stick, and gave a loud "Hi!"

The obvious difference in the responses of husband and wife to the same situation sets the structural pattern for the rest of the story. Very little happens in the way of a plot. They go to a restaurant, talk, and leave, but in the interim, their essential differences are underscored. George is adventuresome, matter of fact, authoritarian, parochial, non-romantic; Fanny is fearful, enthusiastic, accepting, romantic; and these differences will create problems after the honeymoon is over; an essential lack of communication will develop, perhaps similar to the kinds expressed in "Marriage a la Mode," "The Stranger," and "The Escape."

William and Isabel in "Marriage a la Mode" love one another, but they have been unable to communicate their needs to each other, and they have grown estranged. In the early years of their marriage, William had been happy in their little white house with blue curtains and a window box of petunias, but Isabel had been lonely, "pining for new people and new music and pictures." Then Isabel had met Moira Morrison and gone with her to Paris and come back a "new" woman. They had moved into a new and modern house in the suburbs, and Isabel was constantly surrounded by her artist friends, and William had become an appendage, necessary only to provide the house and the food and the pleasant surroundings, and now William is unhappy, continually filled with a dull, persistent gnawing, a constant ache. After one particular week-end "visit" to his home, William writes Isabel a letter, pouring his feelings out to her. Isabel reads the letter in the company of her friends, and not knowing how to respond laughs until her friends insist that she read the letter to them. She does, and they ridicule it. Now Isabel crushes the letter in her hand and goes to her room, filled with confused feelings. She thinks what a loathsome thing it was to read William's letter aloud, and she wants to answer it; but her friends call her from below, and the moment of crisis passes; she decides she'll write to William later, "And, laughing in the new way, she ran down the stairs." Neither are happy in the new relationship, but it will not change.

Nor will the relationship between husband and wife in "The Stranger" change. Their needs are different; they have not been able to communicate those needs, or to respond positively to them. Mr. and Mrs. Hammond are older than William and Isabel; they have been married a longer time; and Mr. Hammond has not realized quite so persistently that his wife is a stranger to him. As the story opens, Mr. Hammond is standing on the wharf waiting for his wife's ship to dock. There has been a delay of some kind and he waits anxiously, worried about his wife who has been away for ten months visiting their eldest daughter. When the ship finally does dock, Mr. Hammond is anxious to get his wife away so that he might be alone with her, and he puts off her questions about the children and other household matters. But his wife seems distracted and the more reassurance he seeks from her, the more withdrawn she appears. Finally, she tells him what had happened on board ship, causing the delay. A man had died of a heart attack in her arms. Mr. Hammond is so struck by the revelation that he finds it difficult to move and to breathe. That a man had died in her arms when she had never--"never once in all these years--never on one single solitary occasion" extended to him the same comfort is more than he can bear. He hides his face in her bosom and puts his arms around her, thinking that "they will never be alone together again," not knowing that they never really have been.

The man and woman in "The Escape" are not so well characterized and, therefore, the motivation for their behavior is not so completely revealed. The man appears to be the protagonist because what revelation there is in the story comes to him. More time, however, is spent in the characterization of the woman and the fact of her constant accusations and really paranoid behavior. The man appears long suffering and withdrawn. The episode which forms the basis for this story recounts a situation where the man is left alone for a few minutes to contemplate a tree which appears to be the central symbol of the story. As he looks at the tree he feels that his breathing seems to die away and that he becomes part of the silence, enfolded by it. This experience seems to provide some meaning for his life. Whereas before the episode with the tree he had felt hollow, parched, withered, made of ashes, afterwards he feels such a heavenly happiness that he wishes that he might live forever, in spite of the fact that his wife continues in her endless accusations.

"Marriage a la Mode," "The Stranger," and "The Escape" are basically stories of husbands who are frustrated in their relations with their wives, as is "The Man Without a Temperament," but in the latter story Robert Salesby's frustration takes a much more specific form and it is for a much more specific reason; Mrs. Salesby is ill, with a heart condition,[8] perhaps dying, and all around Mr. Salesby are reminders of his manhood. His sexual desires are held so strictly in check that he acts like a robot and appears completely unconcerned and unfeelinged. The essential pathos of the situation which finds a man and woman in love but unable to express their love is underscored because it is underplayed, and the symbolic act at the end which finds the man killing a mosquito and bloodying his fingers while his wife lies alone, already corpselike, brings together all elements of the story into a startling revelation of total meaning. The other characters in the story underline the man's frustrated sexual desires and pain. There are the two Topknots, spinster sisters, who sleep together and eat together, their two coils of knitting "like two snakes, slumbering besides the tray" that holds their food. There is the American Woman with her little dog, Klaymongso, curled in her lap, who sits protected from the great purple plant that hungrily watches her, while she plays up to it, "giving herself little airs." There is the servant girl, who behaves seductively, mocking Robert Salesby, "Vous desirez, Monsieur?" There are the three little girls who stand naked to the waist while they bathe and who shriek and hide when they see Robert Salesby; and there are the honeymoon couple, who exude sexuality:

> They were a very dark young couple--black hair, olive skin, brilliant eyes and teeth....And he kept mopping his forehead, rubbing his hands with a brilliant handkerchief. Her white skirt had a patch of wet; her neck and throat were stained and deep pink. When she lifted her arms big half-hoops of perspiration showed under her armpits; her hair clung in wet curls to her cheeks. She looked as though her young husband had been dipping her in the sea, and fishing her out again to dry in the sun and then-- in with her again--all day.

In contrast to this young woman, Mrs. Salesby appears ghostlike. She moves with light dragging steps, slowly; her voice is light and low, like a sigh. She sleeps, half-sitting, banked up with pillows, her white hands crossed on the sheet, silvered over in the moonlight.

But, if there are frustrated husbands, there are also frustrated wives. Isabel and Mrs. Hammond are unhappy and one might speculate that some kind of frustration caused the woman in "The Escape" to develop paranoic tendencies. Mrs. Salesby constantly seeks reassurance that she is not too much of a burden to her husband, knowing that she is, but not being able to change things or to recapture the past. She is as much caught in the cage as he is, as much enveloped in the circular trap of his signet ring which he is constantly turning and which she turns at the end of the story.

Andreas Binzer and his wife in "A Birthday" are prototypes of the later Stanley Burnell and Linda of the New Zealand stories, "Prelude" and "At the Bay." The title of "A Birthday" refers to the birth of a son to Andreas and Anne Binzer. The story moves from early morning to late morning when the child is born. Because his wife is in labor, Binzer has slept in the spare room on a narrow bed. This inconvenience has been a bother to him. His usual practice of putting his watch by his bed has been impossible. Instead he has had to put it under his pillow. As he listens to the watch, his mind begins to tick with it, counting off his well-established habits. Binzer is a creature of habit. Disorder of any kind disturbs him. The broken Venetian blind disturbs him. He thinks he will have to find someone to fix it. His selfish lack of concern for his wife becomes more apparent in an interior monologue: "Anne could do it herself if she was all right. So would I, for that matter, but I don't like to trust myself on rickety step-ladders." His excessive concern for his own well-being, his overbearing pride, his insecurity that reveals itself in a concern for appearance and in excessive guilt feelings, his fastidiousness, his complete lack of concern for others except as they function to maintain his well-being are skillfully revealed through his thought processes and ironically tagged "sensitivity": "I'm too sensitive for a man--that's what's the matter with me. Have been from the beginning, and will be to the end."

This is one of the first stories where Mansfield uses setting to build atmosphere and to contain a major metaphor. The story starts on a clear day. Than a storm blows up while Anne Binzer is in the throes of labor. The storm parallels the child birth: "...the sea swung heavily in rolling waves. Wind crept round the house, moaning drearily." Later the storm gets worse. The wind gusts: "The waves swelled up along the breakwater and were whipped with broken foam." Binzer is inconvenienced by the storm. "That means I'm boxed up here all day." Soon a wailing cry from upstairs merges with the sound of the wind. "The wind caught it up in mocking echo, blew it over the housetops, down the street, far away from him." Later the wind drops, the whole house is still, and the doctor comes to announce the birth of a boy.

The building storm helps to create an atmosphere of foreboding which leads to Binzer's perusal of his wife's picture. Church bells in the distance make him feel tender and he looks at the picture, remembering the vitality and joy his wife had had before their marriage. He kisses the picture. But the wailing cry borne away from him causes him to feel helpless and guilty once again. These guilt feelings eventually result in a manifestation of the death wish. As he continues to look at the picture he imagines the smile to be secret, even cruel. Finally he wants to hide the picture, or destroy it. "There was no good in beating about the bush. Anne looked like a stranger--abnormal--a freak--it might be a picture taken just before or after death. ✓Then, as a result of his need to absolve himself from all guilt, he imagines his wife to be dead so that he might truly suffer the attendant anguish. "My beloved wife has passed away!" But, when he hears of the birth of a son (the storm is over; things are back in order) his guilt feelings dissolve. "Well, by God! Nobody can accuse _me_ of not knowing what suffering is," he says.

Anne Binzer is never seen, but her presence in the house is pervasive, and what her life must be like with Andreas for a husband is a persistent subtheme in the story. What she was like before and after marriage is revealed through Binzer. Before their marriage she was happy and spirited, joyous, full of laughter. But marriage had changed her. Binzer says, "She had lost all her go in two months." They have been married four years and have three children. All the activities of the house are geared to Andreas' pleasure and interests, and there is no suggestion that there will be any change.

Linda and Stanley Burnell in "Prelude" and "At the Bay, provide a more detailed study of a marriage. Linda, almost invalided from childbearing reflects:

> Yes, that was her real grudge against life; that was what she could not understand. That was the question she asked and asked, and listened in vain for the answer. It was all very well to say it was the common lot of women to bear children. It wasn't true. She, for one, could prove that wrong. She was broken, made weak, her courage was gone, through childbearing. And what made it doubly hard to bear was, she did not love her children. It was useless pretending. Even if she had had the strength she never would have nursed and played with the little girls. No, it was as though a cold breath had chilled her through and through on each of those awful journeys; she had no warmth left to give them. As to the boy--well, thank heaven, mother had taken him....

But this function, seen as one imposed by a natural order, does not destroy her love for Stanley. An exploration of her thoughts and fantasies reveals that this love exists alongside equally strong feelings of hate: "For she really was fond of him, she loved and admired and respected him tremendously. Oh, better than anyone else in the world ....He was the soul of truth and decency...." But there is another feeling, hatred, just as real as the love, each sharp and defined, one as true as the other: "She could have done her feelings up in little packets and given them to Stanley. She longed to hand him the last one [the hatred], for a surprise. She could see his eyes as he opened that. . . " Through Linda, also, questions of life and death are examined, not only through the sexual role, but on a larger, more philosophical level: "She hugged her arms and began to laugh silently. How absurd life was--it was laughable, simply laughable. And why this mania, she thought, mocking and laughing."

Stanley provides the contrast of a male vitality and aggressiveness, the unquestioned acceptance of life and the order of life. Dominant and demanding, he shapes the pattern and the climate of family life to his specifications and understanding of what a family should be. But he has, like Linda, a human capacity to harbor strong opposing feelings and needs. He is alternately aggressive and dependent, self-assured and anxious, free and frustrated, child and adult.

Jonathan Trout, Linda's brother-in-law, provides another view of the same human problems. His character is almost a synthesis of Linda's and Stanley's. Sensitive and perplexed over the meaning and purpose of life and a failure as a provider when compared to Stanley, he, nevertheless, like Linda, is endowed with the ability to laugh at himself, and to enjoy and experiment with life in a way that Stanley, for all his strength, is not able to do. This capacity, along with the fact that he has produced two sons, Rags and Pip, stimulates in Stanley a mistrust of Jonathan. To Stanley, Jonathan is strong enough to be a threat; to Linda, he is weak enough to be pitied.

Women, whose lives are dominated by their men fill the pages of the early _Pension_ stories. It is a role that the narrator feels is ignominious and one which she is struggling to avoid. The German women have no interests except family concerns: husbands, sex, children, and like the Hausfrauen in "Frau Brechenmacher Attends a Wedding,"

"At Lehman's" and "The Child Who Was Tired" they are most often pregnant, swollen and spent, weary and aged beyond their years.

But spinsterhood is no answer. Mansfield provides a gallery of middle-aged spinsters, some of whom are sexually frustrated, all of whom are alienated from the mainstream of life. The two Topknots and the American Woman in "The Man Without a Temperament," Miss Brill in the story by that name, Ada Moss in "Pictures," Constantia and Josephine in "The Daughters of the Late Colonel," the unmarried daughters in "Father and the Girls."

Miss Brill is an impoverished middle-aged spinster, living in France, working occasionally as a tutor in English and as a reader for a very old gentleman. Her life is composed of a series of insignificant events which culminate in her weekly visits to the Jardins Publiques, the high point of her week. The slight plot line in the story reflects the inconsequentiality of her life. She goes to the public gardens, listens to the band, watches the people, overhears a conversation which disturbs her, and returns home. An aura of pathos pervades the story. Miss Brill has no life of her own, but must enter into the lives of the people whom she watches, as a spectator watching the drama of life taking place on a stage. Indeed, the major metaphor of the story involves the dramas that Miss Brill creates about the people whom she sees. She creates situations and dialogues to fit her naive imaginings. It occurs to her that she is watching as though she were part of an audience at a play, and then she has a further understanding, that she, too, has a role in the larger drama. She is part of the performance. The thought delights her. She is "An Actress!"

But her delight ends in despair. She overhears a boy and girl, who in her imagination she had endowed with characteristics that made them hero and heroine in a play to be enacted in her mind, speak dialogue that she had not created. The boy calls her stupid and the girl laughs at her fur piece, and Miss Brill is crushed. On her way home she does not buy her Sunday treat, a slice of honeycake, at the baker's. She climbs the stairs to her dark room, enters the room, small as a cupboard, and sits down on the red eiderdown that covers the bed. Finally she unclasps her fur piece and quickly puts it inside its box, but as she puts the lid on, she thinks she hears something crying. The fur piece, of course, is to be identified with Miss Brill. When she takes it out of the box and shakes out the moth powder and gives it a good brushing, attempting to rub life back into it and when she puts it back into the box and hears it cry, the situation parallels her own activities as she readies herself to go out and then returns to her own dark little box.

Ada Moss of "Pictures" is a kind of Miss Brill, but not quite. Cheerful in the face of threatening disaster, she lapses into comforting fantasies until she creates a final role, a distasteful one, but carried off in regal style. Ada Moss is almost an extension of the character of Viola presented in the earlier "The Swing of the Pendulum." Indeed, it is easy to see Viola after some twenty-five years as being an Ada Moss and Ada Moss some twenty-five years before as being a Viola. The stories open in a similar manner. In both a landlady comes in to insist that the rent be paid, and both respond by creating fantasies. But Ada Moss is not twenty and there is no Casimir, only a very stout gentleman who offers a kind of comfort for the night and not for a lifetime, and Ada Moss ventures into the prostitution that Viola had considered as a possibility. And being older, she realizes that a prostitute is not always a courtesan.

Josephine and Constantia in "The Daughters of the Late Colonel" are brilliant creations. Middle-aged, they appear at times to be teenagers and at times to be senile, so that in their characterization Mansfield is able to present the spectrum of women's lives, indeed, from birth to death. In bed, Josephine assumes a fetal position; Constantia resembles a corpse. A gamut of emotions ranges from the absurd to the pathetic, and time is treated as a merger of past and future in the present. Dominated all their lives by their father, when he dies they are cut loose. Their time and habits are bound by the thumping of his stick; when it stops the clock ticks, "What now? What now?" Purposeless, unfullfilled, they know, there is something more. They have always known. Stirrings within them have driven them to assume strange postures. Constantia, especially, the younger, the least aggressive, had been compelled by the moon when it was full to lie on the floor "with her arms outstretched, as though she was crucified," while "horrible dancing figures" on a carved screen leer at her. Totally naive she had not recognized that the motivation for her behavior lay in sexual longing. At the end of the story the sun shines on them, beckoning, but they hesitate, and the sun retreats behind a cloud, and they are lost forever.

Familiar with the remarkable achievement in "The Daughters of the Late Colonel," a reader is frustrated to find "Fathers and Girls" incomplete. The spinster daughters, Edith and Emily, and the situation in which they find themselves have only just begun to be presented when the story breaks off and the reader left suspended, curious.

These middle-aged women have adolescent longings although their lives are metaphorically ended, and the pathos is that they have never lived. The old people, too, come to the end of their lives either questioning their achievement or withdrawing from the question, taking comfort in the old patterns that have sustained them. They, too, live outside of the mainstream, most of them in homes with their children, where they can see the problems, but are impotent to correct them. The grandmother in "New Dresses" cannot really help Helen except to buy her a new doll. The grandmother and the grandfather in "The Voyage" can provide a home for their orphaned grandchild, but they face death;

Ma Parker in "The Life of Ma Parker," cannot even find a place to cry until it rains and then it appears that the whole earth cries with her; the old woman in "The Canary" can only mourn the death of her bird who had provided her with love and a reason for living; old Mr. Neave in "An Ideal Family" is too tired to continue in the old patterns and he has become alienated from his family: "He'd been forgotten. What had all this to do with him--this house and Charlotte, the girls and Harold--what did he know about them? They were strangers to him. Life had passed him by." The Boss in "The Fly" can only reenact the drama of his life and when the fly dies, he knows his own life must end; and Mrs. Fairchild in "Prelude" and "At the Bay" can only continue in the old patterns, imposing order in the arrangement of furniture and by the ritual of everyday activities.

Seldom are Mansfield's plots spectacular; her characters extraordinary; or their feelings manifested in overtly violent behavior. Exceptions are "The-Child-Who-Was-Tired," "The Woman at the Store," "Millie," and "Ole Underwood." The dream aura cast over "The-Child-Who-Was-Tired" creates an element of unreality, causing the murder to be seen as a symbolic act. "The Woman at the Store" and "Millie" are less successful stories. Both lack a clear focus, causing the behavior of the characters to appear unmotivated, the plots contrived. "The Woman at the Store" appears to be about a woman who was driven by loneliness and despair to murder her husband, but the framework for the story, the other characters, and particularly the narrator seem out of place, not integrally related to the whole, lacking a real function. The motivation for Millie's behavior is never clarified. A roughened farm woman, she is childless, but she maintains that it doesn't bother her that she has no children, and there is no reason provided for the reader either to believe or disbelieve this statement. Later, when she meets the injured boy, who is accused of murder, maternal feelings spring up. Still later, a kind of blood lust emerges from her as she joins in the cry to apprehend the boy. But no reasons are provided for any of her actions. A lack of adequate foreshadowing results in a lack of credibility. "Ole Underwood" is more successful; again, because an inner reality is merged with an outer reality, creating one large scene which beats with tension. The pulsating rhythm provided by the syntax of the sentences, the beating of Underwood's heart, matched with the gusty movements of the wind lead to the final episode of the story which is shrouded in an ambiguity that is adequately prepared for. The scene may be real, may be hallucinatory. It does not really matter, because the two orders of reality have been merged. It is significant that these four stories are early stories and that when Miss Mansfield found her metier she never returned to extraordinary characters or situations.

One story, "Bank Holiday," stands almost as a metaphor embodying themes and characters. There is no single protagonist; rather all the people gathered together at a fair create a composite picture of man.

> And up, up the hill come the people, with ticklers and golliwogs, and roses and feathers. Up, up they thrust into the light and heat, shouting, laughing, squealing, as though they were being pushed by something, far below, and by the sun, far ahead of them—drawn up into the full, bright, dazzling radiance to. . .what?

But, created characters made live, are given their vitality by skillful characterization, where all the elements of the story function to present a character, where, as Professor Berkman says, "Every detail of presentation is selected to convey the emotional timbre of a central character, an intensification of the individual to which the situation itself is subordinate."[9] (163-164) The presentation of the character is a matter of technique, of the use of point of view, in an over-all design, and in order to see exactly how it is done it is necessary to examine more closely Mansfield's particular use of these elements; it is necessary to discover her particular techniques.

Chapter Five

POINT OF VIEW

With the disappearance from modern fiction of the author-commentator as view-point character and with the conscious awareness of modern writers that view point is an integral part of any story creating the perspective and many of the complexities, the technical device of point of view has come into increasing prominence as an element of fiction meriting careful study. Given this fact, it is surprising the Mansfield scholars, knowing that she used a wide variety of viewpoints, experimenting with them all, and finally creating a perspective entirely her own, have shown so little insight into her use of the first person narrator in her early stories, insisting that the narrator is Mansfield herself and that the lack of subtleties in the stories are the result of the author's own immature perspective. If, however, as I have indicated earlier, the first person narrator in the Pension stories is recognized as a complex character, interacting with the other characters, the stories can be recognized as considerably more subtle than they are usually considered to be. It is first necessary to appreciate the fact that seven of the stories collected in In a German Pension are related to one another in much the same way as the stories collected in Anderson's Winesberg, Toomer's Cane, and Joyce's Dubliners. The seven stories, taken together, present a gallery of people presented as typically German and a narrator, a young Englishwoman whose involvement in what might be called the German colony undergoes a developmental pattern. Further, the first person narrator is the protagonist in each of the stories. In each she is pitted against one or more of the Germans. It is true that in each of the stories certain sub-themes develop, but the major struggle remains one between the narrator and the other people.

In "Germans At Meat," for example, the Germans are characterized by means of their behavior at table. It is significant that the word is meat, not meal. The connotations suggest a kind of brutality, perhaps even butchery, a blood lust. A comparison, however, is immediately set-up. The narrator is a vegetarian. The entire story takes place at the dinner table where the English narrator, along with all of the others, is taking a cure somewhere in Germany. The central symbolic situation involves the food. The story begins with the sentence, "Bread soup was placed upon the table." Not vegetable soup, not clear soup, but "bread" soup, something heavy and filling. The Germans are very interested in food; the narrator is not. The note of conflict is begun early. The narrator attempts to insert "just the right amount of enthusiasm into her voice," as she comments, "How interesting," in answer to Herr Rat's declaration, "I am a good cook myself!" Later it is revealed that the narrator, though married, has paid no attention to what might be her husband's favorite meat. Herr Rat is not married. His egocentricity and selfishness are quickly revealed. "I have had all I wanted from women without marriage." Through the meal, a five course dinner, including the bread soup, veal with sauerkraut and potatoes, beef with red currants and spinach, stewed apricots, and cherry cake with whipped cream, the Germans comment on the amount of food consumed by the British. "Do they really eat so much?...Soup and baker's bread and pig's flesh, and tea and coffee and stewed fruit, and honey and eggs, and cold fish and kidneys and hot fish and liver?"

The narrator's fastidiousness is contrasted with the vulgarity of the Germans. Herr Rat blows upon his soup as he eats; the traveler from North Germany speaks of his inability to retain sauerkraut; the widow picks her teeth with a hairpin and introduces the subject of childbirth; the traveler spears his potato with a knife; Herr Hoffman speaks of sweating and wipes his face and neck and cleans his ears with the dinner napkin. Whenever possible the narrator attempts to change the subject away from unpleasantries:

"...but now I have eaten so much of it that I cannot retain it. I am immediately forced to--
"A beautiful day!" I cried....
....
"Five healthy babies--though after the first one was born I had to--
"How wonderful!" I cried.

German criticism of the narrator is implicit. Both separately and together they are an overbearing force she cannot resist. When the British are accused of eating too much, a fact the narrator has not the strength to refute, all eyes turn to the Englishwoman. "I felt I was bearing the burden of the nation's preposterous breakfast--I who drank a cup of coffee while buttoning my blouse in the morning." Being put on the defensive she attempts to show her ability. "Ah, that's one thing I _can_ do," said I, laughing brightly. "I can make very good tea!" But they ridicule her revelation of the secret to warm the teapot.

The essential hostitlity and overweaning pride of the Germans is finally expressed in terms of national conflicts. "You have got no army at all--a few little boys with their veins full of nicotine poisoning.... Don't be afraid....We don't want England....We really want you." The narrator bristles, sitting upright, "We certainly do not want Germany, I said."

Except for the broad strokes of characterization, few subtleties are involved in this one story. The narrator ends by retreating, but in dignity, closing the door behind her.

"The Baron," the next story in the collection, is a variation upon the same theme. Again, food is symbolic, but in this one more attention is paid to sickness. The Baron is sick; all the guests are sick, and the narrator is drawn unknowingly into an even greater sickness. At the beginning of the story it is clear that the narrator is not "properly" impressed by royalty as the Germans are. A German baron is at the pension. (Baron--barren?) Everyone looks at him in awe, but he keeps strictly to himself, the first to enter the dining room, the last to leave, but alone at every meal, sitting with his back to the company, never speaking to anyone, never even entering the salon where the guests gather to converse. He comes every year for his nerves, and the guests are waiting for the time when he will honor someone by speaking to him. He is a small man, slight, with scanty black hair and beard and a yellow complexion, with an air of sickness about him. When the narrator first notices him he is absorbed in eating a whole lettuce leaf, nibbling as a rabbit would. The narrator at first doesn't understand the guest's snobbishness, but, later, she, too, entertains visions of the time when the baron will speak to someone. "Surely he will honor the Frau Oberregierungerat or the Frau Feldleutnantswitwe <u>once</u> before he goes." But it is the narrator who is so honored. On the day when the baron is scheduled to leave he shares an umbrella with her and answers the question. "I sit alone that I may eat more," said the Baron..."My stomach requires a great deal of food. I order double portions, and eat them in peace." "And what do you do all day?" the narrator persists. "I imbibe nourishment in my room," he replies. When they arrive back at the Pension, the unusual occurrence of the baron accompanying someone nearly causes a riot. Two of the guests send gifts to the narrator honoring her exalted position. But the next day the baron is gone, and "Sic transit gloria German mundi."

In "The Sister of the Baroness," Mansfield plays another variation upon the same themes, but the narrator is drawn even more intimately into the overall sickness. In this story the narrator feels closer to the Germans, using the pronoun "we" during much of the narration.

> Each guest who came into the dining room was bombarded with the wonderful news. "The Baroness von Gall is sending her little daughter here; the Baroness herself is coming in a month's time." Coffee and rolls took on the nature of an orgy. We positively scintillated: we gorged on scandals of High Birth generously buttered.

But despite the narrator's feelings of belonging, the manager and guests persist in reminding her that she is a foreigner. They take the picture of the Kaiserin Elizabeth from over her bed to hang over the sofa of the royalty. The narrator comments: "I felt a little crushed. Not at the prospect of losing that vision of diamonds and blue velvet but, but at the tone--placing me outside the pale--branding me as a foreigner."

The child comes, accompanied by a woman who says she is the Baroness' sister. She is friendly, smiling and conversing. Everyone is delighted: "Absorbing days followed. Had she been one whit less beautifully born we could not have endured the continual conversation about her, the songs in her praise, the detailed account of her movements. But she graciously suffered our worship and we were more than content."

The poet from Munich and the student from Bonn are especially taken with the sister of the baroness. The poet writes verses to her; the student takes her walking. The narrator finds herself caught up in the romantic ferver. She reads love poems and tries to write poetry, but she is not satisfied with the results. "Did my wild rose then already trail in the dust? I chewed a leaf and hugged my knees." Then a magic moment comes. She overhears the student and the sister of the baroness where they are talking in the summer house. A second-hand romance, the narrator thinks, is better than none; so she listens. But the magic moment is lost for the narrator, and she throws down her volume of Morike's poems when she hears the student explaining that he cannot kiss the girl, even though he longs to, because he is suffering from severe nasal catarrh. Shortly thereafter the magic moment is broken for everyone else. The Baroness arrives and reveals that the girl is an impostor. She has no sister; the girl is the daughter of her dressmaker. In this way Mansfield underlines the gullibility and foolishness of the Germans, but it is quite clear also that the narrator has been gullible also, and has behaved foolishly.

Whereas in these three stories the narrator has either been overpowered, desirous of becoming part of the larger group, or intimately drawn into the group, in "Frau Fisher," she rejects the group of German women and what they consider a woman's proper role. German women are concretized in the person of Frau Fisher, a sexually frustrated widow. The landlady of the pension is also a widow with five marriageable daughters, and the narrator, of course, is separated from her husband. The only man who figures as a character in this story is Herr Rat, whom the reader remembers from "Germans at Meat." But he is, as the narrator remarks, "a shorn Samson." In this story the narrator's conception of a virgin purity is contrasted with the coarse fecundity of the German woman. Frau Fisher attempts to draw the narrator into a conversation about her sexual needs: "My dear, I am a woman of experience, and I know the world. While he is away you have a fever in your blood....At home you cannot bear the sight of that empty bed--it is like widowhood. Since the death of my dear husband I have never known an hour's peace."

The narrator protests, "I like empty beds," and later she declares, "I consider childbearing the most ignominious of all professions." But Frau Fisher will not listen: "Handfuls of babies, that is what you are really in need of." When she is ready to leave Frau Fisher squeezes the hand of the narrator and promises that she will come back to finish the conversation, "But," the narrator comments, "I did not squeeze back."

"The Modern Soul" opens with a man squeezing the narrator's hands, and she not only squeezes back, metaphorically speaking, but she eventually becomes very angry and takes vengeful action before she withdraws from the situation. Somewhat different in plot movement, "The

Modern Soul" is arranged in a tripartite structure. In the first episode the narrator is sitting with a German professor in the garden. He is just back from practicing his trombone in a pine tree forest. He offers her cherries, which she refuses. "I prefer watching you eat them." He responds by commenting upon the feminine sensibility which prefers "etherealized sensations." But, all cherries have worms, he says, and "if one wishes to satisfy the desires of nature one must be strong enough to ignore the facts of nature." The phallic implications of the wormy cherries are clear, but the narrator remains detached. Then two ladies appear, one old and scraggy, the mother Frau Godowska, the other young and thin with mauve sweet peas in her hair, the daughter, Fraulein Sonia. The Herr Professor is taken with the young one, calling her a modern soul, a tigress with a flower in her hair. The narrator wants to leave, but the professor notes, "I think they would consider it a little 'marked' if you immediately retire to the house at their approach, after sitting here alone with me in the twilight." The narrator shrugs, but remains. When the two women come up, Frau Godowska is complaining about her hay fever and Fraulein Sonia is making sweeping gestures, carried away by a rose growing in the garden. The professor introduces the narrator. "She is the stranger in our midst. We have been eating cherries together."

The second episode is concerned with a musicale which is being given by some guests for the benefit of afflicted Catholic infants. The professor plays his trombone and Sonia performs a recitation. "She implored us not to go into the woods in trained dresses, but rather as lightly draped as possible, and bed with her among the pine needles." Afterwards, Fraulein Sonia invites the narrator for a walk. Although it is not clear here, it becomes apparent in the third episode that Fraulein Sonia wants to stake a claim on the Herr Professor and to make the narrator aware of it.

The third episode concerns the conversation between the two women during their walk. The narrator is matter of fact, even somewhat fractious, as Fraulein Sonia waxes poetic and romantic. Her problem, she says is her mother, who constantly brings up common, ordinary problems, when she longs to do wild passionate things. The narrator is not sympathetic. She suggests, in order: 1) that the Fraulein leave her mother; 2) that she marry her to the Herr Professor. The latter suggestion upsets the modern soul so much that she cries out: "You, you ....The cruelty. I am going to faint. Mama to marry again before I marry--the indignity. I am going to faint here and now." And she does. Annoyed, the narrator leaves her there, and still angry, she tells the Herr Professor and then refuses to accompany him back to where Fraulein Sonia lies. The man protests: "I cannot be so indelicate as to attempt to loosen her stays." "Modern souls oughtn't to wear them," the narrator replies.

The next morning Fraulein Sonia and the Herr Professor have gone off together on a day's excursion into the woods. "I wondered," is the narrator's final comment. In view of the imagery in the story, it seems clear that the narrator is wondering whether Sonia is, again metaphorically speaking, about to eat cherries with worms.

In "The Luft Bad," the narrator notes at the outset that people look ridiculous at the bath, strolling around on the beach, nearly naked, and concludes at the end of the story that she is not in the least ashamed of her legs. Like the other Pension stories discussed here, the major metaphor running through this one is sickness: "And in all weather we take the air--walking, or sitting in little companies talking over each other's ailments and measurements and ills that flesh is heir to." Throughout the story the narrator exhibits an extreme self-consciousness about her appearance, and the reader is reminded that in no story has she ever revealed the reason for her being at the pension or the nature of her illness. As is usual, at the end of the story she withdraws to hide behind her husband's umbrella.

"The Advanced Lady" is the last of the stories in the Pension collection, using the first person narrator. It concerns an excursion made by the company to an inn in the country. In this one the narrator is pitted against "the advanced lady," a woman writer who is writing a novel about the "Modern Woman," who is the "incarnation of comprehending Love." Given the narrator's rejection of this role for women, it is understandable that she carries on a continual verbal skirmish with the lady novelist, proclaiming at the end, "Ignorance must not go uncontradicted."

The persistent satiric tone of the first person narrator in the Pension stories is the result not only of the sharp attacks on the crudity of the Germans, but also of the perspective taken by the narrator. Mansfield causes her to maintain a certain distance on herself, so that her feelings, thoughts, and actions are also objects of the satire. This is the same method that is used in "Pension Seguin," "Violet," and "Bains Turcs," stories that were conceived together and submitted to the New Age under the titles, Epilogues I, II, and III. In "Pension Seguin," the narrator, the same young woman, is tired and apprehensive after looking all morning for a room, when she arrives at the Pension Seguin. A servant lets her in and as she sits waiting for the landlady she notes in a sardonic manner that there are a superfluous number of white mats dominating the decor of the room. The sardonic attitude is not inconsistent with the position taken immediately afterwards that the mats are "signs and tokens of virtue and sobriety." It is obvious that the narrator doesn't think much of crocheted mats, but she is tired and she latches on to them to help convince herself that she has found a quiet place to stay. But even the rationalization has a touch of sardonic humor. The narrator might be fooling herself, but she knows that she is: "A woman with such sober passions," thought I, "is bound to be quiet and clean, with few babies and a much absent husband." The same kind of humor continues and manifests itself in her flight of fancy: "And I began to dream of unpacking...in the delicious autumn air that smelled of apples and honey," and, after the landlady arrives, in her response to the landlady's statement that the former occupant of the room had been summoned by his dead father. The narrator hopes that the Hamlet-like apparition is at rest again. This humor leads to the narrator's comment on appearance versus reality, and this comment is as much rationalization as is the earlier response. The paragraph begins by referring to the apparition:

> I have always viewed with a proper amount of respect and abhorrence those penetrating spirits who are not susceptible to appearance. What is there to believe in except appearances? I have nearly always found that they are the only things worth enjoying at all, and if ever an innocent child lays its head upon my knees and begs for the truth of the matter, I shall tell it the story of my one and only nurse, who, knowing my horror of gooseberry jam, spread a coat of apricot over the top of the jam jar. As long as I believed it apricot I was happy, and learning wisdom, I contrived to eat the apricot and leave the gooseberry behind. "So you see, my little innocent creature," I shall end, "the great thing to learn in this life is to be content with appearances, and shun the vulgarities of the grocer and the philosopher."

This paragraph, together with the wry humor in the story provides its unifying element. The landlady, of course, turns out to be anything but virtuous and sober, and the place anything but quiet. The dramatized episodes that follow become exemplums contradicting the appearances until the final point is made that Madame Seguin did not crochet the mats.

In "Violet," Mansfield makes use of the same place, the same narrator, and the same kind of sardonic humor. Again the narrator takes a perspective on herself which allows her to become the object of the satire. The story opens with the narrator's thoughts about proverbs, which are unctuous and irritating, but nevertheless true. Still, "what comfort can it be to one steeped to the eyebrows in clouds to ponder over their linings." Nevertheless, her room in the morning light is lovely, a fact not to be denied, but rather turned into a fancy. Her room is "bright with sunlight as if every golden-haired baby in Heaven were pelting the earth with buttercup posies." This fancy delights the narrator and turns her thought to an imagined interview with one Katherine Tynan. In the interview the narrator takes the position that proverbs are true. But she finds herself thinking that the role she assumes is a coarse one and she is "an impossible creature." The gentle, tender, and brooding Katherine Tynan prevails in the fantasy, having the final say, "But if you were Saint Francis, the bird would not <u>mind</u> being in your hand. It would prefer the white nest of your hand to any bush." The aura created by the imagined Katherine carries over to the reality and the narrator springs from her bed and goes to the window. The charming little houses below remind her of children and children's games and she imagines a lovely creature, Yvette. "She spends her mornings in a white lace boudoir cap, worked with daisies, sipping chocolate...."

This kind of imagining continues until the dream is interrupted by the reality of a servant on a balcony beating rugs and an old gentleman in a window opposite who shoots "a jet of spittle out of the window."

Sobered, but still rationalizing, the narrator reflects on sentiments that she calls pious and smug about the world being fine "if it were not for the people." Then she goes for a walk which allows her to regain the image of children playing, and she imagines that she is amusing herself, as a child does, playing a solitary game. But the child's game is again interrupted by a meeting with an old friend, Violet Burton. At first the narrator is friendly because it is obvious that Violet is glad to see her, but a remark by Violet causes the narrator to withdraw:

"But What are you here for?"

". . .Nerves."

"Oh, impossible, I really can't believe that."

"It is perfectly true," I said, my enthusiasm waning. There is nothing more annoying to a woman than to be suspected of nerves of iron.

Wrapped in her own problems, Violet is really not aware of the narrator and the narrator continues to assume a pose of indifference. "Why do you persist in denying your emotions?" Violet demands to know. "I keep them tucked away," the narrator answers, "like little pats of jam." "There you are again!" Violet exclaims. "Emotions and jam!"

It is not that the narrator doesn't have emotions obviously. The first part of the story proclaims them strongly and indicates her propensity for daydreams. It is just that she does not want to nibble on Violet's jam. But one bite whets the appetite, and although she "doesn't know how to sympathize," she is curious, "Do go on." But the romantic secret that Violet finally reveals amounts to nothing. "Is that all?" I cried. "You can't mean to say that's all?" And again the narrator's fancy is broken. This is why the fountain at the end of the story laughs not at Violet but at the narrator, at her habit of creating balloons of fancies made to be pricked by the pin of reality.

"Bains Turcs" repeats many of the same themes that are explored in the Pension stories. At first glance it may appear that the narrator in this story is not the protagonist, but merely an observer, an object at whom the German woman rails, as audience for the two blond women, and a sounding board against which the final statement reverberates. This kind of reading of the story would make the German lady the protagonist whose desires are revealed at the end as motivations for her speech and behavior in the bath. The nasty comments that she makes about the two blond women, pictured as prostitutes, can be seen to be sour grapes, motivated by her own frustrations. It is possible, however, to argue that the narrator plays the same role in this story as she had in the others, and that the drama that is played out before her is an object lesson of acute interest to her as she seeks to find the role she must play. The German woman follows the narrator about like a grotesque shadow, reflecting what she might become.

These stories were written in 1913. Earlier, in 1910, Mansfield wrote two stories that used a first person narrator in much the same way. "The Journey to Bruges" recounts the adventures of a young woman who travels by train and boat to Bruges. She is not merely an observer, although she has no real interaction with any of the other characters. She seems loose; she is unsure of herself. She spends a great deal of time running around on the train platform. On the train she is in a compartment with four young men who carry on a light conversation around her. On the boat everybody speaks in French phrases. The young woman goes to her cabin and then to the deck and then back to her cabin. Her wanderings seem aimless. She moves detached. She seems on the outside, living other people's lives, in a manner similar to Miss Brill of the later story. The failure of any real point to emerge from this story is the result of the failure of the story and not of the use of point of view. One gets the idea that the youthful Mansfield was trying to capture a microcosm as she did very shortly thereafter in the Pension stories. Indeed, one paragraph in the story provides the base for such a microcosm:

> In the shortest sea voyage there is no sense of time. You have been in the cabin for hours or days or years. Nobody knows or cares. You know all the people to the point of indifference. You do not believe in dry land any more--you are caught in the pendulum itself, and left there, idly swinging....

But, although one can imagine how the story might have been integrated around a central point, it is not. The focus wavers; the touch is unsure.

"A Truthful Adventure," which makes use of the same narrator, is a better story. It is composed of a series of juxtaposed incidents designed to show the inability of people to do anything but what they are used to. In this one the narrator is sitting in the waiting room of a hotel reading a guide book to Bruges which tells of the peace and calm of the town which enchants the eye and inspires the soul. The narrator is much taken with the description, and while waiting, dreams of the peaceful times that she will spend there: "At the evensong I shall lie in the long grass...and look up at the elm trees--their leaves touched with gold light and quivering in the blue air--listening the while to the voices of nuns at prayer in the little chapel...." The hotel keeper, a lady, comes in to tell the narrator that there is no room for her. She is influenced by the fact that the young woman has no luggage with her, but when she learns that the narrator plans to spend some time in Bruges, she finds an empty room for the girl. Her cleverness and mercenary attitude, of course, contrast with the view of Bruges given in the guide book, as does the dining room. The narrator is the only guest. A tired waiter holding a limp napkin serves her. The walls hold many mirrors which reflect empty tables. Her room, pink and vulgar, also contrasts with the ideal. But the narrator is not daunted. She climbs into bed and starts to dream again of the quiet house and the old typical servant. Her reveries are broken immediately, however, by the sound of voices. She can hear every word of a trivial argument taking place between a husband and wife in the room next to hers. They are visitors, too, and the woman is moaning about her tired and inflamed feet and the man grumbling about visiting art galleries.

The next day the narrator tries to hire a little boat that the guide book had suggested, but she is badgered into hiring a guide also and then into allowing a fat couple to accompany her. Later, after the fat lady has fallen into the water, the narrator escapes. "They may think me as drowned as they please," thought I, "I have had quite enough of canals to last me a lifetime."

The next juxtaposed incident is the climactic one. The narrator is lying under a tree, doing nothing and feeling guilty about it, when she recognizes an old school friend with her husband. They try to get the narrator to tour Bruges with them, but the thought horrifies her and she invents an excuse. They try to engage her in familiar arguments, saying, "You know, after the strenuous life in London, one does seem to see things in such a different light in this old-world city." The narrator answers ironically, "Oh, a very different light indeed," and shakes her head at the sight of the familiar guide book emerging from the man's pocket.

The narrator in "An Indiscreet Journey" is a young woman very similar to the narrator in the stories discussed above. Her tensions and problems are much the same, although there is no question that the narrator in "An Indiscreet Journey" is the protagonist of that story. The casting of the story in the first person allows for the abrupt and jarring transitions and the tone of frenzy and hysteria that pervades the story. There are only two Mansfield stories where the narrator is not the protagonist--"The Young Girl" and "The Woman at the Store"-- and both stories would have been better had they been cast in another point of view. As discussed earlier, the narrator in "The Young Girl" is an ambiguous figure, whose position and function can be justified only if she is seen as a woman and thus a segment of the pattern of life, but there is no argument to justify the point of view used in "The Woman at the Store." The first person narrator in that story is another young woman, but the reader is not clear about her sex until the feminine pronoun is used in association with her rather late in the story. She is probably the wife of one of the men, although this is never made clear, and she is the sister of the other. These three people are making a journey on horseback through the rough New Zealand country, and they come across a house where a woman is living with her daughter. They stop for the night. The brother, Jo, is starved for female company, and despite the haggard appearance of the woman, makes arrangements to spend the night with her. The daughter is sent to sleep in the store with the narrator and her husband. Later, the daughter reveals through a drawing that the mother has killed her husband. The next morning the narrator and Jim leave, leaving Jo behind who shouts to them that he will catch up with them later.

Much has been made of the so-called "naturalistic technique," which Mansfield employs in this early story. It was written for the magazine _Rhythm_ which set pity and brutality and a carefully wrought plot with adequate foreshadowing as its esthetic goal. But, although the editors of _Rhythm_ like it, it is really a poor story. Mansfield seems to go out of her way to emphasize the ugliness and the brutality, and although there is foreshadowing, it is blatant. The effect of the denoument on the narrator is awkwardly handled and lacks credibility. In fact, the narrator gets in the way of the most interesting part of the story, the developing Mansfield style that creates tone and movement. The story begins well, the naturalistic details used to functional advantage; the syntax and word choice, especially the verbs, creating an oppressive atmosphere: "All that day the heat was terrible. The wind blew close to the ground; it rooted among the tussock grass, slithered along the road, so that the white pumice dust swirled in our faces, settled and sifted over us...." But the narrator intrudes, breaking the spell. Details are not allowed to speak for themselves: "Hundreds of larks shrilled; the sky was slate colour, and the sound of the larks reminded me of slate pencils scraping over its surface."

In only five more stories does Mansfield attempt the first person narrator, all are told by men, three are incomplete, four make use of a "fallible" narrator. The exception is "Poison," told in the first person by the protagonist about a time when he was a young man of twenty-four, innocent and naive, having an affair with an older woman and having his idealistic views shattered by her behavior. The point of view makes the story credible and provides the ironic tone. The woman is seen through a kind of double vision, through the eyes of the young man and through the perspective of the older one. This provides a certain complexity for an otherwise fairly simple story.

The much lauded use of the fallible narrator in "Je Ne Parle Pas Francais" is really not much different from the use of the narrator in the _Pension_ and related stories, discussed above. In all of them more is revealed about the narrator than the narrator knows about himself. The difference is of degree and complexity. Raoul Duquette is more complex than the naive young Englishwoman of the _Pension_ stories and "Je Ne Parle Pas Francais" is a much more subtle and profound statement. Duquette's dramatic sense, his habit of creating roles for himself and other people, the parallel metaphor that life is a stage which creates the microcosm in which the drama is played, the play within a play involving Mouse and Dick Harmon, all combine to create the feeling of immediacy and intimate knowledge that one gains from "Je Ne Parle Pas Francais."

The incomplete stories, "Daphne," "A Married Man's Story," and "A Bad Idea" give evidence of having been conceived to parallel "Je Ne

Parle Pas Francais" in style and movement. "A Married Man's Story" is typical of this kind of effort. The story opens on a kind of interior monologue to reveal a most unpleasant narrator, whose character was perverted by childhood experiences in much the same way that Duquette was perverted by his experiences with the African laundress. Like "Je Ne Parle Pas Francais," "A Married Man's Story" builds slowly, the narrator's background and present responses dovetailed. The narrator of the latter story is writing his story, choosing his words and phrases carefully in the same manner as Duquette. Gradually an ominous tone develops until the reader wonders what horrible thing the narrator is planning for his quiet and uncomplaining wife.

"The Canary," which Murry says is Mansfield's last completed story is a straight dramatic monologue, as is "Late at Night" but they are both more sketches than stories. "Late at Night" is told by a woman who feels she is getting along in years and has not yet had a chance to love, to express herself, to come into flower. She has sent a pair of socks to a man and he has answered in a malicious letter. The focus of the piece wavers. It is not clear whether the story is ironic or the woman simply pathetic. "The Lady's Maid" and "Two Tuppenny Ones, Please" are both kinds of dramatic monologues. The protagonists of each speak lines as though in a play, but the speeches of the other characters are not given. However, the nature of their responses is clear from the dialogue presented. The situations are similar to what one would hear if he heard one side of a telephone conversation. Both stories are very slight. What characterization there is comes, of course, solely through the speeches. "The Black Cap" is a small drama with dialogue and characters and stage directions. The first scene presents a husband and wife in a conversation which reveals that the wife is leaving her husband. The scene involving the woman on the way to the station is presented by means of dramatic monologue, which is sustained until the meeting with the lover; then the dialogue picks up again. The lover has lost his hat and he wears a borrowed black cap. She thinks he looks ridiculous and feels that if he cannot see the absurdity he is not the man for her. This scene leads to another monologue in the taxi which returns her home. There is a neat revelation of the woman's character throughout, but the whole piece is slight. These sketches (it is difficult to call them stories) have the appearance of being experiments in uses of point of view. It is almost as though Mansfield was deliberately trying to see whether points of view different from the usual ones in short fiction could be made functional. In "Spring Picture," for example, she shifts from third person to first person and back again to third person in a three page story. The fact that she makes such experiments indicates that she was continually aware of point of view as a device in fiction; the fact that there are so few departures from the usual first and third person categories suggests that she was not satisfied with the results.

The great bulk of Mansfield's stories are told through the third person, but there are significant variations upon it. Only once, in "Blaze," does she use a completely objective third person view. Most of the stories either focus through the consciousness of the central character or characters or employ the peculiar shifting viewpoint, called multipersonal by Berkman, which in Mansfield's hands can be considered innovative to the point of standing as a Mansfield signature.

Five completed stories--"See-Saw," "The Wrong House," "Sixpence," "The Singing Lesson," "A Cup of Tea"--and three incompleted ones--"Honesty," "Mr. and Mrs. Williams," and "A Man and His Dog"--make use of an omniscient narrator who has a voice separate from that of any character in the story. In each of these stories the narrator's voice provides ironic commentary and the stories themselves are primarily ironies of situation. In "Sixpence," for example, the narrator's voice opens the story and makes continual comment upon it. The story concerns Mr. and Mrs. Bendall, their little boy Dicky, and a visitor, Mrs. Spears. The narrator begins: "Children are unaccountable little creatures. Why should a small boy like Dickey, good as gold as a rule, sensitive, affectionate, obedient, and marvelously sensible for his age, have moods when, without the slightest warning, he suddenly went 'mad dog,' as his sisters called it, and there was no doing anything with him?" Dicky has one of his moods at a time when Mrs. Spears is visiting. Mrs. Bendall apologizes and seems helpless in the light of Dicky's stubbornness. Mrs. Spears insists that the only way to handle such behavior in children is to punish them or hand them over to their fathers for whippings. But Dicky has never been punished or whipped. Mrs. Spears insists that mischievous behavior is a child's way of showing that he needs a whipping. The narrator comments that Mrs. Bendall is "a weak little thing and this impressed her very much." Later, when Mr. Bendall comes home, Mrs. Bendall insists that he whip Dicky. Mr. Bendall has had a hard day, and his frustration in the face of his wife's insistence that he do something that he's never done before together with his anxieties brought home from the office combine to cause him to want to beat somebody, even Dicky. He gets through with the task and afterwards is filled with guilt and attempts to alleviate the situation by giving the boy sixpence. "But," the narrator's voice comments to finish the story, "could even that--could even a whole sixpence--blot out what had been?"

The narrator's voice in "The Singing Lesson" is more subtle, but it is still there and it controls the irony. The opening sentence of the story pictures the protagonist, Miss Meadows, striding down the cold corridors of the school in which she is singing mistress, "with despair--cold, sharp despair--buried deep in her heart like a wicked knife." The word _wicked_ indicates the presence of the narrator's voice. Without it the sentence might have flowed through Miss Meadow's consciousness; with it, the irony is begun, for Miss Meadows does not have enough distance on herself or her problem to provide the needed ironic overtones. She might be aware that she harbored a knife in her heart, but not a "wicked" knife. The second sentence continues the narrator's voice, a description of the girls "rosy from the air and bubbling over with that gleeful excitement that comes from running to school on a fine autumn morning." Again, the narrator's presence is needed because the girls are bright and happy and Miss Meadows is in no condition to notice. Indeed, when the story moves away from the narrator to focus on Miss Meadows, it is clear that everything she sees and everything she does is colored by her immediate emotions. Miss Meadows has received a letter from her fiance breaking off their engagement and she is filled with dignified and overly dramatic rage and deep but proud despair. The singing lesson that she conducts mirrors her feelings, objectifies her emotions. While she is filled with despair, she conducts the girls in "A Lament," where "every note was a sigh, a sob, a groan of awful mournfulness." Later, after she has received a telegram of recantation from her fiance, she conducts them in a "warm, joyful, and eager" song, and, the narrator comments, "this time Miss Meadows' voice sounded over all the other voices--full, deep, glowing with expression." Without the narrator's presence, the story might have become sentimental; with the narrator's presence, Miss Meadows' emotions are seen as overdramatic, the story as ironic.

"Honesty," is an interesting fragment concerning Rupert Henderson and Archie Cullen, two men, living together who are so different that they are characterized by an omniscient narrator as a python and a rabbit. Again the narrator's voice controls the ironic tone.

> Wasn't it possible to see Rupert and Archie as the python and the rabbit keeping house together? Rupert that handsome, well-fed python with his moustaches, his glare, his habit of uncoiling before the fire and swaying against the mantelpiece, pipe and pouch in hand. And Archie, soft, hunched, timid, sitting in the lesser armchair, there and not there, flicking back into the darkness at a word but emerging again at a look--with sudden wholly unexpected starts of playfulness (instantly suppressed by the python). Of course, there was no question of anything so crude and dreadful as the rabbit being eaten by his housemate....

The story breaks off shortly after and the reader is left curious as to just how Rupert will go about "eating" his housemate.

Two stories, "The Stranger" and "The Voyage," make use of a separate narrator to introduce the characters and situation, before moving to a focus on and through the protagonists. It is questionable whether the narrator's voice is necessary in the first two paragraphs of "The Stranger." The narrator provides an overall view, like a camera focusing in, with accompanying voice commentary, first on the crowd, then on the central figure of Mr. Hammond. But the story could have begun with the third paragraph, in a typical Mansfield _in medias res_ beginning: "But what a fool--what a fool he had been not to bring any glasses! There wasn't a pair of glasses between the whole lot of them." There is nothing said by the voice of the narrator in the first two paragraphs that is not provided for indirectly in the rest of the story. The comment, for example, that Mr. Hammond "was something between the sheepdog and the shepherd," states a fact that is later amply demonstrated through his behavior. The same is true of the first paragraph of "The Voyage." In this one a narrator uses language and metaphors inconsistent with the child's view which is later established. Several small changes could have made the viewpoint consistent and the story would have been better for it.

Some of the early stories are flawed as a result of lapses in the viewpoint established. "A Birthday," for example, makes use of the third person focused through the consciousness of Andreas Binzer. For the most part this viewpoint is consistent and functional, revealing dramatically more about Binzer than Binzer knows about himself. But passages which enter the consciousness of the servant girl and one passage into the mind of Doctor Malcolm are jarring departures and serve no useful purpose. Likewise, in "Frau Brechenmacher Attends a Wedding," departures from the viewpoint character allow the focus to waver and weaken the story as does satiric comment made by a separate narrator. It is not necessary, for example, that the narrator tell the reader that the bride who is dressed in a white dress decorated with stripes and bows of colored ribbons looks like a cake ready to be cut and served to the bridegroom. The image patterns in the story make that fact obvious. The point made immediately afterward is much more effective because it is indirect. The bridegroom, we are told, is dressed in clothes much too large for him, and the reader is left to make the connection for himself that soon the suit will be too small and the husband will have to be stuffed into it like Herr Brechenmacher.

The point of view used in "Something Childish But Very Natural" is, for the most part, beautifully handled and maintained. Henry's romantic attitudes and poetic nature help to set the whole fairy-tale tone of the story. His attitudinizing demands the poetic diction used, just as his fantasies about Edna and himself demand the fanciful imagery of birds, butterflies and flowers, with which the story is filled, to sustain the dreamlike and fleeting quality of their relationship. The insertion of the loveletters reproduced in toto does seem to break the point of view established, however, as does the entry into a kind of composite consciousness early in the story: "Their eyes were not frightened--they looked at each other with a sort of desperate calmness. If only their bodies would not tremble so stupidly!" In later stories, Miss Mansfield makes the entry into a composite consciousness part of a repetitive pattern and functional to the narrative, but here the lapse in viewpoint is abrupt and jarring.

In three stories, "Marriage a la Mode," "The Escape," and "A Dill Pickle," the narrator enters into the consciousness of two characters rather than one. In "Marriage a la Mode," the viewpoint is functional.

Equal time is spent upon William and Isabel who are dual protagonists in the story. In "The Escape," however, the man seems to be the protagonist involved in the central conflict and participating in the revelation. It is, therefore, hard to justify the entry into the consciousness of his wife and the inordinate amount of time spent on her. This awkward handling of point of view results in a lesser story that lacks clear focus and complete integration of all its elements. The shift in viewpoint in "A Dill Pickle" occurs at the very end of the story. Up to the last two paragraphs the story has stayed within the consciousness of the protagonist and to good advantage, since the story concerns her responses and a crisis in her life. The fact that the man in seen wholly from the outside functions to characterize him as unthinking, unfeeling, somehow a little less than human. The entry into his mind at the end of the story reveals no more than this and is consequently unnecessary. Indeed, the simple irony underlined at the end of the story detracts from the complex situation developed throughout the story and weakens it.

But the stories that are weakened by an inconsistent use of point of view are few in number. For the most part Mansfield uses point of view with great skill to direct the reader's responses by providing a perspective which immerses the reader in the situation and gives him an intimate knowledge of the characters. In his biography, <u>Katherine Mansfield</u>, Antony Alpers mentions her gift of impersonation which allowed her from an early age to mimic family and acquaintances. In her use of point of view Mansfield makes use of this "gift of impersonation." The narrator becomes the character (or characters in the multi-personal view) and everything seen is seen through the eyes of the characters. Everything described is described in the language and syntax peculiar to the characters.

In the stories, for example, which use a child as viewpoint character, short sentences reflect the attention span of a child; the language used is a child's language free from complexities; the images and metaphors are those peculiar to children. In "How Pearl Button Was Kidnapped," for example, the child swings on a "little gate," while the winds play "hide and seek," blowing dust like a cloud of pepper. The woman is as "warm as a cat." A "great big piece of blue water creeps over the land." Policemen, seen at a distance are "little blue men." But the children are not all the same. Although sentences consistently remain short, language and metaphors are different, characterizing the different children. Pearl Button is fanciful, poetic; Fenella, in "The Voyage," is more prosaic; rolls of luggage are "sausages;" the air smells of "paint and burnt chop-bones and indiarubber." The child-who-was-tired sees a distorted world. "As she sat at supper the Man and the Frau seemed to swell to an immense size as she watched them, and then become smaller than dolls, with little voices...." Her world is dreary, her dreams in black and white.

In the stories which use an adolescent or young woman as viewpoint character, the tone is nervous, fluttery, excited, gay, or anxious, agitated, wavering, melancholy, depending on the mood of the protagonist in a given situation. "Her First Ball" begins:

> Exactly when the ball began Leila would have found it hard to say. Perhaps her first real partner was the cab. It did not matter that she shared the cab with the Sheridan girls and their brother. She sat back in her own little corner of it, and the bolster on which her hand rested felt like the sleeve of an unknown young man's dress suit; and away they bowled, past waltzing lamp-posts and houses and fences and trees.

But soon the mood shifts with the changing situation: "Leila gave a light little laugh, but she did not feel like laughing. Was it--could it all be true? It sounded terribly true. Was this first ball only the beginning of her last ball after all? At that the music seemed to change; it sounded sad, sad; it rose upon a great sigh." Like the children, the young women are carefully distinguished. Although they all indulge in day dreams and fantasies, Leila is a romantic innocent, Sabina in "At Lehman's" is a "magical child," Viola in "The Swing of the Pendulum," is a role-playing pseudo-sophisticate.

In "The Swing of the Pendulum," radical changes in tone effected by the use of point of view mirror Viola's many moods. At the beginning of the story her room is drab, "tumbled and grimed." The flowers exude a sickly perfume. Later, when Viola's mood shifts, the room is "full of sweet light and the scent of hyacinth flowers." Even the furniture appears "different--exciting." Her initial and later responses to the stranger provide another example of the swinging pendulum of her many moods and roles. First he has an "infectious" smile; he looks "sane and solid." Later, when she feels her control of the scene is threatened, her viewpoint changes. He does not seem "quite so jolly;" his eyes are set too close together; he looks "silly."

The multipersonal view which Mansfield made peculiarly her own extends the viewpoint from a single character to a group. The narrator hovers just outside the consciousness of the characters, shifting from one to another and sometimes to a composite consciousness, causing the reader to become familiar not only with a central character or characters but also with a host of minor characters. This method, of course, enlarges the scope of the stories, and is the viewpoint used in almost thirty of the stories including the masterful New Zealand stories involving the Burnell family, as well as the excellent and frequently anthologized "The Man Without a Temperament," "The Daughters of the Late Colonel," and "The Garden Party."

The opening of "Prelude" illustates the method. The initial statement: "There was not as inch of room for Lottie and Kezia in the buggy," is a composite judgement of all the people already in the buggy, of Pat, the driver, who had tried to place them on top of the luggage and failed; of the grandmother, whose lap was already full; of Linda Burnell, the mother, who "could not possibly have held a lump of a child on hers for any distance; of Isabel, the oldest daughter, who sits, superior, on the driver's seat next to Pat; perhaps even of the "absolute necessities," the hold-alls, bags and boxes, already piled upon the floor of the carriage. Then the view quickly shifts to Lottie and Kezia who stand alone on the lawn and their dismay is felt: "Hand in hand, they stared with round solemn eyes first at the absolute necessities and then at their mother." Linda's next statement, shrouded in ambiguity provides a note of irony. "We shall simply have to leave them. That is all. We shall simply have to cast them off." The word them might, of course, refer to the children or the "absolute necessities." The irony of the situation causes Linda to laugh with a laugh that borders on the hysterical. But happily for all concerned a Mrs. Samuel Josephs makes her appearance, waddling down the garden path, and offers to keep the children until evening. The grandmother considers, (It is apparent that Linda is in no condition to) and agrees. "Yes, it is really quite the best plan. We are very obliged to you, Mrs. Samuel Josephs. Children, say 'thank you' to Mrs. Samuel Josephs." And the little girls, subdued, repeat, "Thank you, Mrs. Samuel Josephs." The carriage rolls off, but the viewpoint hovers over it for a time, revealing the feelings of the major characters as they leave. Isabel is "bursting with pride," her nose turned up at all the world; Linda is "prostrated;" the grandmother is rummaging about in her reticule for something to give her daughter. Then the view shifts back to the lawn, to Kezia biting her lip to keep from crying and Lottie, carefully finding her handkerchief before she sets up a wail. In this opening scene the characters come alive, caught by just the right detail to delineate and differentiate them one from another. As the first episode continues it focuses on Lottie and Kezia and the Samuel Josephs children who tease the little girls as they eat. The viewpoint shifts from one child to another and finally rests in the last paragraph of the section on Kezia.

> But Kezia bit a big piece out of her bread and dripping, and then stood the piece up on her plate. With the bite out it made a dear little sort of a gate. Pooh! She didn't care! A tear rolled down her cheek, but she wasn't crying. She couldn't have cried in front of those awful Samuel Josephs. She sat with her head bent, and as the tear dripped slowly down, she caught it with a neat little whisk of her tongue and ate it before any of them had seen.

It is this shifting view from one character to another, the easy movement in and out of the consciousness of the characters that provides the reader with an intimate knowledge of the Burnell family. Through the use of other families, the Samuel Josephs and the Kembers, the position and the character of the Burnell family is established. They are closely knit, educated, well-to-do, middleclass. Through the shifting viewpoints of the members of the family, its distaff emerges--its beginning in Tasmania, the loss of the father, the death of the oldest boy in the mines of Australia. Through the consciousness of the younger members of the family patterns of similarity in character and motivating forces are apparent in three generations so that the future of the family is glimpsed. In this way, Mansfield is successful in making the Burnell family as much of a character as any one member of it, doing in two stories what often takes a full length novel to accomplish.

The use of the multipersonal view also gives an overriding sense of time, not only in a historical context, but also as immediate, personal time. Linda, alone upstairs hears the children playing. Later in the morning, when Mrs. Fairchild reminds Linda that the children should be checked on, she replies, "Oh, Kezia has been tossed by a bull hours ago." The next paragraph shifts tense and scene abruptly. "But no, Kezia had seen a bull through a hole in a knot of wood...but she had not liked the bull frightfully...." There is a gradual shift in tense from immediate past into present while Kezia explores the garden and wanders along the drive until she meets Linda in front of the house, bringing together two different streams of thought in a significant moment of encounter. Through this shifting sense of time and perception, a pattern of the order of activities and household routines is created. Throughout the two stories there is careful provision made for every activity, for every character, and a continuity is created and maintained. In "At the Bay," for example, the opening scene where sheep move along the beach before sunrise is brought again to mind at the end of the story when Rags reveals that they had awakened Jonathan, and the reader has an intimate awareness of a whole series of causes and effects. If Jonathan had not been swimming before Stanley got to the beach the whole course of events in the lives of the characters on that particular day might have been different.

The multipersonal view also serves to create a constantly shifting perspective of the major characters. Through Linda the reader is made aware of depths and areas in Stanley's personality that would not be evident otherwise. Mrs. Fairchild is seen through the crosshairs of both Linda and Beryl and emerges more complete than she would have otherwise. At the same time the juxtapositioning of two divergent views of the same character makes a significant comment on the nature of the observer. In one scene in "Prelude," for example, Linda looks at her mother:

> She thought her mother looked wonderfully beautiful with her back to the leafy window. There was something comforting in the sight of her that Linda felt she could never do without. She needed the sweet smell of her flesh, and the soft feel of her cheeks and her arms and shoulders still softer. She loved the way her hair curled, silver at her forehead, lighter at her neck, and bright brown still in the big coil under the muslin cap. Exquisite were her mother's hands, and the two rings she wore seemed to melt into her creamy skin. And she was always so fresh, so delicious.

In this passage Mansfield provides not only a description of Mrs. Fairchild and Linda's love and need for her mother, but also she allows Linda herself to reveal her own abiding sensuality, a sensuality that does not find expression in her other relationships.

The exchange which takes place between Jonathan and Stanley in the opening of "At the Bay" and the double perspective that is used, functions to create a tension in the reader similar to the tension felt by the characters. Stanley bounding into the water, exulting that he is the first one there, finds Jonathan already there. Jonathan hails him ironically: "All hail, Thou Mighty One!" challenging him. But Stanley does not make the expected response and Jonathan challenges him again. "I had an extraordinary dream last night," he shouts. A long time passes before Stanley stoops to reply to Jonathan's nonsense and the reader is waiting, expectant. The rapid shifts between the consciousnesses of the two men create a fast pace and a certain annoying confusion which both men feel. And the use of the delayed response interwoven with the unspoken thoughts of the two men creates confusion, tension, and exasperation in the reader.

Mansfield's ability to assume various voices consistent with the various characters makes it possible for her to begin characterization and delineate the situation in very little space. The opening paragraph of "The Man Without a Temperament" introduces Robert Salesby and quickly catches his tension and detachment:

> He stood at the hall door turning the ring, turning the heavy signet ring upon his little finger, while his glance traveled coolly, deliberately, over the round tables and basket chairs scattered about the glassed-in verandah. He pursed his lips--he might have been going to whistle--but he did not whistle--only turned the ring-- turned the ring on his pink, freshly washed hands.

His inner tension, reflected in the rhythmic repetitive phrases, his posture, poised for action but in arrested movement, his strength, held in check by sheer will power, are soon contrasted with the weakness and languidity of his wife:

> Light dragging steps sounded across the hall, coming towards him. A hand, like a leaf, fell on his shoulder. A soft voice said: "Let's go and sit over there--where we can see the drive. The trees are so lovely." And he moved forward with the hand still on his shoulder, and the light, dragging steps beside his. He pulled out a chair and she sank into it, slowly, leaning her head against the back, her arms falling along the sides.

The tension created by the relative positions of these two characters is never released, but emphasized continuously not only by their every action and thought but also by the thoughts and behavior of the people around them, by the hotel setting, and the landscape itself. The spinster topknots as grey and speckled as their drink and food, the sexually frustrated American Woman playing up to the great purple plant and crying out with no one to hear, "Have you seen this moon?" the marvelously fecund honeymoon couple, making love to each other across the table, the sterile hotel cluttered with objects contrasted with the total sensuality of the plants in full bloom, serve as a backdrop against which the drama of the Salesbys is played. The method of "oblique impersonation," as Alpers calls it, reveals each of the characters and the total situation with such thoroughness and depth that by the time the climax is reached the reader understands the full pathos of characters caught in a moment of time, arrested by life itself.

Like "Prelude," "The Daughters of the Late Colonel" begins in a composite consciousness: "The week after was one of the busiest weeks of their lives. Even when they went to bed it was only their bodies that lay down and rested; their minds went on, thinking things out, talking things over, wondering, deciding, trying to remember where. . ." The composite consciousness where Mansfield enters the minds of the two sisters simultaneously serves to emphasize their likenesses at the same time that it provides motivation for their behavior, for the fact that there are two of them is important thematically. They have been able to indulge each other's vagaries, to cleave to one another for comfort, to join together in a common concern to appease their father. They eat together, shop together, sleep together, and at the end, choose one another, for they know nothing else and they are fearful. But if they are alike in some ways there are also significant differences to differentiate Constantia from Josephine, and so the hovering narrator enters the minds of each to delineate the differences. And the hovering narrator enters the minds or stays just outside the minds of the other characters to show their responses to the two sisters and their positions in the household. "Proud young Kate," the servant girl, sees them as two old tabbies to be controlled for her pleasure, slapped down in the same way she slaps down the "white, terrified blancmange" on the table. Nurse Andrews uses them to provide a leisurely interlude between jobs and takes advantage of their hesitations. Cyril, provides a note of normalcy for the absurd household. He does his best to cope with his aunts and to get away as quickly and as gracefully as he can. Only Colonel Pinner remains a mystery, outside of the scope of the hovering narrator, and it is right that he remain a mystery. He is a reality in the minds of his daughters and whether that reality conforms to an objective reality in the world of fact is never revealed.

"The Garden Party" is a New Zealand Story, but one featuring the Sheridans rather than the Burnells. The Sheridan family includes a mother and father, three daughters, Laura, Meg, and Jose, and a son, Laurie. The primary focus in the story is through the consciousness of Laura who is the single central character, but enough is revealed of the other members of the family to account for Laura's behavior and her need to establish her own set of standards. Again, the story opens from a composite consciousness:

> And after all the weather was ideal. They could not have had a more perfect day for a garden party if they had ordered it. Windless, warm, the sky without a cloud. Only the blue was veiled with a haze of light gold, as it is sometimes in early summer. The gardener had been up since dawn, mowing the lawns and sweeping them, until the grass and the dark flat rosettes where the daisy plants had been seemed to shine. As for the roses, you could not help feeling they understood that roses are the only flowers that impress people at garden parties; the only flowers that everybody is certain of knowing. Hundreds, yes, literally hundreds, had come out in a single night; the green bushes bowed down as though they had been visited by archangels.

Thus immediately the family is introduced before it is even seen. They are well-to-do, comfortable, a little superior, self-satisfied, likeable. Mrs. Sheridan says over the breakfast table, "I'm determined to leave everything to you children this year. Forget I am your mother. Treat me as an honoured guest." But she cannot keep her hand out of the arrangements and the daughters accept and love her as she is, somewhat distracted, flighty, in some areas insensitive. The man has come to put up the marquee, but Meg has wet hair and Jose is not dressed, so Laura has to go, and it is right and acceptable, because Laura is "the artistic one," and away she flies, holding a piece of bread and butter. Laura concurs in the family's feelings that she is the artistic one: "She loved having to arrange things; she always felt she could do it much better than anybody else." But when she gets outside, the workmen look so impressive that she feels out of place, is embarrassed about the bread and butter that she carries, and tries to recover by assuming the role that her mother would play. But it fails--she sounds "so fearfully affected" that she is ashamed, and she stammers "like a little girl." The workman who speaks to her is pleasant and friendly and Laura recovers somewhat: "How very nice workmen were! And what a beautiful morning! She mustn't mention the morning; she must be business like. The Marquee." But she cannot entirely escape her upbringing. She points with the hand that does not hold the bread and butter and she thinks the workman is not speaking quite respectfully to her. But along with her acceptance of the convention, there is her concurrent desire to escape it to something better, something more democratic. It bothers her that one of the workmen seems to imply that it is an extravagance to have a band, too; when one of the workmen pinches a piece of lavender and inhales it, she thinks "how extraordinarily nice" workmen are, so much nicer than the "silly boys" she dances with. It is the fault she decides of "these absurd class distinctions," which she tells herself she doesn't feel, "not a bit, not an atom," and she falls easily into the role: "Just to prove how happy she was, just to show the tall fellow how at home she felt, and how she despised stupid conventions, Laura took a big bite of her bread-and-butter as she stared at the little drawing. She felt just like a work-girl." The setting is so pleasant, the house warm and attractive, the people good-humored and gentle, the preparations for the party moving at such a fast pace with everyone caught in them, that the announcement of the death of a man, the father of five children, startles the reader as it does Laura. But the reader understands, as Laura does not, that it is not in the nature of things to stop a garden party because a man down the way whom one doesn't even know has been killed, especially when he lives in one of the mean little cottages that were, according to the composite family view, "the greatest possible eyesore" among people whose lives were "disgusting and sordid." Jose accuses Laura of being extravagant and absurd and her mother refuses to listen. Mrs. Sheridan has been trying on a hat and when Laura comes in she places it on Laura's head, insisting that the hat is just right for her. But Laura persists, refusing to look at herself in the mirror, until Mrs. Sheridan loses patience and speaks sharply. Laura turns to leave the room and by accident sees herself in the mirror. She looks so lovely in the hat that she finds it easy to put aside her disturbing thoughts and the party goes on.

Afterwards, when the family sits together discussing the garden party the business of the dead workman is brought up by Mr. Sheridan, tactlessly Mrs. Sheridan thinks. But then Mrs. Sheridan has a "brilliant" idea. They will make up a basket of leftover party food to send to the bereaved family and Laura will take it down. Laura senses that there might be something wrong with taking leftover party food to a funeral, but her mother will not let her speak. On the road outside of her own garden gates, Laura is still wearing the hat but her mood has changed and with it the tone of the story. Whereas before everything had been bright, cheery, gay, it is dusk now, and everything is shadowy and gloomy. She thinks that it was a mistake to have come; she feels out of place. The house where the funeral is being held is in sharp contrast to the Sheridan's house, and the woman who conducts Laura in has an oily, ingratiating voice. She brings Laura to view the dead man.

To Laura he appears sleeping, remote and peaceful, wholly given up to a dream of his own. She thinks that he is "wonderful, beautiful ....Happy . . . happy . . . ." But still she thinks she ought to cry and to say something. She gives out a "loud, childish sob," and says, "Forgive my hat." Outside again, she meets Laurie who has come to meet her. She is still crying, but she maintains that the experience was "simply marvelous," and she continues, "Isn't life, . . . isn't life--" but she is unable to continue and Laurie's answer, "<u>Isn't</u> it, darling?" ends the story.

In her own romantic way, Laura has idealized death, and in her youth, she feels she has found the answer to life. But she is still wearing her hat, and she is going back to the remains of the garden party, and the dead man has still left behind a wife and five children.

Chapter Six

DESIGN

To the inexperienced reader of short fiction, it must seem that nothing ever happens in the modern short story. A conversation takes place at dinner; a family moves to a new house; a family spends the day at the beach; a man visits a woman and they talk; a woman meets a man in a restaurant and they talk; a man has tea with his wife, goes for a walk, has dinner with her, and sees that she is safely in bed; two spinster sisters try to decide whether to fire the maid; a girl goes to her first dance; a family gives a garden party while a funeral is taking place; a man accidently kills a fly. Plot, as one used to know it and still finds it in occasional popular fiction, has disappeared. The old plot line that could be charted--rising action, climax, falling action--has given way to a line that doesn't rise very much and then stops somewhere and remains hovering. Interest lies not on what happens but on why it happens, an altogether different thing. In this kind of story details function to do more than set the scene; objects, characters, incidents and their positions make a tangential point; nothing is apparent, everything implied; the structure creates a metaphor, the metaphor reveals the meaning. This is the kind of story that Katherine Mansfield wrote.

"The Wind Blows" exhibits the typical structure and uses all the characteristic devices. On the surface level the story concerns an adolescent girl, Matilda, who wakes up one morning, nervous and tense. While the wind blows outside, she readies herself to go to her music lesson. Before she gets away she has a small argument with her mother. She has her music lesson, goes home, meets her brother and goes for a walk with him to the sea. They stand together and watch a ship in the water. Then she imagines a time in the future when she and her brother will be leaving their home on just such a ship.

The story begins _in medias res_. There is no formal introduction, no formal exposition; no formal setting of scene. Just, "Suddenly--dreadfully--she wakes up." The positioning of words in the sentence, the punctuation, the harsh consonants grouped together suggest the jarring quality of the awakening and the anxiety it creates. But more than this; the very act of awakening sets the area of thematic concern. The next sentences move the reader into Matilda's consciousness:

> What has happened? Something dreadful has happened. No--nothing has happened. It it only the wind shaking the house, rattling the windows, banging a piece of iron on the roof and making her bed tremble. Leaves flutter past the window, up and away; down in the avenue a whole newspaper wags in the air like a lost kite and falls, spiked on a pine tree. It is cold. Summer is over--it is autumn--everything is ugly. The carts rattle by, swinging from side to side; two Chinamen lollop along under their wooden yokes with the straining vegetable baskets--their pigtails and blue blouses fly out in the wind. A white dog on three legs yelps past the gate.

DESIGN

> It is all over! What is? Oh, everything! And she begins to plait her hair with shaking fingers, not daring to look in the glass. Mother is talking to grandmother in the hall.

The tension created in the first sentence describing the exterior detail is carried over into the interior monologue. Short sentences filled with repetitive phrases continue the abrupt movement, beating out the anxiety pattern. The wind that she hears outside is emphasized by the use of the present participle in the verb forms. It is "shaking," "rattling," "banging" things around outside, causing her bed on the inside to tremble. Although no mention is made of her overt behavior, it is clear that she rises from the bed and goes to the window to look outside. Everything that she sees is described in terms of the movement of the wind which reflects the tension within her: "It is all over." Her inability to define the pronoun reference indicates that her anxiety feelings are undifferentiated, as they will remain for her, but not for the reader, for the story proceeds to locate the specific area of anxiety and to comment on it. That she does not dare to look in the mirror is a significant detail in the pattern that will be established, making credible and acceptable her fantasy which ends the story.

The business of the house goes on around her, continuing the sweeping and shaking movement of the wind, while in her mind she tries to attend to a minor movement of a Beethoven piece, but the "trills" turn out to be "long and terrible like little rolling drums," as the wind outside shapes her responses. Again, although no mention is made of her overt behavior it is clear that she is dressing, preparing to leave for her ten o'clock music lesson. The business of the household going on around her--the teacloth on the clothes line being torn to shreds, someone at the door--someone on the telephone, together with her own inner tension cause her to think, "How hideous life is--revolting, simply revolting." Ready to leave now, she discovers that her hat elastic has snapped. She decides to wear her old tam and slip out before her mother sees her in it, but she doesn't make it, and her mother calls to her to come back immediately; but "She won't. She won't. She hates mother. 'Go to hell,' she shouts, running down the road."

Outside she is stung and beaten by the wind and the dust it carries. She hears the roar of the trees moving in the wind and the sea sob: "Ah! . . . Ah! . . . Ah-h!" The cry appears to come also from within her. But Mr. Bullen's drawing room is quiet, a haven from without and within. She likes the room; it has a masculine feel and smell. The picture hanging over Mr. Bullen's piano is a romanticized image of "a dark tragic woman draped in white, sitting on a rock, her knees crossed, her chin on her hands;" it comes to represent an idealized version of herself, the image that she would not have seen in the mirror had she dared to look in it. Close to Mr. Bullen, her fingers tremble; her heart beats loudly; she identifies the source: "It's the wind."

When he speaks kindly to her she feels that she must cry, she leans her head on his shoulder, murmuring "Life is so dreadful," but the conflicts of adolescence are expressed in a merging of pleasure and pain, and "she does not feel it's dreadful at all." He comforts her, reinforcing her idealized image of woman.

Back in her room, the wind continues, constant. She feels that her bed is frightening, lying there "sound asleep." Then her brother calls to her to come take a walk. They stand together and she looks at herself and her brother in a mirror: "Her face is white, they have the same excited eyes and hot lips. Ah, they know those two in the glass. Goodbye dears; we shall be back soon." The mirror image and the romanticized figures in the mirror are separate from the young people who stand before it.

They walk, blown by the wind, their voices carried away by it. On the water she sees a big black steamer cutting through the waves. "The wind does not stop her." The ship is making for an open gate between pointed rocks. The imagery used here recalls the photograph of the woman in the piano studio. It is a vehicle to carry her away from the wind. Then she imagines that she and her brother are on board the ship and she sees them as she had seen the mirror images. They are older; the wind is down; they are being carried away over the tumbling water. Then the ship disappears and with it her vision, leaving "The wind--the wind."

In this story, the wind, as major metaphor, becomes a concrete objectification, what might be called the objective correlative, of Matilda's anxieties. The trembling and frightened bed, the idealized image of womanhood expressed in the photograph, the mirror images are symbols functioning within the major metaphor, delineating the area of anxiety, the sexual stirrings of adolescence.

The plot lines of the great bulk of Mansfield stories are similar to the plot of "The Wind Blows." Employing an _in medias res_ beginning they move to what Professor Berkman calls an "apparently casual interlinking of incidents to form a texture through which the real intention of the writer shines."[1] The trick is to find the _causal_ relationship which is usually delineated by means of the juxtaposition of objects, events, and characters, image patterns which move to the symbolic, time manipulations, and, oftentimes, the merging of various levels of the real.

The _in medias res_ beginnings function to plunge the reader immediately into the situations providing him with a certain psychological set. As Alpers says, "...the reader, treated from the beginning as someone who already knows the scene and people well, is tricked into familiarity with them before he has time to feel lost."[2] Sometimes the stories begin with dialogue in the manner of a stage play: "Max, you silly devil, you'll break your neck if you go careening down the slide that way...." "'Good-evening,' said the Herr Professor...." "Two

purl--two plain--woolinfrontofthe needle--and knit two together."
More often they begin with something similar to a stage direction before the dialogue begins: "Eight o'clock in the morning. Miss Ada Moss lay in a black iron bedstead, staring up at the ceiling...." "In the afternoon the chairs came, a whole big cart full of little gold ones with their legs in the air...." "When she opened the door and saw him standing there she was more pleased than ever before...." "Mr. and Mrs. B. sat at breakfast in the cosy red dining room...." Sometimes they open within the consciousness of a character: "If there was one thing he hated more than another it was the way she had of waking him in the morning...." "The week after was one of the busiest weeks of their lives...." "Of course he knew--no man better--that he hadn't a ghost of a chance, he hadn't an earthly...." Plunged immediately into a story in this way, without time to accomodate himself to a new situation, the reader is thrown into an imbalance which he must immediately work to set straight and he has no means except that which the story provides. The frame of mind in which the reader is set motivates him to account for what happens.

Once in the story the reader is moved through a series of incidents, carried along with the action, and it is no more than action until he discovers causal relationships. In "The Fly," for example, the reader is introduced to a man called only the Boss, watches him entertain a former employee, called Old Woodifield, hears old Woodifield mention the Boss' dead son, and then watches the boss torture and kill a fly. In "Honeymoon," the reader is introduced to a couple on their honeymoon who go to a restaurant and listen to music. In "The Voyage," the reader watches a child, Fenella, being taken by her grandmother to her home. The father, whose wife has just died, brings them to the ship. They set sail and then go to bed. In the morning they arrive at the grandparents' house. In "Prelude," the reader watches a family move from one house into another and follows various members of the family during a week's activities. In "At the Bay," the reader watches a family spend the day at the beach. There is not much in the action itself to help the reader gain his balance.

But before long a reader begins to notice certain positionings that form repetitive patterns that begin to suggest possible relationships. In "The Fly," he notices that old Mr. Woodifield is consistently described as a baby, although he is aged and sick, and that Mr. Woodifield is persistently contrasted with the Boss, five years older, but still rosy and strong. He notices that the Boss is immensely proud of his possessions, most of them recently obtained, and that his geniality is an expression of his feelings of superiority. He notices that Mr. Woodifield's perfectly normal response to his own dead son is set next to the Boss' strange detachment. After Old Woodifield leaves, and the reader is brought into the consciousness of the Boss as he reflects on his son and his relationship with him, the reader notices that what the boss says about himself is in strange contrast to what he appears to be. He says that life had no other meaning except for his son and that when he heard of his son's death six years ago, he had left the office a "broken man, with his life in ruins." But the reader knows that he does not look like a broken man and his life does not appear to be in ruins. When the boss begins to play with the fly, birth imagery begins to appear and the reader remembers that Woodifield was described as a baby. As the fly struggles to recover from the persistent blobs of ink the boss drops on him, the reader begins to get the notion that perhaps the fly is a symbol for man and his struggle is man's struggle. But the reader is bothered by a persistent question: what role does the boss play? In the little drama with the fly he appears to be a god, giving life and taking it away. Might this action, the reader wonders, be a typical behavior pattern, and he finds, upon reflection, that it is. The Boss is given no other name. He is Boss, authority, the father figure not only to his former employee, Woodifield, but to his present employee, the bent and withered Macey. Now the reader remembers the little drop of whiskey the Boss had given to Woodifield, insisting that it wouldn't hurt a child, although whiskey is forbidden to the aged man. Could the Boss have dropped similar metaphoric blobs of ink on his son, the reader wonders. And upon reflection the reader discovers that it is perhaps so. The Boss had insisted that the son follow in his footsteps, provide meaning for his own life. But now there emerges an apparent contradiction. If, the reader reasons, the fly represents struggling humanity and consequently Woodifield, Macey and the son, then what has the Boss to do with the fly, for he is obviously a man, too? Now the birth and death imagery that pervades the story emerges more clearly in relationship to the symbolic meaning of the fly, for flies are not only as Berkman says, created in multitudes, but they also fly, they can soar through the heavens, they can escape earth bound reality, if only for a time, for they, too, must die. There is birth and youth and old age and death; there is struggle, but along with the struggle, there are moments of flight, desires, hopes, aspirations. The Boss had dared to hope that he could accomplish his own immortality through the life of his son; but a greater power had dropped a blob of ink on the son and on the Boss. Realizing the son's death for the first time, the boss acts out a symbolic drama, himself assuming the god role, releasing his feelings of inadequacy and hostility on the fly and accomplishing at last a realization of his own mortality. Now, the reader sees that everything in the story falls together in a moment of revelation in the last sentence. "For the life of him [the boss], he could not remember." The words, "for the life of him" are chosen carefully, for at this moment he has an intimate, though unconscious knowledge of his own approaching death. And for the reader, things are set back in balance.

One of the major structural devices which allows the reader to locate causal relationships is juxtaposition, the setting together of characters, events, and objects, and thus causing to emerge by means of the juxtaposition a meaning larger than the characters, events, or objects, taken separately. When Mansfield uses juxtaposition, she offers no word of explanation. Two (or more) things are simply placed one by another until a repetitive pattern emerges that is charged with significance.

In many of the stories meaning is derived in part from the juxtaposition of people: the innocent Katie is set next to the knowing Eve in "Carnation;" the excited and seeking Bertha Young against the calm and contained Pearl Fulton in "Bliss;" Sabina against the pregnant woman, swollen with child in "At Lehmann's;" the young girl against the narrator, her mother, and the ancient withered creature in "The Young Girl;" and in much the same kind of pattern that reveals the effect of life on women in various stages of development, Kezia is set next to Beryl, Linda, and Mrs. Fairchild in "Prelude" and "At the Bay." Often people's attitudes are juxtaposed to give structure to a story. In the <u>Pension</u> stories the attitudes of the young British narrator are juxtaposed with the attitudes of the Germans; In "A Dill Pickle," the contrasting attitudes of the man and the woman reveal their past, present, and future; in "Honeymoon," the difference in attitudes between the husband and wife bode ill for the future. Sometimes a person's feelings are revealed as they are juxtaposed against scenes, objects, or backdrops. The wind is the concrete embodiment of Matilda's trepidations in "The Wind Blows;" the storm parallels Binzer's inner turmoil as well as his wife's labor pains and delivery in "A Birthday;" Bertha Young imagines herself to be like the pear tree in the garden in "Bliss."

Settings are juxtaposed with settings to reveal meaning: the houses of boxes with the open sea in "How Pearl Button Was Kidnapped," the empty house with the furnished house in "Prelude," and in the same story, the paddock where the duck is killed with the dining room where it is eaten; London with the country in "Something Childish But Very Natural." Events are often juxtaposed with events to give structure to a story. Some plots are composed of a series of juxtaposed incidents, often without transitions, as in "A Truthful Adventure," "See-Saw," "Spring Pictures," and "An Indiscreet Journey." The games the children play are juxtaposed with the adult games in "At the Bay." Appearance is juxtaposed with reality: what Miss Brill thinks she is versus what she is, what Raoul Duquette tells about himself versus what he reveals through a series of images that he uses to describe himself; what the little governess carries as self-image versus what she appears to be to other people (including the reader). Fancy is juxtaposed with fact, the dream with the real, as in "Something Childish But Very Natural," "The Child-Who-Was-Tired," "The Wind Blows," "Taking the Veil," and "The Tiredness of Rosabel." Beauty is juxtaposed with ugliness, stasis with action, the serious with the absurd. Indeed, the multipersonal viewpoint is a kind of juxtaposition, as various viewpoints are juxtaposed, one with another.

In "The Garden Party," the "bread and butter" Laura is juxtaposed with the "business-like Laura," the aristocratic Laura with the bourgois Laura; the happiness and gaity and affluence of the Sheridan house is juxtaposed with the grief and poverty stricken death house; Laura's feelings and reactions are juxtaposed with the feelings and reactions of the other members of the Sheridan house; and finally Laura's comment that life is "simply marvelous" is juxtaposed with the real situation. In "The Man Without a Temperament," the real is juxtaposed with the memory, sensuality with sterility, summer with winter, illness with health, clock time with something more permanent and enduring.

"The Doll's House" is composed of a series of juxtaposed incidents, people, attitudes, objects, viewpoints. The composite consciousness opens the story in such a way that one can imagine the Burnell family standing around, the adults dismayed at the disruption of the household the gift can cause:

> When dear old Mrs. Hay went back to town after staying with the Burnells she sent the children a doll's house. It was so big that the carter and Pat carried it into the courtyard, and there it stayed, propped up on two wooden boxes beside the feed-room door. No harm could come of it; it was summer. And perhaps the smell of paint coming from the doll's house ("Sweet of old Mrs. Hay, of course; most sweet and generous!")--but the smell of paint was quite enough to make anyone seriously ill, in Aunt Beryl's opinion. Even before the sacking was taken off. And when it was . . . .

Now the view shifts to that of the children, as the house and their reaction to it are described. It is a perfect little house, complete in every detail. The whole house-front swings back and "there you were, gazing at one and the same moment into the drawing room, the kitchen and two bedrooms. That is the way for a house to open! Why don't all houses open like that?" The composite children's view goes on to establish the doll's house as a microcosm to be compared with real houses, especially the Burnell house. How much more exciting it seems to them to open a house this way and get a complete view of everything it harbors than to peer through "the slit of a door into a mean little hall with a hatstand and two umbrellas!"

The happiness of the children is so complete that their cries of joy are like cries of despair. "They had never seen anything like it in their lives." Now the viewpoint focuses in on Kezia: "But what Kezia liked more than anything, what she liked frightfully, was the lamp." The father and mother dolls are sprawled stiff as though they have fainted; the children dolls are asleep upstairs, but they are really too big. Only the lamp is perfect. "It seemed to smile at Kezia, to say, 'I live here.' The lamp was real."

It is determined that while the doll's house is in the courtyard, the children may invite some of their schoolmates, "two at a time" to come and look at the house: "Not to stay to tea, of course, or to come traipsing through the house. But just to stand in the courtyard and look at the house quietly." Isabel is to tell the children about the house first, because she is the eldest. The next day the children are excited, hardly able to contain their pride. At recess groups of little girls crowd around the Burnell children, all except the Kelveys, who "knew better" than to come anywhere near the Burnells.

The attitude of the adult Burnells, the feeling that the doll's house would disrupt the order of the home, the invitation to the children to come and stand quietly but not to come inside, the revelation that the family is not too happy with the fact that there is only one school and their children will have to mix with the children of everyone in the town, including the storekeeper's and the milkman's, the drawing of the line at the Kelveys because a line had to be drawn somewhere, the attitude of the children reflecting the attitude of the adults as they walk past the Kelveys with their heads in the air, and the results of that attitude, the malicious and cruel treatment of the Kelveys by the children, define the Burnell home and delineate it as a kind of doll's house, where the mother and father dolls are stiff as though they have fainted and the children "really too big," for the house.

The Kelveys are the daughters of a washerwoman and a man whom everybody said was in prison, "a gaolbird." They are dressed in odd bits of garments given to their mother by the people for whom she worked. Lil, the older, is stout and plain, our Else, the younger is a "tiny wishbone of a child, with cropped hair and enormous solemn eyes--a little white owl." She never smiles; she hardly ever speaks. "She went through life holding on to Lil, with a piece of Lil's skirt screwed up in her hand. Where Lil went our Else followed." And whenever our Else wants anything she gives a tug on Lil's skirt and Lil stops. Although outsiders, "The Kelveys never failed to understand each other."

Now, as Isabel tells the other children about the doll's house, the Kelveys hover on the edges of the group and endure the sneers of the children. As Isabel talks she feels more and more proud and superior; only Kezia feels that she is not making enough of the little lamp, and twice Kezia interrupts Isabel to urge her to tell about the little lamp.

Days pass and the children come to see the doll's house. At recess they sit around talking about it, with the Kelveys always hovering as near as they can get. Finally Kezia asks her mother whether she can invite the Kelveys, but her mother dismisses her without an appropriate answer. At last the day comes when everybody except the Kelveys has seen the house and interest in the house has flagged among the children, who turn their attention to tormenting the Kelveys.

The scene is a masterful one, juxtaposing as it does the attitudes of the adults reflected in the cruel behavior of the children:

> The children stood together under the pine trees, and suddenly, as they looked at the Kelveys eating out of their paper, always by themselves, always listening, they wanted to be horrid to them. Emmie Cole started the whisper.
>
> "Lil Kelvey's going to be a servant when she grows up."
>
> "O-oh, how awful!" said Isabel Burnell, and she made eyes at Emmie.
>
> Emmie swallowed in a very meaning way and nodded to Isabel as she's seen her mother do on those occasions.
>
> "It's true--it's true--it's true," she said.
>
> Then Lana Logan's little eyes snapped. "Shall I ask her?" she whispered.
>
> "Bet you don't," said Jessie May.
>
> "Pooh, I'm not frightened," said Lena. Suddenly she gave a little squeal and danced in front of the other girls, "Watch! Watch me! Watch me now!" said Lena. And sliding, gliding, dragging one foot, giggling behind her hand, Lena went over to the Kelveys.
>
> Lil looked up from her dinner. She wrapped the rest quickly away. Our Else stopped chewing. What was coming now?
>
> "Is it true you're going to be a servant when you grow up, Lil Kelvey?" shrilled Lena.
>
> Dead silence. But instead of answering, Lil only gave her silly shamefaced smile. She didn't seem to mind the question at all. What a sell for Lena! The girls began to titter.
>
> Lena couldn't stand that. She put her hands on her hips; she shot forward. "Yah, yer father's in prison!" she hissed spitefully.
>
> This was such a marvelous thing to have said that the little girls rushed away in a body, deeply, deeply excited, wild with joy. Someone found a long rope, and they began skipping. And never did they skip so high, run in and out so fast, or do such daring things as on that morning.

In the evening while Isabel and Lottie go upstairs to dress Kezia thieves outside "to swing on the big white gates of the courtyard." Then in the distance she sees two little dots in the road. The dots come nearer and nearer and turn into the Kelveys. When she sees them Kezia stops swinging. She slips down from the gate as though she is going to run away and then hesitates. The Kelveys approach nearer, "and beside them walked their shadows, very long, stretching right across the road with their heads in the buttercups." This image of the shadows of the Kelveys with their heads in the buttercups is juxtaposed with Kezia's decision. She climbs back on the gate, waiting for them, and she speaks first. The Kelveys are so astounded that they stop. Kezia invites them to come in and look at the doll's house. Lil knows better; she blushes and shakes her head. "Why not? Kezia demands to know. "Your ma told our ma you wasn't to speak to us," Lil answers. But Kezia will not be put off. "That doesn't matter," she says, and then, "Don't you want to?"

Lil knows better, but our Else is younger and wants to see the doll's house. She gives a tug on Lil's skirt and the two little girls follow Kezia to the courtyard. But before Kezia is finished pointing out the house's attractions, before even, she has pointed out the little lamp, her aunt Beryl's voice is heard, cold, and furious. She chastizes Kezia and sends the Kelvey's away, shooing them out "as if they were chickens." Her action puts out the lamp of the Burnell house. Kezia, strongly identified with the lamp throughout the story, representing the light of a stronger wisdom, the truth of human relationships, just disappears. No further mention is made of her in the story, not even to say that she disappears. But the Kelveys go on and stop down the road and our Else smiles a "rare smile," and utters the first words she has used in the story. "I seen the little lamp." The lamp, Kezia, our Else with the owl eyes, are the only things that are "right," the only things that fit in a house built to accomodate human beings. The story has lifted the side of the Burnell home to reveal it at a glance in the same way that the children were able to see at a glance in a moment of time all that was inside the doll's house when its side was opened.

Causal relationships are also revealed through details charged with symbolic significance, image patterns which move to symbolic levels, and symbolic actions. Details, of course, properly chosen, provide the texture of an experience; sense data grounds the reader in the concrete, convinces him of the reality of a given scene. In her stories, Mansfield causes the reader to become emersed in the sensory. All the senses are evoked, or occasionally, one is omitted to provide a certain quality of distortion when a peculiar angle of vision is needed. Sometimes but not often details of sense impressions are used merely to create a vivid scene, as, for example, in the first section of "Spring Pictures," where the five senses are evoked, one after another in the first five sentences of the initial paragraph:

> It is raining. Big soft drops splash on the people's hands and cheeks; immense warm drops like melted stars. "Here are roses! Here are lilies! Here are violets!" caws the old hag in the gutter. But the lilies bunched together in a frill of green, look more like faded cauliflowers. Up and down she drags the creaking barrow. A bad, sickly smell comes from it.

Sight: of the rain, of the splashing drops, of flowers, of the old hag, of the lilies in a frill of green; touch: of rain drops, warm like melting stars, of the dragging barrow; sound: of the old hag's caw; of the creaking barrow; smell: of the creaking barrow; taste: (tangential, but evoked) of the warm drops like melted stars; of lilies looking like faded cauliflowers in a bad smelling barrow. The scene created in the first section of "Spring Pictures" is little more than that. Later the scene is juxtaposed with other scenes--of a lonely woman, lying in an empty bed: "The huge bed big as a field and as cold and unsheltered; of a woman walking on a beautiful evening, when "the sky is the colour of lilac and the river of violet leaves," and crying. But the images presented do not form patterns; the details do not become symbolic. The only continuity presented is in the circular pattern: the large warm drops of the rain, the tears of the woman. In most cases, sense impressions, details used to create a scene or a setting, function not only as a backdrop, but are made to serve other roles, to create atmosphere, to delineate a character's feelings, or to specify areas of thematic concern. The opening episode of "At the Bay" creates a feeling of calmness and regularity as a shepherd makes his way from the east to the west bringing with him the rising sun, opening a curtain on the morning. The descriptive paragraphs in "Bank Holiday" create a feeling of great vitality and longing:

> It is a flying day, half sun, half wind. When the sun goes in a shadow flies over; when it comes out again it is fiery. The men and women feel it burning their backs, their breasts and their arms; they feel their bodies expanding, coming alive . . . so that they make large embracing gestures, lift up their arms, for nothing, swoop down on a girl, blurt into laughter.

Since most of the descriptions that Mansfield uses in her stories are presented through a character's point of view, they function to reveal the character in a given situation. In "Bliss":

> When she had finished with them [the purple grapes] and made two pyramids of these bright round shapes, she stood away from the table to get the effect--and it really was most curious. For the dark table seemed to melt into the dusky light and the glass dish and the blue bowl to float in the air. This, of course, in her present mood, was so incredibly beautiful. . . . She began to laugh.

In "The Daughters of the Late Colonel":

> Some little sparrows, young sparrows they sounded, chirped on the window ledge. <u>Yeep-eyeep-yeep</u>. But Josephine felt they were not sparrows, not on the window-ledge. It was inside her, that queer little crying noise. <u>Yeep-eyeep-yeep</u>. Ah, what was it crying, so weak so forlorn?

Sometimes the characters are seen against a backdrop where the juxtaposition creates an irony important for meaning. In "The Man Without a Temperament," Robert Salesby and his dying wife are placed in a garden that exudes sensuality:

> The sun was still high. Every leaf, every flower in the garden lay open, motionless, as if exhausted, and a sweet, rich, rank smell filled the quivering air. Out of the thick fleshy leaves of a cactus there rose an aloe stem loaded with pale flowers that looked as though they had been cut out of butter; light flashed upon the lifted spears of the palms; over a bed of scarlet waxen flowers some big black insects "zoom-zoomed"; a great, gaudy creeper, orange splashed with jet, sprawled against a wall.

Since a typical Mansfield story begins <u>in medias res</u>, the reader being plunged immediately into action, there is no initial identification of time or place. Setting is usually something to be absorbed first, recognized as part of a meaningful pattern later. The "Pension" stories take place in a boarding house where people have gathered for a cure. The place itself is not obtrusive. As a matter of fact Mansfield makes very little use of description in these early stories, but gradually it is revealed that the people, including the narrator, are sick in ways other than the physical.

Most Mansfield stories take place in houses or in gardens outside of houses. Sometimes the house itself is significant. In "Prelude," the empty Burnell house is juxtaposed against the newly occupied one. Both impressions come through the eyes of Kezia. The deserted house is seen in terms of its emptiness, emphasized by the description of tiny objects that Kezia finds, a pill box, some stray buttons, some beads, and a long needle. Later Kezia's feelings of wonder turn into terror:

> As she stood there, the day flickered out and dark came. With the dark crept the wind, snuffling and howling. The windows of the empty house shook, a creaking came from the walls and floors, a piece of loose iron on the roof banged forlornly. Kezia was suddenly quite, quite still, with wide open eyes and knees pressed together. She was frightened.

Kezia's first view of the new house is of "its soft white bulk" which lay "stretched upon the green garden like a sleeping beast." Later she carries a lamp into the house where all the members of the family are revealed, positioned according to their roles.

The doll's house in the story by that name functions as a microcosm, reflecting the larger home in which the Burnells live. The confection house in "Sun and Moon" is doomed to melt and with it Sun's visions. But most often it is not houses but rooms within houses that take on significance. A room may serve to characterize, set a mood, or effect some kind of transformation. Mrs. Fairchild's kitchen in "Prelude" mirrors her orderly life. "When she had finished, everything in the kitchen had become a part of a series of patterns." Ian French's room in "Feuille d'Album," is "neat as a pin," "arranged to form a pattern, a little 'still life' as it were," and his life is arranged in as orderly a manner as his room. Raoull Duquette's rooms are filled with expensive items, his closets stuffed with clothes and personal effects none of which is paid for. Rosabel's real room is drab, plain, containing a chipped wash-stand and a single candle. But Rosabel doesn't really see it. Descriptive details are sparse. Yet her dream room is closely detailed, the "great, white and pink bedroom with roses everywhere in dull silver vases, the fire in the fireplace, her beautiful dress spread on the bed."

In "The Swing of the Pendulum," Viola's room changes with her changing moods; in "The Daughters of the Late Colonel," different rooms reflect the different activities which take place in them. The woman's room in "Spring Pictures" is filled with a huge bed which she occupies alone. At the end of "The Man With a Temperament," the Salesbys' bedroom is "painted white with moonlight. The light trembles in the mirror; the two beds seem to float." Mrs. Salesby is on her bed, covered by a net. She is propped up with pillows, "her white hands crossed on the sheet," her cheeks and hair silvered over by the moonlight. Corpselike she occupies her own bed and Mr. Salesby undresses to enter the other.

Windows and mirrors inside rooms take on special significance whenever they are mentioned. In "Prelude," Kezia views the world through a multicolored glass. Later a window serves to transport the reader from Linda's bedroom to the yard where the children are playing. The reader moves with the same ease as the sounds of the children's voices. Rosabel uses her window to transport her to a world of fantasy and beauty. In "The Wrong House," the aged woman looks through a window to see a reflection of what could be her own funeral procession. Stanley opens the blinds with a clatter so that he might take his exercises in the full sunlight. The tearing open of the blinds in "Revelations" jars Monica Tyrell's nerves as she tries to keep out the daylight as long as possible. The barrel organ and the sparrows sound through the window and the sun thieves its way in in "The Daughters of the Late Colonel," but eventually to no avail, for the sisters are unable to step through the windows into a different world.

Mirrors serve to reflect reality as it is or as the character wants it to be. In "Bliss," Bertha Young sees herself in a mirror as a "woman radiant, with smiling trembling lips, with big, dark eyes and an air of listening, waiting for something." In "Revelations," Monica Tyrell sees a tragic reflection in her glass. The young girl, in the story by that name, keeps her compact mirror handy as though to assure herself that she is real. Ada Moss in "Pictures" looks in her glass frequently and her reflection makes a face at her as though to remind her that her fantasies are not real.

Gardens are employed for various effects, often as in "The Man Without a Temperament," to delineate areas of natural reproduction and growth. Kezia rolls and tumbles around in a lush garden before making her way to the aloe tree which blossoms once every hundred years. Bertha Young, although a frigid wife, identifies herself with her pear tree which is in full bloom. It is spring and flowers are growing and bees are buzzing in "Taking the Veil," as Edna, in the spring of her life, indulges in romantic and melodramatic fantasizing, evoking images of the winter and of her old age. In "Something Childish But Very Natural," persistent garden imagery suggests an Eden motif, but Edna withdraws from physical contact with Henry and remains an innocent, while, for Henry, the butterfly that had been Edna turns into a moth.

Other natural elements are important in Mansfield stories: the sun, the moon, the wind, and the sea, periods of calm and storm, light and dark, ebb and flow, spring and fall, summer and winter. The sun, characterized by the rays of light that it emits, is often identified with the male life force, aggressive and urgent; the moon, bathing objects with gentle and silvery beams, is often identified with the female; the wind, beating or tearing, sweeping, gusting is usually used to objectify inner fears and anxieties; the sea with its ebb and flow is both life and death, light and dark; spring, characterized by warming and budding, by the presence of flying insects and birds, can in a moment of fantasy become fall, cold, dark, sterile; summer, characterized by heat and luxurious, almost rank growth, can in memory become winter; rain can, by a deft time manipulation, become snow.

A great many of Mansfield's stories make use of one or more of these natural elements to create a central symbolism which gives shape to the stories. In "Bank Holiday," for example, the world becomes a fair, the people like children, playing in a forbidden garden. They are pushed by the wind and pulled by the sun up a hill, but they do not know why or how or what will be their ultimate end. In "The Dove's Nest," Millie is pictured as a young bird yearning to fly, being seduced by the sun. In "The Wind Blows," the moan of the sea merges with the urgency of the tearing wind to cause Matilda to yearn for an end to the turmoil, for escape to a more ordered world. In "The Garden Party," Laura moves from the party, replete with the aura of spring, to the death house, dark and shadowy. In "The Voyage," Fenella takes a symbolic night journey by water to emerge in the morning facing a new beginning in a fairy tale house.

Most of Mansfield's symbols emerge from the story itself; they are formed from the natural materials that create the texture of the experience. There are, however, a few where objects not intrinsic to the situation are caused to bear a heavy symbolic burden, like the doves in "Mr. and Mrs. Dove." the fly in the story by that name, the fur piece in "Miss Brill," the newspaper account of a poisoning in "Poison," the tree in "The Escape," the dill pickle in the story by that name, the hungry sparrows in "A Surburban Fairy Tale." Although it can hardly be said that these stories lack credibility, with the exception of "The Fly," most of them are lesser stories mainly because the symbolism is less complex. The central symbolism in the fly occurs as the climax of other carefully built repetitive patterns which create depth and complexity.

Another typical element of a number of Mansfield stories which helps the reader to locate causal relationships is the skillful manipulation of time and levels of the real. The stories move easily from present to past or exist in a perpetual present where past time and future time are embodied in the moment; they move easily from fact to fancy, from the real to the dream and often these levels merge to suggest that the real world is both complex and ambiguous.

Rosabel escapes her frustrations into a world of fantasy which is more real and satisfying than her drab life; Frau Brechenmacher attends a wedding and in so doing makes a symbolic journey back into time to relive her own wedding ceremony and its frightening climax; Pearl Button lives a wish-fulfillment dream; "The Child-Who-Was-Tired" cannot separate the real from the dream and will perish from it; Henry and Edna in "Something Childish But Very Natural," try to hold on to the dream and in the process lose it; the narrator in "An Indiscreet Journey" moves through a world characterized by dream motifs--mazes, abrupt transitions, distortions; in "Prelude" and "At the Bay" Kezia dreams her fears and Linda dreams both her fears and her desires to escape; Matilda in "The Wind Blows" projects a dream as a means of escape; the man without a temperament tries to escape the present by reliving the past scenes; the daughters of the late colonel escape into fantasies when the world presses too much upon them.

The movement from the world of mundane reality into dream or fantasy worlds is typically accomplished without accompanying explanation. "The Child-Who-Was-Tired" opens within the child's dream and through the story references to the dream are merged with action in the real world. In "The Wind Blows," elisions accomplish the merging of times. "It's the light that makes her look so awfully beautiful and mysterious. . . . They are on board leaning over the rail arm in arm." The voice of an unidentified spectator asks, "Who are they?" And another answers, "Brother and sister." Then the projected image of the adult Matilda speaks:

> "Look, Bogey, there's the town. Doesn't it look small? There's the post office clock chiming for the last time. There's the esplanade where we walked that windy day. Do you remember? I cried at my music lesson that day--how many years ago! Goodbye, little island, good-bye. . . ."

The merging of time in "The Man Without a Temperament" is accomplished through the juxtaposition of the present moment with Salesby's memories; reconstructed scenes are set in the present tense with the attendant immediacy:

> ...Snow. Snow in London. Millie with the early morning cup of tea. "There's been a terrible fall of snow in the night, Sir." "Oh, has there, Millie? The curtains ring apart, letting in the pale reluctant light. He raises himself in the bed....

"The Daughters of the Late Colonel" presents a graphic example of the remarkable dexterity with which Mansfield handles times junctions. West and Stallman, in their book *The Art of Fiction*, say that "The Daughters of the Late Colonel" is composed of a series of moments, bombarding the reader in a continual present time."[3] The story is composed of twelve episodes. The first episode takes place a week after the death of their father but includes both their memories of the past and their imaginings of the future presented as if in the present. The second section is a scene with Nurse Andrews that took place a week before, but it, too, is dramatized in the present. The third section, a short one, told through the composite consciousness of the sisters, presents a summary of their views, both past and present. The fourth section, again, is of past time told in the present concerning the visit of the minister. The fifth section is a vignette, dramatizing the sisters in the cab following their father's funeral. The sixth section takes place two days after the funeral and dramatizes what happens when they try to clear out their father's room. The seventh section occurs on the same day as the sixth, but includes imaginings of the future, again all told in present time. The eighth section is in the same time period as the sixth and seventh sections, but extends back in their memory to some time in the past when their nephew Cyril had visited. The ninth section continues with an account of Cyril's visit; it is not clear whether the tenth section takes place in the past or the present or, as a matter of fact, the future, because by this time it really doesn't make any difference. The same is true for the eleventh and twelfth sections. What is clear is that the present is an extension of the past and that the future will hold no more for them than the present.

Time proceeds not chronologically, but logically; the only problem is that the sisters' logic is as askewed as their clock, which is "either too fast or too slow." The reader, however, has been carefully introduced to the logic of their thinking and is able to follow it in the same way that he absorbs in a moment all their past, present, and future.

Mansfield's consistent use of the juxtaposition of people, attitudes, objects, viewpoints, times, levels of the real, without making apparent the causal relationships, might cause a reader familiar with the technique to believe that the story "Six Years After," which Murry categorizes as imcomplete, is finished as it stands. In structure the story is very similar to "The Wind Blows." Told through the multipersonal view, it begins in medias res. "It was not the afternoon to be on deck--on the contrary. It was exactly the afternoon when there is no snugger place than a warm cabin, a warm bunk." It is a grey day, cold with a pervasive raw mist, but the husband and wife, married twenty-eight years, are hurrying to their chairs. The multipersonal view moves first into her consciousness, revealing her understanding and acceptance of the fact that her husband has a compulsive need to be outside, even though she would have prefered the cabin, "tucked up with a rug, a hot-water bottle and a piping hot cup of tea." They are walking rapidly, because even after twenty-eight years it is still an effort for him to adapt his pace to hers. The movement into his consciousness reveals that he is concerned about her. He knows she ought to be in the cabin. "But he had come to believe that it really was easier for her to make these sacrifices than it was for him." And she really does not mind. She has adapted herself to his habits, of not tipping adequately, for example, or his inordinate fondness for clothes, which he insists that she rub between her fingers to "feel the quality."

The steamer emerges as a microcosm, "pitching gently, over the grey, unbroken, gently-moving water, that was veiled with slanting rain." The hovering narrator establishes the symbolism:

> It is extraordinary how peaceful it feels on a little steamer once the bustle of leaving port is over. In a quarter of an hour one might have been at sea for days. There is something almost touching, childish, in the way people submit themselves to the new conditions. They go to bed in the early afternoon, they shut their eyes and "it's night" like little children who turn the table upside down and cover themselves with the table cloth. And those who remain on deck--they seem to be always the same, those few hardened men travelers--pause, light their pipes, stamp softly, gaze out to sea, and their voices are subdued as they walk up and down. The long-legged little girl chases after the red-cheeked boy, but soon both are captured; and the old sailor, swinging an unlighted lantern, passes and disappears. . . .

The attitude and responses of the husband and wife, set in juxtaposition with the symbolism of the steamer, suggest that they have submitted themselves to life, accepting conditions as they emerge, but gradually it is revealed that within the wife there is deep grief. She is watching the gulls listlessly flying and thinking how cold and lonely they look. It occurs to her that the scene will be even more lonely when the steamer has passed by and "there will be nothing but the waves and those birds and rain falling." She cautions herself, telling herself not to look, because it will be too depressing, but she cannot help herself, and it seems to her that a lonely presence out there is calling to her, "Mother!" She recognizes the cry of her son, "Don't forget me. You are forgetting me," and it seems as though the weeping is in her own breast. A dual perspective sees her at once sitting beside her husband on the deck of the steamer and holding a child in her arms who has just waked out of a dream: "I dreamed I was in a wood--somewhere far away from everybody,--and I was lying down and a great blackberry vine grew over me. And I called and called to you--and you wouldn't come--so I had to lie there forever." In the past when he had dreamed terrifying dreams she had gone to him, to comfort him, but now she hears his call more often, "at all times--in all places." In her mind she answers him, "I am coming as fast as I can," but the dark stairs that used to carry her to his room now have no ending, and the dream goes on "for ever and ever uncomforted." "Can one do nothing for the dead?" she asks herself, and answers, "Nothing." But in her mind she creates the juxtaposed fantasy: "Surely he will marry--later on--not for several years. Surely one day I shall remember his wedding...." And in her dream the young man who was killed in a way that was a metaphoric nightmare answers her: "Oh, Mother, it's not fair to put these ideas into my head! Stop, Mother, stop! When I think of all I have missed, I can't bear it."

The words carry over from the fantasy to the reality and she speaks them, repeating, "I can't bear it," as the dusk falls "like ash upon the pallid water."

The concluding paragraph draws the symbolic motifs together but does not answer the pressing question of whether she will ever again wake him from the nightmare and comfort him: "And the little steamer, growing determined, throbbed on, pressed on, as if at the end of the journey there waited. . . ."

Time present in "The Daughters of the Late Colonel" is defined, in part, as an excursion in and out of the sisters' fantasies, which they use to help them escape the frustrations of the moment. Time present in "Six Years After" is defined as a point on a symbolic journey where fantasies and dreams are a part of the reality. Fantasies, dreams, role-playing, the metaphor of life as a stage, provide the structure, the shaping force for many of the stories, including "The Swing of the Pendulum," "Psychology," "Miss Brill," "Taking the Veil," and most notably, "Je Ne Parle Pas Francais." The latter story is another of the virtuoso pieces. An exercise in a strickly limited point of view, it is told in the first person by Raoul Duquette, a twenty-six year old Parisian, with aspirations to be a serious writer. As the story opens he is sitting in a little cafe, which he describes as dirty and sad, the kind that caters to workman and soldiers. He begins by announcing that he does not know why he has "such a fancy for this little cafe." It has nothing to distinguish it from others of its kind not even strange types of people whom one could watch and try to understand.

It is not until the second paragraph that one realizes that he is writing and that the contents of the first paragraph are a part of his manuscript, which, indeed, the whole story purports to be. In the second paragraph he declares that he does not believe in the human soul and he moves to a fanciful image: "people are like portmanteaux-- packed with certain things, started going, thrown about, tossed away, dumped down, lost and found, half emptied suddenly, or squeezed fatter then ever, until finally the Ultimate Porter swings them on the Ultimate Train and away they rattle. . . ." This view of the human condition is a dismal one and helps to account for Duquette's behavior in the story. He continues with his writing, describing the owner of the cafe and the attendant waiter, creating roles for them, giving them life. Fully aware of what he is doing, he moves to a statement of the shaping metaphor:

> Do you believe that every place has its hour of the day when it really does come alive? That's not exactly what I mean. It's more like this. There does seem to be a moment when you realize that, quite by accident you happen to come on to the stage at exactly the moment you were expected. Everything is arranged for you--waiting for you. . . Ah, master of the situation! You fill with important breath. And at the same time you smile secretly, slyly, because Life seems to be opposed to granting you these entrances, seems indeed to be engaged in snatching them from you and making them impossible, keeping you in the wings until it is too late....

Life is a stage where people act out the roles alotted them; but there are times when the stage is set for a particular entrance, when the player can be master of the situation. Raoul Duquette lives as though he is on a stage, and he is at once writer and director, and sometimes actor. He is continually aware of himself as separate from himself, constantly viewing himself in mirrors. The first image that appears comes when he is recounting the time previously when he had visited the cafe and one of those exact moments of stage entry had occured. Suddenly, he says, he realized that he was smiling, and he looked up to see himself in the mirror opposite. He was smiling his "deep, sly smile." Seeing himself in the glass he opened his eyes wide. "There I had been for all eternity, as it were, and now at last I was coming to life. . . ." It was quiet in the cafe and as he sat there viewing the snow outside and the waiter strewing straw around the floor he thought that he would not be surprised to see the Virgin

Mary come in, "riding upon an ass, her meek hands folded over her big belly." He had been quite taken with the phrase and had reached over to the next table to procure a writing pad so that he might make a note of it. He sat, rolling the phrase around his mind while he pursued the writings and drawings already on the pad and suddenly his eyes lit on a phrase: "Je ne parle pas francais." This was the moment and it had caught him unaware. He was filled with agony, the kind of agony that took him out of himself. "Just for one moment I was not." But the feeling passed and he was filled with exhileration. "No second-rate mind could have experienced such an intensity of feeling so . . . purely." His need to reassure himself suggests a deep sense of alienation and detachment, which are only suggested here, but which will be explored later. Now, he is reminded that he has no patience with people who "can't let go of things." "I have made it a rule of my life never to regret and never to look back." But, it is apparent that he cannot help himself. One part of him sits writing and another part of him leaves to run around in the dark, like a lost dog, chasing after a familiar step, crying out, "Mouse! Mouse! Where are you?" But soon the dog is back, his tail between his legs, and the self who sits in the restaurant writing addresses the lost dog: "Lie down then! Lie down! Lie down!"

As he continues, he identifies himself by name, age, and nationality, but he refuses to discuss his family or his background, in a manner that suggests that there are painful memories that must be blocked. "I have no family; I don't want any. I never think about my childhood. I've forgotten it." There is one incident from his childhood that he recounts, however, and, when he does, part of the motivation for his behavior is revealed. It appears that the only affection the ten year old boy had was provided by an African laundress who introduced him to secret and passionate kisses and embraces so that he was in a state of continual physical excitement. This experience has resulted in his complete sensuality and has made of him a commodity to be purchased by anyone willing to pay the price. He speaks of it lightly: "It's extraordinary how one can live without money . . . . I have quantities of good clothes...and nothing is paid for. If I find myself in need of right-down cash--well, there's always an African laundress and an outhouse, and I am very frank and _bon_ _enfant_ about plenty of sugar on the little fried cake afterwards. . . ." He considers his attraction to women strange and describes himself in feminine terms: "Rather charming, plump, almost like a girl." Indeed, everytime he thinks of himself, it is as a woman, or as a fox terrier, beaten, scurrying.

Now he orders a whiskey, saying it is because he is going to write about an Englishman. The whiskey acts as a stimulus for the creation of Dick Harmon out of his memories, who is getting drunk on whiskey and singing a song, "One Fishball." He recalls his behavior as he asked Dick to sing the song again and again: "I would plead, clasping my hands and making a pretty mouth at him." But he recognizes the element of seductiveness and he stops to explain that it had been Dick who had made the initial advances in their relationship. They had met at a literary party and hearing who Dick Harmon was, "an Englishman," making "a special study of modern French literature," Duquette had created a role for himself, "I was a young, serious writer who was making a study of modern English literature." But he discovers that he doesn't have to play out the role and slowly he inserts other lines, revealing himself; even, when he gets no response other than acceptance, exaggerating:

> But I was quite breathless at the thought of what I had done. I had shown somebody both sides of my life. Told him everything as sincerely and truthfully as I could. Taken immense pains to explain things about my submerged life that really were disgusting and never could possibly see the light of literary day. On the whole I had made myself far worse than I was--more boastful, more cynical, more calculating.

Afterwards they spend a great deal of time together, but Dick never volunteers any information about himself and Duquette doesn't ask him. Once a photograph falls out of his wallet and Dick identifies the woman as his mother. During their relationship Duquette creates a role for Dick as a sailor who might at any minute get up and without explanation go off to his ship. And finally he does. He announces suddenly that he is leaving for home the next morning. Duquette is astounded and then hurt: "I felt as a woman must feel when a man takes out his watch and remembers an appointment that cannot possibly concern her, except that its claim is the stronger." Again a reference to a fox-terrier follows Duquette's self image as a women. "And then I stood on the shore alone, more like a little fox-terrier than ever. . . ."

Two days later Duquette receives a letter from Harmon and reads it while he stands in front of a mirror. It occurs to him that he looks like Madame Butterfly, and the reference reflects his feelings that he is a rejected lover. He feels sick. "Having been up for my first ride in an aeroplane I didn't want to go up again, just now."

Months pass and following his injunction that he should never look back or regret the past, he succeeds almost in forgetting Dick Harmon. But a letter arrives. Dick Harmon is coming back to Paris with a woman. He asks Duquette to find rooms for them. "Of course I would. Away the little fox terrier flew." But this time Duquette intends to play another role. He acts it out in front of his mirror:

> "Since you left Paris," said I, knotting my black silver-spotted tie in the (also unpaid for) mirror over the mantelpiece, "I have been very successful, you know. I have two more books in preparation and then I have written a serial story, Wrong Doors, which is just on the point of publication and will bring me a lot of money. And then my little book of poems," I cried, seizing the clothes-brush and brushing the velvet collar of my new indigo-blue overcoat, "my little book--Left Umbrellas--really did create," and I laughed and waved the brush, "an immense senstion!"

The thought occurs to him that he does indeed look the part he has created, and he takes out a notebook and still in full view of the mirror jots down a note: "How can one look the part and not be the part? Or be the part and not look it? Isn't looking--being? Or being --looking? At any rate who is to say that it is not? . . ." But, another self whispers to him, smiling, "You--literary? you look as though you've taken down a bet on a racecourse!"

He almost doesn't get away. He is caught by his landlady to whom he owes money, but he finally makes it to the station. For a minute he thinks that the woman with Dick is his mother and then he realizes that she is not. Dick's behavior, nervous, embarrased, suggests to him that they have come to Paris for an illegal liason, and Duquette slips into another role. "What fun I was going to have! I could have hugged him."

The woman is named Mouse and when she is introduced to Duquette she speaks the phrase, "Je ne parle pas francais." She holds and strokes a fur muff throughout the journey in the taxi. When Duquette suggests that he will drop them at their rooms and then leave, Dick turns white and insists that he accompany them. Now Duquette assumes the role of stage manager and director. He conducts them through the hotel, gesturing, turning on lights, acting in (as the fox terrier) and responding to the drama that is being enacted. When she asks for tea, Duquette feels that the comedy is being overplayed; the touch is too much. He tries to make conversation but is not too successful; finally Dick asks him if he will post a letter to his mother for him and then rushes off to write it, leaving Mouse and Duquette alone. Duquette takes the opportunity to turn the comedy into a melodrama. He asks her if there is something wrong and inserts stage directions into the narrative:

> (Soft music. Mouse gets up, walks the stage for a moment or so before she returns to her chair and pours him out, oh, such a brimming, such a burning cup that the tears come into the friend's eyes while he sips--while he drains it to the bitter dregs. . . .)

He continues to act out his role of sympathetic friend to a tragic heroine, while another part of himself watches the drama. "Ah, why couldn't I tell her that it was months and months since I had been so entertained?" Finally, after Dick has been gone some time, Mouse enters the room and emerges with a letter, which she shows to Duquette. The letter says to Mouse that he cannot continue in their relationship, because it would "kill" his mother. Dick has gone. When Duquette asks whether she will go back home she answers that she cannot because all her friends think her married. Duquette continues to play his role, putting out his hand to comfort her, but she shrinks back and he recognizes that his action has been a "false move." He asks about money and about her plans, recognizing that his false move had broken the spell:

> Yes, I know. My question was the most clumsy, the most idiotic one I could have put. She had been so tame, so confiding, letting me, at any rate spiritually speaking, hold her tiny quivering body in one hand and stroke her furry head--and now, I'd thrown her away.

She answers briefly and asks him to leave. He is disturbed, and for a moment, falls out of his role. "I wanted her back. I swear I was not acting then." He asks if he can come again on the next day and she agrees, but he never goes back. Duquette speaks to the reader of the manuscript he is writing: He could not go back: "It wouldn't be me otherwise." But, he says, he does not fully understand why. Still, memories of her make him break his rule of not looking back. He creates fantasies of what their life together might have been, childish fantasies of sweet innocents playing together or touching cheeks. But he pulls himself out of his fantasies and juxtaposes in a cynical manner what he will do instead: A "dirty old gallant" will come up to the table and "grimace and yap." And then he will hear himself saying:

> "But I've got the little girl for you, mon vieux. So little . . . so tiny." I kiss the tips of my fingers and lay them upon my heart. "I give you my word of honour as a gentleman, a writer, serious, young, and extremely interested in modern English literature."

At the surface level, Duquette is prostitute and pimp, egotistical and parasitic, but stripped of his armor of defense, he is like a dog, begging for acceptance and affection. The constant role playing makes it clear that he had been unable to find a satisfactory ego-identity. Seeing himself as both dog and woman, he recognizes a kinship with Mouse and his inability to help her haunts him. He deserts her, as he had been deserted, and expresses his hostility against himself by acting as a procurer, selling "tiny" girls to old men. He knows that he could not have set up and maintained a satisfactory relationship with Mouse. He says it: "I couldn't have kept it up." What he doesn't understand is why he couldn't use her to his own advantage, but the reader knows that he couldn't because his identification with her is so strong that the pain would have been too great, and he is left with nothing except his own pathetic efforts to give himself an identity by declaring his agony when he came across the phrase, Je ne parle pas francais, an agony that for a moment took him out of himself, a self that in reality he despises, but can do nothing about.

It is finally style that is the distinguishing characteristic, and with Mansfield, it is particularly hard to define. Others have mentioned the poetic quality of her prose. Murry's statement that "her affinities are rather with the English prose-writers," was the first to point the way. Berkman speaks of the "suggestive vibration" of her words,[4] the "lyrical quality" of her descriptive passages and her use of "poetic imagery."[5] Elizabeth Bowen says that she learned "to evolve from noun, verb, adjective, a marvelous sensory notation hitherto undreamed of outside poetry" by creating a style "generated by subject and tuned to mood."[6] Dorothy M. Hoare notes that she records details with a fine and subtle sensitiveness so that "All is not only observed but felt."[7] David Daiches comments on her ability "to extract, and present, the greatest significance from a very limited phase" of experience. So refined was this technique, Daiches continues, that Mansfield "could persuade others...to view as subtle symbol what they otherwise would regard merely as stray fact."[8]

In talking about her style it is more appropriate to use the language of prosody than to use the language of rhetoric, for her better stories are prose poems, making use of every element common to poetry as distinguished from prose except a regular metrical structure. And if one substitutes the more general word <u>rhythmic</u> for the more specific <u>metrical</u>, it is hard to distinguish a good Mansfield story from a poem.

Prosodists, attempting to distinguish poetry from prose, usually make the distinction in terms of expository prose, that which in Herbert Read's terms is predominantly logical, constructive, and analytical as opposed to poetry which is intuitive, imaginative, and synthetic.[9] And, indeed, it is not hard to distinguish the poetic from the discursive. But Mansfield's prose does not usually move discursively from point to point, nor is it usually possible to extract the "substance" of a story which can be considered separately from the language of the story, which Charles B. Wheeler designates as the essential difference between poems and stories.[10] It is true that one can discuss the constituent parts--plot, character, setting, theme--but one can also discuss "The Love Song of J. Alfred Prufrock," extracting the same constituent parts. Matilda in "The Wind Blows," is created by the same process as Prufrock and does not exist except in terms of the language used. John Ciardi, in <u>How Does a Poem Mean</u>, says, "What a poem is, is inseparable from its own performance of itself," and he goes on to say that a poem is not a verbalization but a symbol, rendering meanings that are not paraphrasable. It is a design of images, a metaphor, which speaks of the unknown in terms of the known.[11]

A poem is a palpable presence. It is not an imitation of a reality, but a reality itself. Paul Vallery makes the distinction:

> Watch the reader of a novel plunge into the imaginary life his book shows him. His body no longer exists. He leans his forehead on his two hands. He exists, moves, acts, and suffers only in the mind....
>
> ...Poetry must extend over the whole being; it stimulates the muscular organization by its rhythms, it frees or unleashes the verbal faculties, ennobling their whole action, it regulates our depths, for poetry aims to arouse or reproduce the unity and harmony of the living person, an extraordinary unity that shows itself when a man is possessed by an intense feeling that leaves none of his powers disengaged.
>
> In fact, the difference between the action of a poem and of an ordinary narrative is psychological. The poem unfolds itself in a richer sphere of our function of movement, it extracts from us a participation that is nearer to complete action, whereas the story and the novel transform us rather into slaves of a dream and of our faculty of being hallucinated.[12]

Ciardi, too, speaks of the reader's need to participate in the poem's design. It must act out and cause the reader to act out its rhythms which are physical and emotional constituents of meaning. Tensive and evocative, its language creates a psychological immediacy and a bodily involvement in the total experience.

In speaking of all prose as though it were discursive, logical, analytical, prosodists make a case for the poem as a "significant form," where, in Susanne K. Langer's terms, "the factor of significance is not logically discriminated, but is felt as a quality rather than recognized as a function,"[13] but they ignore pieces of fiction, like Mansfield's, which are non-discursive, highly articulated, dynamic structures, employing images, symbols, and rhythmic patterns in designs that render meanings (often multi-leveled) not by verbalization, but by feeling.

It was a search for significant form and for techniques and a language that would create it that motivated Katherine Mansfield throughout her entire writing career. It was a concept of significant form that led her to praise Chekhov and to criticize John Galsworthy, Edith Warton, and Henry James for pedestrian achievements, for failing to involve the reader's whole being; that led her to hesitate to use the term <u>short story</u> for the kind of fiction she was trying to write; that caused her to eliminate a plot line, to employ images and symbols, to create recurrent patterns, to juxtapose object, characters, incidents in an over-all design that clarified individual details and associated them together to render meaning. And it was a struggle for significant form that made her aware of language that must operate primarily as a means for nonverbal expression, that must communicate directly through image-making and sound patterns to create the palpable present that a poet does.

When they are not contemplating abstractions, men think in images. Recall a sunrise and it comes to you as a picture, not a verbalization. Indeed, verbalization would serve no purpose unless you were trying to describe the sunset which exists intact in your mind, complete in every detail; and if you were trying to cause your audience to experience the sunrise, you would have to verbalize the images, selecting just the right details that would move to the creation of the total picture. And if your memory was of more than the visual, or if it were not memory but a present experience you were trying to describe, and depending on the nature of the experience, your language would have to reflect, besides the visual, also the vocal, the aural, the tactile, and perhaps, even, the olfactory and the kinesthesic.

A sunrise opens section 5 of "Prelude":

> Dawn came sharp and chill with red clouds on a faint green sky and drops of water on every leaf and blade. A breeze blew over the garden dropping dew and dropping petals, shivered over the drenched paddocks, and was lost in the sombre bush. In the sky some tiny stars floated for a moment and then they were gone--they were dissolved like bubbles. And plain to be heard in the early quiet was the sound of the creek in the paddock running over the brown stones, running in and out of the sandy hollows, hiding under slumps of dark berry bushes, spilling into a swamp of yellow water flowers and cresses.
>
> And then at the first beam of sun the birds began. Big cheeky birds, starlings and mynahs, whistled on the lawns, the little birds, the goldfinches and linnets and fan-tails flicked from

> bough to bough. A lovely kingfisher perched on the paddock fence preening his rich beauty, and a <u>tui</u> sang his three notes and laughed and sang them again.

Color, sound, touch, movement. The natural world is close, palpable. The scene moves from darkenss to light, from the heavy to the buoyant. Dawn is sharp and chill. Heavy accents, sharp consonants pervade the two sentences that describe it. The transition sentence turns on anapests: "In the sky some tiny stars floated for a moment and then they were gone." The sound of the creek, light, hurrying, is described in one long sentence, accenting the present participle verbs used in a rushing series. Then, as the first beam of sun appears, the birds are seen positioned, singing.

In her best pieces, every mood, every scene is as carefully controlled and tuned to the purposes of the story. The ending of "The Doll's House":

> When the Kelveys were well out of sight of Burnells', they sat down to rest on a big red drain-pipe by the side of the road. Lil's cheeks were still burning; she took off the hat with the quill and held it on her knee. Dreamily they looked over the hay paddocks, past the creek, to the group of wattles where Logan's cows stood waiting to be milked. What were their thoughts?
>
> Presently our Else nudged up close to her sister. But now she had forgotten the cross lady. She put out a finger and stroked her sister's quill; she smiled her rare smile.
>
> "I seen the little lamp," she said softly.

Repose, silence, painful joy are expressed through the simple, the quiet. Of the one hundred and twelve words in this sequence, excluding the names, more than one hundred are monosyllables and the few multisyllabic words are simple adjectives or adverbs. The movement from the Burnell house to a place of safety is accomplished quickly in a series of anapests (when the Kelveys were well out of sight of Burnells), but their anxiety and the eratic beat it creates is detailed: "they sat down to rest on a big red drain-pipe by the side of the road." Inside the frame of anapests lie four heavy accents clustered together. Then the "l's" and the "n" sounds begin to emerge and lead to the climax in quiet iambs. "I seen the little lamp."

The opening of "An Indiscreet Journey" reflects near hysteria, frenzy. Short sentences in subject-verb-object designs set the rhythm, the pattern of expectation. And played off against the pattern are departures from the usual word order, parenthetical insertions, surprising repetitions, culminating in the abrupt trochees: "Never! Never!"

> She is like St. Anne. Yes, the concierge is the image of St. Anne, with that black cloth over her head, the wisps of grey hair hanging, and the tiny smoking lamp in her hand. Really very beautiful, I thought, smiling at St. Anne, who said severely: "Six o'clock. You have only just got time. There is a bowl of milk on the writing table." I jumped out of my pyjamas and into a basin of cold water like any English lady in any French novel. The concierge, persuaded that I was on my way to prison cells and deaths by bayonets, opened the shutters and the cold clear light came through. A little steamer hooted on the river; a cart with two horses at a

gallop flung past. The rapid swirling water; the tall black trees on the far side grouped together like negroes conversing. Sinister, very, I thought, as I buttoned on my age-old Burberry. (That Burberry was very significant. It did not belong to me. I had borrowed it from a friend.) My eye lighted it hanging in her little dark hall. The very thing! The perfect and adequate disguise--an old Burberry. Lions have been faced in a Burberry. Ladies have been rescued from open boats in mountainous seas wrapped in nothing else....

"You will never get there," said the concierge, watching me turn up the collar. "Never! Never!"

An ominous tone pervades all of "Ole Underwood." From the initial sentence--"Down the windy hill stalked Ole Underwood"--heavy accents, harsh sounds, pulsating beats, form the pattern:

"Ah-k!" shouted Ole Underwood, shaking his umbrella at the wind bearing down upon him, beating him, half-strangling him with his black cape. "Ah-k!" shouted the wind a hundred times as loud, and filled his mouth and nostrils with dust. Something inside Ole Underwood's breast beat like a hammer. One, two--one, two--never stopping, never changing....

The pulsating, staccato rhythm of the rushing wind, the pounding heart, and its repetitive pattern in various forms that sound through the story create a compelling urgency that moves with fearful inevitability to the disturbing end.

A comparison of the initial paragraphs of "Frau Brechenmacher Attends a Wedding" and "The Wind Blows" reveals the consummate skill Mansfield exhibits in manipulating language to suit the individual scene.

Getting ready was a terrible business. After supper Frau Brechenmacher packed four of the five babies to bed, allowing Rosa to stay with her and help polish the buttons of Herr Brechenmacher's uniform. Then she ran over his best shirt with a hot iron, polished his boots, and put a stitch or two into his black satin necktie.

Suddenly--dreadfully--she wakes up. What has happened? Something dreadful has happened. No-nothing has happened. It is only the wind shaking the house, rattling the windows, banging a piece of iron on the roof and making her bed tremble. Leaves flutter past the window, up and away: down the avenue a whole newspaper wags in the air like a lost kite and falls, spiked on a pine tree. It is cold. Summer is over--it is autumn--everything is ugly. The carts rattle by....A white dog on three legs yelps past the gate. It is all over! What is? Oh everything!

Stylistic devices establish mood. Both passages begin with simple sentences, but they each in their own way, anticipate the frustration of the major characters that will emerge from the action. "Getting ready was a terrible business." Trochees and dactyls drag in ominous flatness. "Suddenly--dreadfully--she wakes up." The dactyl becomes an anapest; the down beat moves up with startling rapidity. In "Frau Brechenmacher," the remainder of the paragraph moves through a heavy cataloguing of particulars that make getting ready a terrible business. Frau Brechenmacher's thoughts and actions are logically connected and cumbersome, as burdensome as her occupation. But the opening of "The Wind Blows" illustrates the abrupt confusion of Matilda's waking by a noticeable lack of transitions, an abundance of dashes and halts and by Matilda's free association of everything that assaults her senses, reflecting the illogical connections of her subconscious perceptions. In the first four sentences, seven stops occur in sixteen words, and the "d's" and "p's" and "t's" reverberate. Seven of the sixteen words are verbs or part of verb phrases with the series "has happened" repeated three times. The senses are assaulted on every side in the sentences that follow. The movement is quick and painful. In "Frau Brechenmacher," on the other hand, sensual involvement is slight as Frau Brechenmacher's responses are deadened by her activities, and the reader moves into the vacuum that is her world.

An almost mocking tone is established by the wind that reflects the emotions of Monica Tyrell in "Revelations." "A wild white morning, a tearing, rocking wind" catches her and floats her across the pavement, hurls her from side to side. She is near self-indulged hysteria: "'I'm free. I'm free. I'm free as the wind.' And now all this vibrating, trembling, exciting, flying world was hers."

In all of her successful stories the language that is used is consistent with the scene presented and the viewpoint used, and it is within these limitations that the manipulation of language for poetic effect takes place. In "The Man Without a Temperament," a glimpse of the hotel interior is accomplished as Salesby rushes upstairs:

> And he turned and swiftly crossed the verandah into the dim hall with its scarlet plush and gilt furniture--conjuror's furniture-- its Notice of Services at the English Church, its green baize board with the unclaimed letters climbing the black lattice, huge "Presentation" clock that struck the hours at the half-hours, bundles of sticks and umbrellas and sunshades in the clasp of a brown wooden bear, past the two crippled palms, two ancient beggars at the foot of the staircase, up the marble stairs three at a time, past the life-size group on the landing of two stout peasant children with their marble pinnies full of marble grapes, and along the corridor, with its piled up wreckage of old tin boxes, leather trunks, canvas hold-all, to their room.

His swift movement is created by the sentence structure, the whole passage being a single sentence composed of a series of descriptive passages connected by commas and by the emphasis on the verbs as he moves, "swiftly" crossing the verandah, going "up" the "stairs three at a time," moving "past" the sculpture on the landing and "along" the corridor. His haste prevents his taking more than a fleeting glance as he passes, but the details that stand out associate the hotel with the ancient, cluttered, and decrepit.

A dismal scene evoked through images of touch, sound, sight, and taste, faces Ada Moss when she leaves her apartment in "Pictures," causing her to experience despair. Adjectives cluster around nouns causing subject phrases to rise and verb phrases at the ends of sentences to fall, duplicating Miss Moss's "sinking" feeling, and causing a corresponding kinesthesia in the reader:

> But the person in the glass made a face at her, and Miss Moss went out. There were grey crabs all the way down the street slopping water over grey stone steps. With his strange, hawking cry and the jangle of the cans the milk boy went his rounds. Outside Brittweiler's Swiss House he made a splash, and an old brown

cat without a tail appeared from nowhere, and began greedily and silently drinking up the spill. It gave Miss Moss a queer feeling to watch--a sinking--as you might say.

The opposite effect is achieved in "Her First Ball":

A great quivering jet of gas lighted the ladies' room. It couldn't wait; it was dancing already. When the door opened again and there came a burst of tuning from the drill hall, it leaped almost to the ceiling.

Dark Girls, fair girls were patting their hair, tying ribbons again, tucking handkerchiefs down the front of their bodices, smoothing marble-white gloves. And because they were all laughing it seemed to Leila that they were all lovely.

In this group of sentences the "quivering jet of gas" is set dancing by a sentence composed of two iambs, two anapests, and an unaccented beat: "It couldn't wait; it was dancing already." Then anapests and iambs announce the music, culminating in a variation on the same beat: "it leaped almost to the ceiling." And the actions of the girls accent the beat, repeating dominant patterns of iambs and anapests:

In this way Mansfield uses language to express the non-verbal, as the painter uses color, texture, and line, as the musician uses notes in time patterns. The result of the total effort is the presentation of moments as metaphors, embodying total meaning. All the techniques are functional in the total design and create it.

Chapter Seven

THE ART

"Prelude," Antony Alpers says, "has a peculiar magic."[1] Like a poem, Saralyn Daly says, it compels the reader to move "in the experiences," creating for himself the "larger complex, the characters' and his own interwoven responses, which for the careful reader, will be something near that experience toward which the author's control has led him."[2] Originally titled "The Aloe," and written in 1916, Mansfield revised the story in the summer of 1917, changing its title, and concentrating in her revisions on eliminating the obvious, underlining the suggestive and, as Sylvia Berkman says, muting the whole.[3]

As is usual in Mansfield stories, plot is limited. The story describes a move the Burnell family makes from one house to another. It begins in medias res. The Burnell women are in the buggy. A few pieces of furniture, still to be moved, stand on the walk, Lottie and Kezia beside them, as there is no room for them in the buggy. It is decided to leave the children with a neighbor, Mrs. Samuel Josephs, until they can be brought later by the grocery man in his wagon. Left behind, Lottie and Kezia have lunch with the Stanley Josephs children, and later Kezia explores the empty house. That night she and Lottie are driven to their new house. It is the first time either of the children have been out at night. When they arrive they find the family assembled in the dining room for dinner. Shortly afterwards the children are sent to bed. Then, later, the adults retire. The next day is spent in getting the house arranged and in exploring the garden. Linda is half invalided, and the work of the house and care of the children fall to Beryl and Mrs. Fairchild. One day, when the children are playing with their cousins, Rags and Pip, who live only a mile away, Pat, the new handy man takes them to the pond where he kills a duck for the family dinner. Alice, the maid, cooks it, while she also serves tea to visitors in the drawing room. Later, Linda goes out to view the aloe. In the concluding section Beryl writes a letter to a friend in which she indicates that the family has been living in the new house for a week and that Stanley is bringing two young men home with him for lunch and tennis.

The interest that develops is not in the outcome of a particular situation or in the solution to a particular problem. Interest resides, rather, in the complexities of the characters and in the unravelling skeins of motivations, desires, and thoughts, all expressed through the dramatic presentation of experiences juxtaposed one with another, forming a created moment in time that expands to include past and future.

There is no internal evidence in the story fixing the specific date or geographic location, except that it is not Australia. A general time is fixed by the fact that buggies and candles are used, and the mention of certain plants suggests the New Zealand location. But although setting is not specific, there is a strong feeling of both time and place. There is the time that is measured by the clock and to which the characters respond with daily routines; there is the time of a larger order, that of generations in history; there is time in a larger, grander sense, the time of nature, of the movement of the planets through the heavens, rotating about the sun. A corresponding sense of place is achieved as the family move through prescribed paths and areas. The family moves from one house to another, from city to country; the characters move from one house to another, from city to country; the characters move from house to garden and back again into the house; they move from family rooms to private rooms, and they move from reality to dream to fantasy in the innermost circle of all.

Time and place are parallel, correspondences being set up and maintained. The personal time that governs daily activities is ordered by clock time, which, in turn, corresponds with the movement of the earth around the sun. The planetary motions suggest the larger order of historical time made parallel with the generations of the family delineated in all its tenses, past, present, and future. An absolute time transcends planetary motions, extending beyond the finalities of life and death, and accounts for the individuals' attempts to impose structure, order and meaning to life, to escape the narrow boundaries imposed by life to the freer realms of death, to overcome the restrictions imposed by society. And such is the closely woven complex of relationships in the story that at any specific moment in time, a larger construct of meaning can be derived.

In the space of one short story a reader is caught up in these various aspects of time. He sees a family for the calender space of seven days; he becomes familiar with their daily routines that measure time like a clock, through mealtimes and bedtimes. He sees the years of the past merge in the present moment so that the future is always on the point of becoming one with the present, and sometimes does. The child becomes mother and the mother is child. Generation is followed by generation in one unbroken sequence. The century plant is coming into bloom and will bloom again in another century as it has bloomed in the past. The universe spins on its axis; the planets move about the sun, eternally, through endless space at incredible rates as the sun rises and sets. The hands of the clock move slowly in imitation, and the calendar pages are turned even more slowly, but the different times are simultaneous and exist as one in the human mind, which alone is capable of experiencing abstract time, where measures of time become unnecessary.

It is only in the areas of the geographic and social that time must be marked into segments of motion, in the distance from the city to the country, from the harbor, away from the ocean, up into the steep hills, down into the deep bushy valleys, "a good six and a half miles," that must be traversed in terms of motion and time. The household revolves about the comings and goings of Stanley, who travels a path not unlike that of the sun, and Linda, whose life revolves about him in the getting and producing of children. The position that the family occupies is placed in a present that extends from the past, from the city house, one step above that of the Stanley Josephs, to the larger country house, and then into the future where we feel certain of its continuing growth and prosperity. But a human mind is not bound by the limitations of clock and calendar time and a person can know the hot sun of Australia while at the same time he occupies a space in another country viewing a scene from a kitchen window. A person can exist at once as child and adult while the past, present, and future intergrate and coalesce into another reality.

Within the interior regions of the mind themes are developed; human concerns are presented: problems of human existences, meanings of life and death. People respond in different ways. Some accept life without question and seek only to achieve order and control over the chaos of living; life, for them, is order in this world; death is a continuation of life in the more desirable region of Heaven. The questions of these people concern operational means, the design of routine. Stanley's concern is to provide for his family the best that is available so as to increase his own prestige. Life, for him, is a matter of regulating daily routines. He exercises each morning with vigor; his trip to the office covers six and a half miles and the distance must be covered as efficiently and comfortably as possible. His days and weeks are planned. Even Saturdays and Sundays are organized to take care of what he considers basic human needs, tennis on Saturday, church on Sunday, companionship with Linda in the evenings and on Sunday afternoons. His is a conventional notion of the well-ordered life. But Stanley is both man and child, the master of the house and the object of the care and responsibility of the members of the household, and that there is something wrong with his simplified notion of living is suggested by the panic he experiences when he approaches the house at night and the anxiety he feels in the morning before work.

In contrast, Linda accepts nothing, neither the principle of life, her role, nor Stanley as being the answer to larger problems. Her concept of life is broad. It extends to include all things, even the minute inanimate objects that she invests with her own mobility and awareness in much the same way that she gives life to the children that she bears unwillingly. Her life revolves around the more fundamental questions, of the conflict between the will to survive that is a part of human make-up and the equally strong drive and need for death.

Juxtaposed through the story with Linda's view is that of her mother, who calmly and passively accepts life, people, and herself. She accepts the aloe which blooms but once every hundred years exactly as she accepts the currants in the kitchen garden, as simple things put there for human needs. For Mrs. Fairchild, time is simple. It extends in a straight line from the present back into the past and forward into the future. For her, the line to the past is longer, covering years, while the line to the future must be seen in terms of months. The present is occupied by her efforts to fill the needs of the people around her, ordering things, placing things in pairs, lining jars of jam neatly on shelves. But the juxtaposing of the magnitude of the questions that bother Linda with the reduction of them in Mrs. Fairchild to jars of jam neatly lined on a shelf suggests an involvement in the present motivated by fears of the future, habits taking the place of living.

The juxtaposition of Kezia with both Linda and Mrs. Fairchild raises other questions and reinforces the old ones. So strong are the affinities between Kezia and Linda that at times it is possible to see Kezia as an apparition of the past, Linda as a child. Their fantasies and dreams are interchangeable. Their common fears and love of Mrs. Fairchild unite them. And it is around Kezia and her confrontation with death that a major part of the story revolves. When the duck is killed, she is first thrilled by the sight of blood, and then appalled. She rushes at Pat, putting her arms around his legs and butting her head against his knees, screaming, "Put head back! Put head back!" That she comes to a similar intuitive knowledge of life and death as Linda is made clear in the last of the story when she tiptoes away from the mirror, "far too quickly and airily," rejecting the reflected image in the mirror in the same way that Linda had earlier when she turned her head as she passed the mirror. The bottle cap that flies through the air like the head of the duck does not break, but for Kezia "it had broken the moment it flew through the air," and she picks it up, "hot all over." Kezia understands the reality of death, the excitement and pleasure and her immediate demand that order be restored, by returning the bottle cap, or asking the impossible that the duck's head by replaced, will never suffice to conceal the fact of her pleasure in death. Nor are her defenses against this knowledge any more sufficient for her than thay are for Linda. But like Linda, Kezia knows intuitively that the mirror image is not the real.

This knowledge is denied Beryl. She sees her real self as a shadow. Only the image of her loveliness in the mirror is real. But her concern is stated in different terms. Her problems are those of an adolescent girl, seeking her own identity. She sees herself in terms of her mother, old and complacent, content to shell peas in a pan, or mysterious and rich and good, like Linda. She rejects the fact that she is selfish and vain and flippant and silly, like other human beings, and constantly thinks of herself in terms of a man's adoration and desire. She cries out to herself

"I'm always acting a part. I'm never my real self for a moment."

And plainly, plainly, she saw her false self running up and down
the stairs, laughing a special trilling laugh if they had visitors,
standing under the lamp if a man came to dinner, so that he should
see the light on her hair, pouting and pretending to be a little
girl when she was asked to play the guitar. Why?

She even flirts with Stanley, dressing for him, playing up to him. It is a little ironic that Beryl would have been quite content with Stanley for a husband, but it is difficult to imagine Beryl capable of Linda's maternal concern for Stanley.

The theme of sexual frustrations and anxieties run through the story. Although Linda loves Stanley, he frightens her: "If only he wouldn't jump at her so, and bark so loudly, and watch her with such eager loving eyes. He was too strong for her; she had always hated things that rush at her, from a child." Although she submits to him, she longs to cry out, "You are killing me.... You know I'm very delicate. You know as well as I do that my heart is affected, and the doctor has told you I may die any moment. I have had three great lumps of children already . . . ." But Stanley wants a son.

Beryl longs for a lover, but is unable to do anything about it. Stanley wants to live in the country, successfully isolating her except from the men he chooses to bring home from the office, men whom she has already rejected. "If only she had money of her own," she thinks, longing to be free. Her frustrations are expressed in the songs that she sings: "How many thousand birds I see/ That sing aloud from every tree," and:

Nature has gone to her rest, love,
  See, we are alone.
Give me your hand to press, love,
  Lightly within my own.
Even the moon is aweary . . .

But it is not Stanley who has imprisoned her. Her frustrations arise from a source that she does not fully realize, and her feelings, unrealized and conflicting, prevent her from making a satisfactory ego-identity, from breaking away from her "false self."

Difficulties in the male-female relationship and anxieties that arise are further explored by means of symbols. The aloe functions not only as a symbolic representation of the merger of past and present and the characters of Kezia and Linda, but also as an expression of the sexual fears that Linda exhibits. With its tall, stout, swelling stem, it has special significance for Linda. She particularly likes its long, sharp thorns, she says, expressing the age-old feminine notion of the destructive powers of sex, and the domineering role of the male. For Linda the aloe is power, the power to escape, as money is to Beryl. Linda's dream is especially significant, underlining her deep-seated anxieties and fears:

"How loud the birds are," said Linda in her dream. She was walking with her father through a green paddock sprinkled with daisies. Suddenly he bent down and parted the grasses and showed her a tiny ball of fluff just at her feet. "Oh, Papa, the darling." She made a cup of her hands and caught the tiny bird and stroked its head with

her finger. It was quite tame. But a funny thing happened. As
she stroked it began to swell, it ruffled and pouched, it grew
bigger and bigger and its round eyes seemed to smile knowingly at
her. Now her arms were hardly wide enough to hold it and she
dropped it into her apron. It had become a baby with a big naked
head and a gaping bird mouth, opening and shutting.

In her dream her father laughs, a loud, clattering laugh, and the father is suddenly transformed into Stanley, who is rattling the Venetain blinds. The dream, merging with the real, forms a montage, focusing her fears in two points of time. Furnishing a graphic picture of a childish concept of how babies are born, the dream is juxtaposed with the decapitation of another bird (which the children witness) and with the eventual appearance of the duck on the dinner table. The duck is even given a female gender. Lying "in beautiful basted resignation with its legs tied together," it is compared to Alice: "It was hard to say which of the two, Alice or the duck, looked the better basted." The duck is placed in front of Stanley, who is holding the carving knife, flourishing it, one might say. He takes pride in his carving, "in dividing a chicken or a duck with nice precision." Stanley's associations at this point go to his own father, performing the same act, and he speaks:

"My father would say," said Burnell, "this must have been one of
those birds whose mother played to it in infancy upon the German
Flute. And the sweet strains of the dulcet instrument acted with
such effect upon the infant mind. . . .

The words, ending on the phrase "infant mind," recall the infant that Linda has dropped into her lap in her dream and the effect of the decapitation upon Kezia's childish mind. Stanley's pride in his ability to cut the duck into neat little pieces acts to foreshadow Linda's response, when, later, she leaves the room and goes out, seeking her mother's company, thinking of how frightening Stanley can be, and how she would like to hand him her feelings, done up "in little packets," her hatred last of all. This series of juxtaposed images and events gives depth to the theme of the relationship between the sexes, and presents the complexities of the castrated-castrating aspects of the feminine psyche.

Although it is not stated in the story that Linda is pregnant, there is a suggestion that she either is or will soon be. Stanley's gift of oysters which Linda puts aside is recalled when Alice reads in her dream book that a party in a family way should avoid eating "a probable present of shell fish." Removed, unconcerned in the caring for the children and the household, Linda's one function seems to be a creative one. While her mother and sister busily put the household into order and tend to the children, Linda is most often shown apart, either alone in her room, alone in the garden, away from the dinner table when the family is having dinner, at the other end of the drawing room when Beryl and Stanley play cribbage. Mrs. Fairchild and Beryl dress conventionally and their dresses are described in detail. But Linda does not dress as the other women do. Instead she is draped in a shawl or a blanket. Her outdoor clothes are a cape and a hat with a plume. She is as "mysterious as ever," writes Beryl. The romantic aura thrown about Linda suggests another aspect of the feminine mystique that is bound up in birth-giving, and from which arises the shadowy figure of the mother-goddess who is intimately connected with the moon and the earth. Such ancient goddesses were the expressions of the reproductive cycles of nature, representing fecundity and regeneration, thus embodying in one figure the notions of life and death.

This feeling of legend is underlined by the careful notations of the positions of the moon. It is first seen by Kezia when it is in its first quarter, low in the sky as it rises over the ocean. In Section Four, the moon is high in the sky when Beryl undresses in its light. Later in the story Linda watches two moths: "Round and round they flew; they seemed to bring the silence and the moonlight in with them on their silent silent wings." Then she gets up to seek her mother in the garden and to stand with her under the gibbous moon. The movement of the moon, tied in its various phases to the females in the household, provides an overriding sense of lunar time and a feeling of swelling growth. "The moon that Lottie and Kezia had seen from the storeman's wagon was full, and the house, the garden, the old woman and Linda -- all were bathed in dazzling light." It is at this moment that Mrs. Fairchild comments on the possibility that the century plant will bloom: "I have been looking at the aloe," said Mrs. Fairchild. 'I believe that it is going to flower this year. . . .'"

The same kind of association is carried through the identification of Stanley with the sun. On the first morning in the new house he stands in the exact center of a square of sunlight. Naked, his ginger hair bushy, he comes from his bath glowing and slapping his thighs, hitting himself on his chest in delight and pleasure, acting with what Linda feels is "amazing vigor." The initial identification of Stanley with the sun takes on greater proportions as the household comes to life and everything revolves around him and the urgency of his departure. The horse and buggy must be readied; he must make his daily journey, timed with the appearance and disappearance of the sun in the sky. All day the activities of the house will prepare for his return, and when he comes

> It wanted a few minutes to sunset. Everything stood motionless bathed in bright, metallic light and from the paddocks on either side there streamed the milky scent of ripe grass. The iron gates were open. They dashed through and up the drive and round the island, stopping at the exact middle of the verandah.

A chariot and horses of the sun would seem more fitting to Stanley who comes offering his gifts to Linda "as though he had brought her back all the harvest of the earth."

The theme of orderly progression and sequential time is juxtaposed with a state where order and time are chaotic, haphazard. It begins on moving day and through Linda's consciousness:

> "Yes, everything outside is supposed to go," said Linda Burnell, and she waved a white hand at the tables and chairs standing on their heads on the front lawn. How absurd they looked! Either they ought to be the other way up, or Lottie and Kezia ought to stand on their heads, too. And she longed to say: "Stand on your heads, children, and wait for the storeman." It seemed to her that would be so exquisitely funny . . . .

And it continues with Kezia as she explores the empty house and the discarded objects brought together by chance, and experiences empty space where a bit of fuzz on a carpet tack or a needle in the crack of a floor creates a surrealistic effect. Even the outside world is fantastic and surrealistic as Kezia views it through colored windows:

> Kezia bent down to have one more look at a blue lawn with blue arum lilies growing at the gate, and then at a yellow lawn with yellow lilies and a yellow fence. As she looked a little Chinese Lottie came out on to the lawn and began to dust the tables and chairs with a corner of her pinafore. Was that really Lottie?

As Kezia stands before the windows, the day flickers out and the dark comes, and with it comes panic. The windows of the house shake, the walls and floors creak, a piece of iron bangs on the roof. Kezia stands still, her eyes wide open and her knees pressed together:

> She was frightened. She wanted to call Lottie and to go on calling all the while she ran downstairs and out of the house. Bit IT was just behind her, waiting at the door, at the head of the stairs, at the bottom of the stairs, hiding in the passage, ready to dart out at the back door.

The "its" that rush at Kezia in her fantasies and in her dreams are a part of the same world that exists in Linda's imagination, a world apart from the normal apprehension of reality, where inanimate objects come to life, become "theys" filling empty spaces, demanding something of her, inspiring a fear and an awe, making her turn from the mirror as she passes it, just as Kezia, having been initiated, tiptoes too airily and too quickly away from her knowledge of a dual kind of reality.

Intermingled with the narrative, an exploration of these areas of reality takes place. The journey begins with the storeman at night when everything familiar is left behind, and the dray rattles "into unknown country, along new roads with high clay banks on either side, up steep, steep hills, down into bushy valleys, through wide shallow rivers. Further and further." Then they reach the house and to Kezia the "soft white bulk" of the house, "stretched upon the green garden" looks like "a sleeping beast."

From here on there is a careful room by room description of the house. Kezia is given a lamp to carry and the hall is revealed as square and papered with a wall paper covered with flying parrots. From the hall there is a narrow passage covered with the same wall paper. The dining room has a fireplace and the table is in the center of the room. There the family is assembled, lighted and placed, in a stage-like scene. The windows are bare, but by the next morning Beryl will have hung red serge curtains. The bedrooms are next to be mentioned.

There are four and they are upstairs. Frequent references are made to the windows. The servants sleep downstairs in rooms just behind the kitchen. The kitchen is mentioned next. From its two windows it is possible to see the whitewashed leanto which contains the washhouse and scullery. The nursery also has a fireplace and a table where the children have their meals. It is downstairs. The backstairs are not wide enough for two people to pass side by side. The drawing room is described after it has been put in order. It is long and narrow with glass doors that open to the verandah. The wall paper is cream with gilt roses. There is a piano with a painting hung above it. The other furniture is dark and plain. There is a table near the windows and across from it a rocking chair. There is a mirror above the fireplace.

 The house takes shape in the story as Beryl and Mrs. Fairchild set it in order. The daily routines are established until there emerges a floor plan of the house and yards. The windows and the view from them serve to orient the house to the garden, to the light of the sun and the moon. The packing cases disappear, the curtains go up, the beds are made, pictures are hung, the kitchen is made neat, everything put in pairs and on shelves. Organization and order prevail. Life is organized into daily patterns. The butcher calls; Mrs. Fairchild plans on making jam in the autumn; Stanley plans to bring home men from the office for Saturday lunch and tennis. An unnamed third sister comes to spend the afternoon with her two boys. The children play in the garden, an imitation of life in the house, but that play is only a prelude to their experience when they leave the garden and go down to the creek, for the garden which is detailed with as much care as the house, is the prelude to the dark bush that lies beyond it.

 Kezia explores the well laid out, neatly arranged flowers and orchards, always aware of what lies beyond, of what is on the other side of the drive, the "tangle of tall dark trees and strange bushes with flat velvet leaves and feathery cream flowers that buzzed with flies when you shook them--this was the frightening side, and no garden at all." Driving through it at sunset, Stanley is overcome with panic that does not subside until he has been reassured by the sound of Linda's voice that everything is in order. For it is in Linda that the two realities find accomodation and life is seen as a necessary prelude to death. Her longing is to escape into the darkness:

> She dreamed that she was caught up out of the cold water into the ship with the lifted oars and the budding mast. How the oars fell striking quickly, quickly. They rowed far away over the top of the garden trees, the paddocks and the dark bush beyond. Ah, she heard herself cry: "Faster! Faster!" to those who were rowing.

But this longing for the reality that lies beyond the neat paths, the boxed-in flowers, the organizations of life is in conflict with her instinctual pleasure in life. Her realization of this is saddening. She will go on living, she will continue to have children; and to this knowledge she responds characteristically, mocking herself, her thoughts and her feelings, laughing silently: "How absurd life was—it was laughable, simply laughable."

Like "Prelude," "At the Bay" is organized around time in all its various aspects, the design of the story functioning symbolically as part of the overall meaning which derives from the integration of themes. The story begins at the moment the sun rises over Crescent Bay, and immediately the reader is introduced to the geographical area where the story takes place and to the emotional climate which will prevail.

> Very early morning. The sun was not yet risen, and the whole of Crescent Bay was hidden under a white sea-mist. The big bush-covered hills at the back were smothered. You could not see where they ended and the paddocks and bungalows began. The sandy road was gone and the paddocks and bungalows the other side of it; there were no white dunes covered with reddish grass beyond them; there was nothing to mark which was beach and where was the sea. . . . It looked as though the sea had beaten up softly in the darkness, as though one immense wave had come rippling, rippling—how far?

From the merging images of earth and sea arises the major symbol of the story. Throughout the narrative the activities of the characters will be seen against the background of the rise and fall of the tides of the ocean, and, as in "Prelude," timed with the movement of the sun and the moon through the heavens. Life moves through a path between birth and death and is no more than the rising and setting of the sun; and as the images of sea and earth merge, so life and death are unified; the manifestations of sex, male and female, merge also, so that distinctions disappear.

Through this montage of images sequential and nonsequential time is explored by means of the same kinds of patterns used in "Prelude." Clock and calendar time, the astrological and the geological, are contrasted with time as a function of the human mind. Opening with a panoramic view of Crescent Bay, the first section of the story is presented with a camera-like perspective and progression. The figure of the shepherd who moves in a path along the bay like the path that the sun will follow across the sky, suggests Father Time, the personification of generations of men, seen in a context of suns and planets.

At one end of Crescent Bay, through a gate that is formed by piled up rocks, appears a flock of sheep, followed by a sheep dog. Then, alone in the gateway, appears the shepherd, a bearded man, wearing velvet trousers. As he moves across the scene he whistles a faraway, mournful, and tender song. He passes the shops and bungalows, and as he moves the sun rises, lighting up the scene of the summer colony. He moves on until he reaches another rocky pass. Through this second gate, recalling the notion of the gates of heaven through which the sun comes and goes, shepherd, sheep, and dog disappear as he leads them toward Daylight Cove. Now the door of a bungalow opens and, illuminated by the sun, Stanley Burnell appears. The camera-like eye follows him down to the water. A voice booms over the water, "Hail, Brother! All hail thou Mighty One!" and the action begins.

The first section, which is a prelude to what is to follow, functions remarkably well to introduce the themes of the story. The pattering rushes of the little sheep who are bleating, and the answering voices from deep below the sea are heard by the little children in their dreams, as they will later in the day find fear answering from deep within themselves. The dog, whose natural impulses are to frolic, instead trots beside his master, as he has been trained to do, in much the same way that all the characters will find it necessary to maintain controls over their natural inclinations. The sudden and startling appearance of the eucalyptus tree which stands in front of Mrs. Stubbs' shop suggests not only the meeting that will take place there but also serves, as does the aloe in "Prelude," as a symbol which embraces ideas of both sex (birth) and death. The encounter between the dog and the cat foreshadows the one between Beryl and Harry Kember that will take place later in the moonlit garden. And finally, the dog, running out from the path onto a rocky ledge and venturing too far, discovers death and decay and retreats, as hurriedly as the characters will during the day that follows.

The meticulous record of that day in terms of time and the household routines of the Burnell family provide a summary of the action of the story, the careful delineation of sequential time causing plot to become symbolic action. Stanley, the first to arise, goes to the beach in order to swim in the bay, but he finds his brother-in-law, Jonathan Trout, there before him. After his swim, Stanley returns to the cottage, and dresses while breakfast is being prepared by Beryl and Mrs. Fairchild. He allows twenty-five minutes to have breakfast with them and the children. Linda remains in bed. After much frenzied activity he leaves for work, and the children are sent out to play. The women relax with another cup of tea. At exactly eleven o'clock they all go to the beach, except Linda who sits in the garden while the new baby sleeps. The children play at the beach with their cousins, Rags and Pip; and Beryl, despite her mother's disapproval, leaves the family group to swim with Mrs. Harry Kember. After lunch Mrs. Fairchild and the children take an afternoon rest. Beryl washes her hair and then goes out to play bridge with Mrs. Kember. Alice, the servant girl, has the afternoon off and goes into town to visit with Mrs. Stubbs. After tea the children go out to play in the garden, while Mrs. Fairchild gives the baby his bath. Linda walks in the garden until sunset when Jonathan comes to take the boys home and Stanley returns from the city. After dinner the day has ended for everyone except Beryl, who, late at night, after everyone is asleep, walks with Mr. Kember in the garden. For the reader familiar with "Prelude," it is apparent that even though the Burnells are on vacation the same order prevails in their daily life, for although there has been a time lapse, there have been no significant changes in the characters or their relationships. The reader contributes the picture of dinner and after dinner activities. Linda will walk in the garden because she always has. Beryl will play a game of cribbage with Stanley; Mrs. Fairchild will care for the children and see them to bed. At the proper time she will retire, as will Linda and Stanley. When everyone else is asleep, Beryl will lean out of her window in the moonlight waiting for a lover. People are unchanging; time is constant; both continue on an unbroken line that extends from the past into the future through the point of present time.

But within this sequence of events which take place in the span of one day, Mansfield provides knowledge of another time, one not bound by ordinary rules of motion and space but rather existing apart from perception or the record of time's passing. Thus, immediately when Jonathan calls to Stanley "Hail, Brother!" the reader experiences a dislocation from normal sequential time. The reader has been watching the scene the whole time; he has seen Stanley emerge from the bungalow; he has believed along with Stanley that he is the first to arrive, but Jonathan's voice, totally unexpected, booming over the water, destroys the whole time sequence. Time has doubled back; another door has been opened; another character has emerged and made his way to the water. The time in which this has happened is unexperienced and unhistorical, since the author has not provided the necessary sense data to fill in the interval. One of the results of this disruption of the normal time-sense is the creation of tension which is unrelieved until near the end of the story when the reader learns from Rags that Jonathan had heard the sheep as they passed that morning, and time-sense is restored to the normal of the perceived and the recorded.

Another, and more striking, example of the disruption of the normal time-sense, when time is stripped of its ordinal and metrical qualities, occurs in the scene with Linda in the garden under the manuka tree. From the garden there is an abrupt shift in geographical place that ignores the ordinary relationships of distance, time, and motion:

> . . . Now she sat on the veranda of their Tasmanian home, leaning against her father's knee. And he promised, "As soon as you and I are old enough, Linny, we'll cut off somewhere, we'll escape. Two boys together. I have a fancy I'd like to sail up a river in China." Linda saw that river, very wide, covered with little rafts and boats. She saw the yellow hats of the boatmen and she heard their high, thin voices as they called . . .
>
> "Yes, papa."
>
> But just then a very broad young man with bright ginger hair walked slowly past their house, and slowly, solemnly even, uncovered. Linda's father pulled her ear teasingly, in the way he had.
>
> "Linny's beau," he whispered.
>
> "Oh, papa, fancy being married to Stanley Burnell."

The reader's imagination accomplishes the sudden movement into past time because Linda's does, but simultaneously the reader is led to experience events that never took place, a time past existing only in Linda's imagination. The high, thin voices of the boatmen are recalled to a present "Yes, papa," that is a past time existing in Linda's memory, then shifting into the present, "Well, she was married to him."

As a result of this manipulation and merger of time, the reader experiences a release from normal sequential time-perception. The ordinal and metrical limitations are destroyed, and when they cease to exist, so do the boundaries which separate the real from the unreal and life from death.

The opening paragraph of the story in which sea and earth are merged is a metaphorical statement of the mutability of time and life. In the microcosm the members of the Burnell family react to the symbolic situation and setting with varying degrees of awareness and acceptance. In "Prelude," the house and garden are surrounded by the dark bush and the story moves back and forth between them. In "At the Bay," the action moves in and out of the house to the sea and seashore. The characters continue the same concerns, seeking answers to the same questions. Linda, considering the manuka tree and its myriads of yellow blossoms, thinks: "Why...flower at all? Who takes the trouble--or the joy--to make all these things that are wasted, wasted. . . It was uncanny." Time poses an additional problem. If only one has the time to look, she thinks, but "Along came Life like a wind and she was seized and shaken; and she had to go. O dear, would it always be so? Was there no escape?" Even her sex imposes limitations. "It was all very well to say it was the common lot of women to bear children. It wasn't true. She, for one, could prove that wrong." But life is also seductive. When her infant son, lying on the grass beside her, turns to her and smiles, she is overcome with a feeling that she does not understand--"it was something far different, it was something so new, so . . ."

Jonathan presents a variation on the same theme. "But as it is," he says to Linda, "I'm like an insect that's flown into a room of its own accord. I dash against the walls, dash against the windows, flop against the ceiling, do everything on God's earth, in fact, except fly out again." And like the moth or butterfly he thinks, "The shortness of life! The shortness of life!" "I've only one night or one day, and there's this vast dangerous garden, waiting out there, undiscovered, unexplored." In her thoughts Linda responds to what Jonathan has said to her. She watches the setting sun and recalls thoughts that other sunsets had aroused in her, of a jealous deity who would turn the earth into a vast graveyard through which she would be driven this way and that. But the experience of the morning with her son has had its effect, and this sunset arouses thoughts of a different sort, "of something infinitely joyful and loving."

The scene of the morning is repeated. Linda is in the same hammock but instead of the baby, Jonathan is beside her on the grass, intoning, "I'm old--I'm old." She bends down to look at him as she had done with the baby, and she encounters not the tender beauty of new life, hope, and promise, but a stark reminder of old age and death. Jonathan rises and then stoops to kiss her fingers. He must go to find the children he says, and then, "he was gone."

Because of the sequence in which the events of the day have been presented the reader knows already the effect his appearance will have on the children:

> Suddenly Lottie gave such a piercing scream that all of them jumped off the forms, all of them screamed too. "A face--a face looking!" shrieked Lottie.
>
> It was true, it was real. Pressed against the window was a pale face, black eyes, a black beard.
>
> "Grandma! Mother! Somebody!"

The altered time-sequence causes the reader to reappraise the reaction of the children to his appearance. Their fear is not only the result of the over-active imaginations of the young, but also the result of an intuitive awareness of death itself.

Earlier in the day Kezia had sought knowledge that would enable her to cope with her ignorance and fear of death, but her grandmother could offer no answers and together they evaded the appalling facts of existence by substituting a nonsensical game in which affection and love take the place of knowledge. The competition between them is for a meaning that ultimately escapes them.

The same kind of substitution is used by Stanley who is shown always engaged in competitive battles. He must be the first one in or his morning swim is ruined. He sets up a situation and then engages the whole household in a race against time to find his cane. Linda breaks a rule and is penalized. He does not tell her goodbye. Beryl avoids the same penalty by assuming a position of safety in a public place which puts Stanley in a vulnerable position. He has to wave goodbye or else lose to public opinion. But he recoups his losses by buying a pair of gloves like the ones worn by Wally Bell. Stanley brings the gloves home like a trophy, but guiltily. "You don't think it was wrong of me, do you?" he asks Linda.

Jonathan also engages in a certain kind of game. His role-playing is a game of masquerade to hide the fact of his dissatisfaction with a life that imprisons him. Beryl's play-acting serves the same purpose, but she is, also, her own audience. Her mind becomes a kind of movie-screen upon which her imagination projects one romantic image after another which she responds to and applauds. Life is sad for her to think about; it is something to be saved from. Her games of make-believe substitute for the evasive knowledge and meaning of life. She is only a few steps removed from the children who are capable of seeing a piece of green glass as a beautiful emerald as big as a star. Throughout the story the games that engage the children are juxtaposed with adult behavior and from the similarities that become apparent emerges the idea that all of life is a game of make-believe with rules and penalties and rewards. And these games have as much reality as the more concrete aspects of life, for the most concrete thing in life is death and that is unexperienceable.

Throughout the story descriptive passages and juxtaposed events reflect the fear and fascination with the idea that life and death merge on some awesome plane that transcends human experience. A rock pool becomes a microcosm:

> Over there on the weed-hung rocks that looked at low tide like shaggy beasts come down to the water to drink, the sunlight seemed to spin like a silver coin dropped into each of the small rock pools. They danced, they quivered, and minute ripples laved the porous shores. Looking down, bending over, each pool was like a lake with pink and blue houses, clustered on the shores; and oh! the vast mountainous country behind those houses—the ravines, the passes, the dangerous creeks and fearful tracks that led to the water's edge. Underneath waved the sea-forest—pink thread-like trees, velvet anemones, and orange berry-spotted weeds. Now a stone on the bottom moved, rocked, and there was a glimpse of a black feeler; now a thread-like creature wavered by and was lost. Something was happening to the pink, waving trees; they were changing to a cold moonlight blue. And now there sounded the faintest "plop." Who made that sound? What was going on down there? And how strong, how damp the seaweed smelt in the hot sun. . . .

The sea is reduced to a rock pool; the summer colony to reflections in the pool. Beneath the water there is a glimpse of an unknown. Because of the reduction the questioner seems to have greater than human perception. Paradoxically, the reduced image implies a view larger than life.

Juxtaposed with this description is another, of the real bungalows and of the Trouts' dog, Snooker, who is asleep on the steps of one of the bungalows, but who looks as though he is dead and waiting for a cart to pick him up. This suggestion of mortality sets the tone for the conversation to follow between Mrs. Fairchild and Kezia, as the scene gradually shifts to an interior wall and a human voice sounds: "What are you looking at, my grandma? Why do you keep stopping and sort of staring at the wall?" In the conversation that follows the question is made more specific. Kezia speaks decidedly: "__You're__ not to die."

The manuka tree with its prodigious blossoms that will fall and be scattered and brushed aside as "horrid little things" is a metaphorical representation of Linda's perplexed questions about the purpose of life. She sees herself as a leaf to be blown and scattered about and feels there is no escape for her. The question is reduced to the personal. Why is she doomed to the role of producing children that she is as unmindful of as the manuka tree is of the perfect and beautiful blossoms that will soon fade and decay? But there is at least a partial answer. Life offers to Linda a whole range of sensual pleasures that are greater than her need for knowledge of the meaning of life. The sight of the baby, his smile, the hope, the tenderness and pleasure that he inspires will suffice as reward enough to insure that she will continue in the patterns dictated by life. Death and the escape it offered a moment before is banished from her mind. And, once again, as in "Prelude," the presence of a mythical being, an earth goddess, hovers in the background behind the image of the mysterious and remote Linda in the garden. She seems the instinctive creator with her infant son in the grass beside her, surrounded by the shimmering colors of the heavens above and nature in full flower. She seems mother of both the gods and the race of man over whom they rule. To both she offers solace. To Stanley, who has made his rounds of the day and returns to her embrace as the sun god returns to the embrace of the earth and to Jonathan who plainly bears the mark of mortality.

As in "Prelude," Linda, as well as the other characters, has another significance. Her position in the family represents a stage of maturity that is half-way between youth and age. One of the three daughters of Mrs. Fairchild, she and Beryl are set in contrast to the third sister, the mother of Rags and Pip, who remains unnamed and unexplored. To a certain extent in "At the Bay," Linda's eldest daughter, Isabel, is also unexplored. Kezia and Lottie, the second and third children, are more fully treated. The concerns of Kezia are paralleled by Linda's, and Lottie's reflect those of Beryl. In the treatment of the two boys, Rags and Pip, Mansfield provides characterization enough to suggest the same set of similarities between them and Stanley and Jonathan. The juxtapositioning of characters in what amounts to an almost one to one relationship gives an added dimension of time to the story. Because of it arises the feeling that the author is presenting the adults as they were as children and simultaneously with the children, the adults they will become. This use of characters in symbolic positions within the family gives rise to the sense of continuity of family history that goes back into the past and projects itself into the future. Along with the sense of life, the family is also given a sense of distinctiveness by the use of contrasts and similarities with other families and groups.

On the beach, the Stanley Josephs offer a neat contrast to the Burnells. Through their appearance and behavior, the Samuel Josephs family is characterized as vulgar and bad-mannered. Their "lady-help" blasting on a whistle as she hands out dirty paper parcels, the washbasin of fruit-salad turned brown, the children, playing like savages, are in direct contrast to Mrs. Fairchild, sitting gentle and genteel in her lilac cotton dress and black hat, fastidious and quiet as she watches her grandchildren playing in the water. The Burnell children no longer play with the Samuel Josephs children or even go to their parties, the well-behaved Kezia remembering a time when they had come to the conclusion that the behavior of the Samuel Josephs children was senseless, with their pinching and cheating, running and racing.

The Kembers offer a study in degrees of respectability. Mrs. Fairchild does not approve of Beryl's association with an older woman who is considered "fast" by the other women and who does not maintain a "proper" relationship with her servants. Though she has money, Mrs. Kember with her emancipated way with men, is a scandal in the community of middle class women who maintain a traditional concept of the respectable woman's role in society. Mrs. Kember cares nothing for her house, does not have children, and behaves toward men as though she were one of them. Unmarried and younger, Beryl is more accepting of Mrs. Kember. She is fascinated by the notions of freedom and women's rights that Mrs. Kember espouses, and her curiosity is stronger than the repulsion the older woman arouses in her.

Alice's visit with Mrs. Stubbs functions in much the same way as does Beryl's encounter on the beach. It, too, helps to set the family in a point of time when the rights of women were seen as a threat to the sanctity of the home and the role of women as the guardians of tradition, which a single standard for male and female conduct threatened to destroy. "Freedom's best," says Mrs. Stubbs, and Alice laughs, but the thought makes her feel awkward, and she longs for the security of her own kitchen in the Burnell home.

So Beryl, and her counterpoint in age, Alice, explore the unknown region of sex and are puzzled as the three younger children who are pictured silhouetted against the sky like three minute explorers with their sand pails and shovels, who will meet the boys at the beach and dig for treasure and be persuaded to accept a fantasy of an emerald for the truth of a piece of green glass.

Beryl's attempts to discover herself are juxtaposed with Lottie's efforts to match the achievements of her older sisters. Lottie is always being left behind, and Beryl fears that she will be left behind--unmarried. Lottie's climbing over the stile is as uncertain as Beryl's attempts to find herself. Which leg and where does she sit down? Lottie is puzzled. A little later at the beach Beryl will be as bewildered by strange and horrible confusion as she begins to see in Mrs. Kember a caricature of her husband. Lottie retreats during the day, once, in horror, before a wave, "an old whiskery one," and later in the afternoon she panics, screaming at the sight of a man's face in the window; just as Beryl freezes in horror when a man appears outside her bedroom window and after her encounter with Harry Kember retreats into the security of her bedroom and her fantasy life.

The whole of "At the Bay" takes place in a day's time, and for Beryl it is a day of disquieting discovery and frustrated attempts to find a life and a lover of her own. Early, at breakfast, Stanley is aware that something is wrong with Beryl. She is unmindful of him and cross with Kezia. Her mood changes when she stops the coach and has the chance to talk and laugh with one of the passengers. She is happy to have Stanley leave, to be free of his demands and authority. This feeling is shared by all the women. "Oh, the relief, the difference it made to have the man out of the house. Their very voices were changed as they called to one another; they sounded warm and loving as if they shared a secret." At the beach, Beryl disregards her mother's wishes and moves beyond the family circle to join Mrs. Harry Kember.

With the older woman Beryl is both seductive and seduced. Fascinated by what she sees as masculine qualities in Mrs. Kember, she becomes shy, then reckless. Defiant of the other women on the beach, she undresses boldly and goes into the water with Mrs. Kember. "Enjoy yourself," Mrs. Kember tells her, and Beryl experiences a moment when her perceptions are altered in a fast series of images that merge animal and human, male and female forms. Mrs. Harry Kember "in her black waterproof bathing-cap, with her sleepy face lifted above the water, just her chin touching," is an image of Satan, constantly shifting forms, in a manner that is for Beryl both horrible and fancinating.

But Beryl is not threatened. Later that night, in her bedroom, she recalls the day, and in her imagination puts Mrs. Kember's words, "You are a little beauty," on the lips of a lover. She tries to dismiss the narcissistic fantasy which makes her both lover and loved one, but only a lover can save her. She remembers the advice, "Enjoy yourself," and in the midst of another fantasy a real man appears. At first he seems no more than a part of her fantasy, a projection of herself. But Harry Kember is not an apparition. She goes out to him and then is frightened:

> What was she doing? How had she got here? the stern garden asked her as the gate pushed open, and quick as a cat Harry Kember came through and snatched her to him.
> "Cold little devil! Cold little devil! said the hateful voice.
> But Beryl was strong. She slipped, ducked, wrenched free. "You are vile, vile," said she.
> "Then why in God's name did you come?" stammered Harry Kember.
> Nobody answered him.

Kember becomes a horrible caricature of a fantasy lover, and, as Beryl vanishes, the episode seems like the sea in the concluding section, disturbed by a dark dream.

The theme of identity and sexual conflicts which is introduced early in the story finds another expression through Linda. She recalls her father and his promise. "As soon as you and I are old enough, Linny, we'll cut off comewhere, we'll escape. Two boys together." But Linda does not escape. Instead Stanley appears and she substitutes a husband for a father, and the promise of realizing her dreams and ambitions is not fulfulled. The conventional demands on a woman are successful in suppressing any outward show of the complex of masculine and feminine drives from which the sense of identity and uniqueness of the individual is derived. Her child, the boy, holds a hope for the realization of the masculine side of her which has never found expression, but the boy, capable of quite forgetting his mother, rolls away in pursuit of his own interests.

Another facet of sexuality is seen in Alice's visit with Mrs. Stubbs, which again is an account of a young girl's seeking knowledge from an older woman. Alice is no more successful than Beryl. What she learns is unacceptable and terrifying.

In the opening section of the story the tree in front of Mrs. Stubb's shop is described as "something immense," like an "enormous shock-haired giant with his arms stretched out." It is toward this gum tree that Alice hurries when she is frightened of being on the road alone. She is hardly inside the shop when Mrs. Stubbs shows her a photograph of herself seated in an armchair alongside of giant fern-trees, a mountain, a waterfall, and a Grecian pillar. She is going to have it enlarged, Mrs. Stubbs says. Indeed, her constant dwelling on size suggests phallic implications. "Size...Give me size. That was what my poor dear husband was always saying." The mention of her late husband combines the notion of sex and death in a manner that is dramatized by the photograph of the man wearing a dead white rose in his buttonhole. "Cold mutting fat," Alice thinks. The image of the man swollen with dropsey and Alice's fascination by and response to the word <u>liquid</u>, occurring in the atmosphere of sexuality first introduced by Beryl, creates an experience that is similar to the one between Beryl and Mrs. Kember. Again sex loses its boundaries of male and female. The edema of the dead man and the edema of pregnancy have been correlated in Alice's mind. She burns to know what has been drawn from him. With the answer, "liquid," she jumps away from the notion of birth as quickly as a cat. The words under the dead man's photograph, "Be not afraid," seem offered in response to the fear that Alice has displayed. But it is not enough. Through Alice's eyes, Mrs. Stubbs goes through a series of transformations similar to the ones Beryl had seen Mrs. Kember undergo. "Freedom's best," says Mrs. Stubbs, recalling Mrs. Kember's words to Beryl, "Enjoy yourself." But Alice titters and feels queer. She longs to be safe, protected from the dangers of sex, life, and freedom.

"At the Bay" was written four years after "Prelude," but Murry was right to print it in the collected stories immediately following the earlier story. The stories exist separately, but read together, they provide a richer experience. "Prelude" serves not only as an introduction to the Burnell household but also to presage certain themes suggested in the first but developed more fully in the second. Foreshadowed events are realized. Linda's baby is born; Beryl's lover appears; Kezia has grown in her knowledge to the point that her feelings are translated into words; some of Stanley's ambitions are realized, but that he is less satisfied is evidenced by his crossness with other people. But alongside of the development are also some of the static qualities of life. The same family is seen in another and new environment, and although there has been a time lapse, some things have not changed for them. Stanley is still concerned about his journey into the city. Kezia still plays with her food. Linda still spends her time in the garden thinking. Beryl's fantasy lover has been transplanted from country to seashore. Nor has the competition between Beryl and Alice changed with the change in scene. Mrs. Fairchild still minds the children. There are the same three meals a day, the same gametimes and bedtimes, all governed by the passage of the sun across the heavens, the sun that rises and sets and in its movement illuminates the human drama, revealing the struggle and the contentment, the pleasure and the pain, the birth and the death as one ongoing process, holding the meaning of life.

Mansfield was, of course, right in her choice of words to describe herself in her last *Journal* entry. "A child of the sun." Close to the time of her death, she had to know intuitively that the phrase would contain at once the summary of her philosophy of life and the measure of her achievement.

NOTES

Chapter One

[1] *Journal of Katherine Mansfield*, ed. J. Middleton Murry (New York, 1940), p. 254.

[2] *Journal*, p. 150. Mansfield's ellipses. Since Mansfield makes much use of the ellipsis in her writing, I have followed the pattern of spacing out her ellipses (thus: . . . .) and of placing mine closer together (thus: ....).

[3] *Journal*, p. 212.

[4] *Katherine Mansfield's Letters to John Middleton Murry, 1913-1922*, ed. J. Middleton Murry (New York, 1951), p. 566. Hereafter referred to as *Letters to Murry*.

[5] *The Letters of Katherine Mansfield*, ed. J. Middleton Murry (New York, 1929), p. 27. Hereafter referred to as *Letters*.

[6] *Letters*, p. 503.

[7] *The Scrapbook of Katherine Mansfield*, ed. J. Middleton Murry (New York, 1940), p. 177.

[8] *Journal*, p. 201.

[9] *Letters to Murry*, p. 560.

[10] *Letters to Murry*, pp. 588-589.

[11] *Letters*, p. 292.

[12] *Scrapbook*, p. 233.

[13] *Letters*, pp. 299, 363, 458-59.

[14] *Letters*, p. 74.

[15] *Journal*, pp. 135-136.

[16] *Letters to Murry*, pp. 18, 161.

[17] *Journal*, p. 151.

[18] *Journal*, pp. 13-14.

[19] *Journal*, pp. 198-199.

[20] *Novels and Novelists*, ed. J. Middleton Murry (Boston, 1959), pp. 19-20.

[21] *Letters to Murry*, p. 598.

[22] *Letters to Murry*, p. 149.

[23] *Novels and Novelists*, pp. 41-42.

[24] *Novels and Novelists*, pp. 50-51.

[25] *Novels and Novelists*, p. 92.

[26] *Novels and Novelists*, pp. 99-100.

[27] *Journal*, pp. 93-94.

[28] *Journal*, p. 71.

[29] *Letters to Murry*, p. 447.

[30] *Letters to Murry*, pp. 620-621.

[31] *Journal*, p. 97.

[32] *Letters to Murry*, p. 415.

[33] *Letters to Murry*, p. 447.

[34] *Journal*, pp. 187-189.

[35] *Letters to Murry*, p. 189.

[36] *Journal*, p. 141.

[37] *Journal*, p. 217.

Chapter Two

[1] (New York, 1965), p. 23.

[2] *Novels and Novelists*, p. 106.

[3] *Letters*, p. 245.

[4] *Letters*, p. 432.

[5] *Letters*, p. 436.

[6] *Letters*, pp. 491-492.

[7] *Letters to Murry*, p. 415.

[8] *Letters to Murry*, p. 477.

[9] *Novels and Novelists*, p. 163.

[10] *Novels and Novelists*, p. 179.

[11] *Novels and Novelists*, p. 57. She concludes in her review that *The Arrow of Gold* must be an early novel, because others by Conrad are much better.

[12] *Letters to Murry*, p. 46.

[13] *Novels and Novelists*, pp. 41-42.

[14] *Novels and Novelists*, p. 137.

[15] *Letters to Murry*, p. 393. There is little doubt that she felt that she was right. A letter to him written about a year later, on December 18, 1919, says that there is something false about his book, *The Evolution of an Intellectual*. "This intellectual reasoning is never the whole truth. It's not the artist's truth--not creative. If man were an intellect, it would do, but man ISN'T (p. 435)."

[16] *Journal*, p. 121.

[17] *Journal*, pp. 96-97.

[18] *Journal*, pp. 236-237.

[19] *Scrapbook*. pp. 255-256.

[20] *Letters*, p. 204

NOTES

[21] *Novels and Novelists*, p. 92.

[22] *Letters*, p. 401.

[23] *Novels and Novelists*, p. 264.

[24] *Novels and Novelists*, p. 198.

[25] *Letters to Murry*, pp. 564-565.

[26] *Letters*, p. 215

[27] *Letters*, p. 312.

[28] *Letters*, p. 364.

[29] *Novels and Novelists*, p. 227.

[30] Note found in Mansfield's copy of *Aaron's Rod*, in her handwriting, printed as an addendum to *Novels and Novelists*, p. 308.

[31] *Novels and Novelists*, pp. 29-30.

[32] *Novels and Novelists*, p. 126

[33] *Novels and Novelists*, p. 176.

[34] *Letters to Murry*, p. 380.

[35] *Novels and Novelists*, pp. 114-115.

[36] *Journal*, p. 67.

[37] *Novels and Novelists*, p. 211.

[38] *Letters*, pp. 74-75.

[39] *Letters to Murry*, p. 26.

[40] *Novels and Novelists*, p. 118.

[41] *Letters to Murry*, p. 544.

[42] *Novels and Novelists*, pp. 50-51.

[43] *Letters*, p. 361.

[44] *Letters to Murry*, p. 211.

[45] *Letters to Murry*, p. 603.

[46] Introductory note.

[47] *Novels and Novelists*, pp. 3-4

[48] *Novels and Novelists*, p. 137.

[49] *Novels and Novelists*, pp. 304-306.

[50] *Novels and Novelists*, pp. 107-109.

[51] *Novels and Novelists*, pp. 307-308.

[52] *Novels and Novelists*, pp. 273-274.

[53] *Novels and Novelists*, pp. 234-235.

[54] *Letters*, pp. 477-478.

[55] *Letters*, p. 434.

[56] *Letters to Murry*, p. 608.

[57] *Letters to Murry*, pp. 120-121.

[58] (New Haven, 1951), p. 135.

[59] *Journal*, p. 151

[60] *Letters*, pp. 491-492.

[61] *Letters to Murry*, p. 19.

[62] *Journal*, p. 64.

[63] *Scrapbook*, p. 198.

[64] *Journal*, pp. 202-209.

[65] *Letters*, p. 387.

[66] (London, 1954), pp. 130-132.

[67] Berkman, p. 43.

[68] *MLN*, L (1935), 397.

[69] *Critique*, V (1962), 70.

[70] Daly, pp. 28-29.

[71] *Letters*, p. 481.

Chapter Three

[1] *Journal*, p. xiv.

[2] *Poems* (New York, 1924), introductory note.

[3] *Letters*, p. 210.

[4] The children's verses written in 1907 are an exception. In fact, one wonders why they have not been reprinted with appropriate illustrations for the children's market.

[5] Only a few of Mansfield's poems were published during her lifetime and these in *Rhythm* and *The Athenaeum*, under a pseudonym.

[6] *Poems*, introductory note.

[7] Collier Edition (New York, 1962), p. 19.

[8] Alpers, pp. 130-131.

[9] Alpers, p. 295.

[10] *The Complete Works*, ed. G.P. Lathrop (New York, 1883), III, p. 13.

[11] Poe's review first appeared in *Graham's Magazine* for May, 1842.

[12] *The Philosophy of the Short Story* (London, 1901).

[13] For a more detailed discussion see my *Hawthorne and the Modern Short Story* (The Hague, 1966). "The short story derives from the romantic tradition. The metaphysical view that there is more to the world than that which can be apprehended through the senses provides the

rationale for the structure of the short story which is a vehicle for the author's probing of the nature of the real. As in the metaphysical view, reality lies beyond the ordinary world of appearances, so in the short story, meaning lies beneath the surface of the narrative. The framework of the narrative embodies symbols which function to question the world of appearances and to point to a reality beyond the facts of the extensional world. There is, however, a group of stories which does not fit the definition that I propose. They are brief, closely wrought, and unified, but they do not have the depth or complexity provided by a symbolic structure. These stories I categorize separately under the title of simple narrative. The structure of the simple narrative is as different from the structure of the short story as the structure of the prose romance is from the structure of the novel." (p. 141).

[14] Popular opinion probably demands the inclusion of the name, de Maupassant. However, it seems to me that the majority of his stories fall into what I categorize as the simple narrative. See Note 13 above. It is likely that Mansfield would agree with this categorizing.

[15] Quoted in What is the Short Story?, eds. Eugene Current-Garcia and Walton R. Patrick (Chicago, 1961), p. 59.

[16] What is the Short Story?, p. 60.

[17] What is the Short Story?, p. 61.

[18] What is the Short Story?, pp. 73-74.

[19] (New York, 1924), p. 362.

[20] A Story Teller's Story, p. 351.

[21] A Story Teller's Story, p. 351.

[22] A Story Teller's Story, p. 353.

[23] A Story Teller's Story, p. 358.

[24] A Story Teller's Story, p. 359.

[25] (New York, 1942), p. 242.

[26] Memoirs, p. 243.

[27] Daly, p. 25.

Chapter Four

[1] Berkman, p. 159.

[2] Daly, p. 23.

[3] Alpers, p. 320.

[4] H. E. Bates, The Modern Short Story, (London, 1941), p. 129.

[5] Kezia is a major character not only here but also in "Prelude" and "At the Bay." An earlier story, "The Little Girl" has as protagonist a child named Kezia in the Murry edition of Mansfield's stories. However, although a prototype, she is not the same character, and had first been called Kass. Kass is terribly fearful of her father, a manifestation of her fear being a stutter (cf. Helen in "New Dresses"). She has a recurrent dream of a butcher with a knife coming at her. But once when her mother is ill, her father takes her to bed with him and she finds that he is not so bad after all.

⁶Another exception occurs in "Something Childish But Very Natural," where the point of view character is a male adolescent and where the view of the female is filtered through the male consciousness. Parts of this story will be discussed later in this chapter.

⁷The first person narrator stories in the Pension collection are generally considered to be inferior to the other stories in the collection because, it is said, the voice of the narrator, which is identified as Mansfield's voice, is obvious, causing the satire to be too sharp, too biting. If, however, the narrator is considered to be a character in her own right, these objections are seen to be baseless. I shall return to this subject in Chapter Five.

⁸Commentators invariably say that Mrs. Salesby has consumption, but the story suggests a heart condition. Mrs. Salesby even mentions the fact that she does not want to move because of her heart.

⁹Berkman, pp. 163-164.

Chapter Six

¹Berkman, p. 153.

²Alpers, p. 216.

³Ray B. West and Robert Woolster Stallman, eds., The Art of Modern Fiction (New York, 1949), p. 213

⁴Berkman, p. 100.

⁵Berkman, p. 156.

⁶"Introduction," Stories by Katherine Mansfield, ed., Elizabeth Bowen (New York, 1956), p. xii.

⁷Some Studies in the Modern Novel, (Port Washington, 1966), p. 149.

⁸The Novel and the Modern World, (Chicago, 1939), pp. 73, 75.

⁹English Prose Style (London, 1947), passim.

¹⁰The Design of Poetry (New York, 1966), p. 24.

¹¹(Boston, 1959), p. 668 and passim.

¹²The Art of Poetry, trans. Denise Foeliot (New York, 1958), pp. 210-211.

¹³Feeling and Form (New York, 1953), p. 32.

Chapter Seven

¹Alpers, p. 216.

²Daly, p. 73.

³Professor Berkman makes an extensive analysis of the revisions in her book, pp. 83-102.

Bibliography of Works Cited

Alpers, Antony. *Katherine Mansfield*, (London, 1954).

Anderson, Sherwood. *A Story Teller's Story*, (New York, 1924).

_____. *Memoirs*, (New York, 1942).

Bates, H. E. *The Modern Short Story*, (London, 1941).

Berkman, Sylvia. *Katherine Mansfield*: A Critical Study, (New Haven, 1951).

Bowen, Elizabeth. "Introduction." *Stories by Katherine Mansfield*, (New York, 1956).

Ciardi, John. *How Does a Poem Mean*, (Boston, 1959).

Conrad, Joseph. *The Nigger of the Narcissus*, (New York, 1962).

Current-Garcia, Eugene and Walton R. Patrick, eds. *What is The Short Story?* (Chicago, 1961).

Daiches, David. *The Novel and the Modern World*, (Chicago, 1939).

Daly, Saralyn R. *Katherine Mansfield*, (New York, 1965).

Hawthorne, Nathaniel. *The Complete Works*, ed. G. P. Lathrop, (New York, 1883).

Hoare, Dorothy M. *Some Studies in the Modern Novel*, (Port Washington, 1966).

Langer, Susanne K. *Feeling and Form*, (New York, 1953).

Mansfield, Katherine. *Katherine Mansfield's Letters to John Middleton Murry*, John Middleton Murry, ed., (New York, 1951).

_____. *The Journal of Katherine Mansfield*, (New York, 1927).

_____. *The Letters of Katherine Mansfield*, ed. J. Middleton Murry, (New York, 1929).

_____. *Novels and Novelists*, (Boston, 1959).

_____. *Poems*, (New York, 1924).

_____. *The Scrapbook of Katherine Mansfield*, (New York, 1940).

_____. *The Short Stories of Katherine Mansfield*, (New York, 1937).

_____. *The Short Stories of Katherine Mansfield*, (New York, 1967).

Matthews, Brander. *The Philosophy of the Short Story*, (London, 1901).

Read, Herbert. *English Prose Style*, (London, 1947).

Rohrberger, Mary. *Hawthorne and the Modern Short Story*, (The Hague, 1966).

Schneider, Elizabeth. "Katherine Mansfield and Chekhov," MLN, L (1935), 394-397.

Sutherland, Ronald. "Katherine Mansfield: Plagiarist, Disciple, or Ardent Admirer." *Critique*, 1934.

Valery, Paul. *The Art of Poetry*, trans. Denise Foeliot. (New York, 1958).

West, Ray B. and Robert Woolster Stallman, eds. *The Art of Modern Fiction*, (New York, 1949).

Wheeler, Charles. *The Design of Poetry*, (New York, 1966).

INDEX

Anderson, Hans Christian, 29
Anderson, Sherwood, 31, 33-34, 56, 73
Austen, Jane, 17
Babel, Isaac, 31
Bennett, Arnold, 16
Brett, Dorothy, 3, 14
Bronte, Emily, 24
Bunin, Ivan, 19, 31
Chaucer, Geoffrey, 19, 21
Chekhov, Anton, 2, 12-14, 16, 21-22, 31, 33
Conrad, Joseph, 9, 17, 24-25, 31
Crane, Stephen, 31, 33
Dickens, Charles, 19, 20, 24
Dostoevsky, Feodor, 19, 20-21
Eliot, T. S., 19, 20
Faulkner, William, 31
Forster, E. M., 5
Galsworthy, John, 17
Gibbons, Arnold, 22
Gogol, Nikolai, 29
Grimm Brothers, 29
Hawthorne, Nathaniel, 29-31, 33
Hemingway, Ernest, 31
Hoffman, E. T. A., 29
Irving, Washington, 29
James, Henry, 31
Joyce, James, 8-9, 31, 56, 73
Kafka, Franz, 31
Koteliansky, S. S., 1, 19
Lawrence, D. H., 6, 13, 16, 19, 31
Mann, Thomas, 31
MANSFIELD, Katherine
   Esthetics, 8-22
   Journal of Katherine Mansfield, 1-7, 11-12, 14-22, 23, 143
   The Letters of Katherine Mansfield, 2-7, 8-9, 12-13
   Katherine Mansfield's Letters to John Middleton Murry, 1913-1922, 1-7, 9-10, 12-22
   Novels and Novelists, 4-5, 8-10, 12-22
   Philosophy of life, 1-8
   Poetry, 23
   The Scrapbook of Katherine Mansfield, 2, 12-22
STORIES
   "A Bad Idea," 83
   "A Birthday," 66-67, 87, 101

"A Cup of Tea," 56, 57, 85
"A Dill Pickle," 58, 59, 87, 88, 101
"The Advanced Lady," 78
"A Man and His Dog," 85
"A Married Man's Story," 83, 84
"An Ideal Family," 6, 71
"An Indiscreet Journey," 58, 62-63, 82, 101, 109, 120-121
"A Surburban Fairy Tale," 41-42
"At Lehmann's," 50-51, 69, 80, 101
"At the Bay," 6, 14, 24, 42, 45, 46-47, 55, 66-68, 71, 91-92, 101, 133-143
"A Truthful Adventure," 81-82, 101
"Bains Turcs," 78, 80-81
"Bank Holiday," 71-72, 106, 108
"The Baron," 74-75
"The Black Cap," 84
"Blaze," 56, 57, 85
"Bliss," 6, 56, 57, 62, 101, 106, 108
"The Canary," 71, 84
"Carnation," 50, 51-52, 101
"The Child-Who-Was-Tired," 44-45, 69, 71, 88, 101
"Daphne," 83
"The Daughters of the Late Colonel," 69, 70, 89, 92-93, 106, 107, 108, 110-111
"The Doll's House," 42, 45, 102-105, 107, 120
"The Dove's Nest," 24, 53, 109
"The Escape," 64, 65, 66, 87-88
"Father and the Girls," 53, 69, 70
"Feuille d'Album," 62, 107
"The Fly," 71, 99-100, 109
"Frau Brechenmacher Attends A Wedding," 45, 68, 87, 121-122
"Frau Fisher," 56, 76
"The Garden Party," 49, 53, 89, 93-95, 102
"Germans At Meat," 73-74
"Her First Ball," 49, 89, 123
"Honesty," 85, 86
"Honeymoon," 63, 101
"How Pearl Button Was Kidnapped," 35, 36-37, 38, 41, 88, 101
In A German Pension, 6, 50, 56, 57, 68, 73-78, 83, 101
"Je Ne Parle Pas Francais," 58, 61, 83, 84, 107, 112-117
"The Journey to Bruges," 81
"The Lady's Maid," 84
"Late at Night," 84
"Life of Ma Parker," 62, 71
"The Little Governess," 55
"The Luft Bad," 56, 78
"The Man Without A Temperament," 7, 65, 69, 89, 92, 102, 106, 107, 110, 122
"Marriage a la Mode," 62, 64, 65, 87-88

"Millie," 71
"Miss Brill," 4, 16, 69, 81
"The Modern Soul," 56, 76-77
"Mr. and Mrs. Dove," 6, 63, 109
"Mr. and Mrs. Williams," 85
"Mr. Reginald Peacock's Day," 62
"New Dresses," 42-44, 70
"Ole Underwood," 71, 121
"Pension Sequin, 78-79
"Pictures," 69-70, 108, 122-123
"Poison," 58, 61, 83
"Prelude," 24, 42, 43, 46-47, 66-68, 71, 89-92, 101, 106, 107, 119, 124-133, 134, 136, 138, 139, 142-143
"Psychology," 58
"Revelations," 58, 59, 108, 121
"See-Saw," 38-39, 85, 101
"The Singing Lesson," 85-86
"The Sister of the Baroness," 56, 75-76
"Sixpence," 85
"Six Years After," 111-112
"Something Childish But Very Natural," 50, 53, 87, 101, 108
"Spring Picture," 84, 101, 105-106, 107
"The Stranger," 16, 64-65, 86-87
"Sun and Moon," 3, 40-41, 107
"The Swing of the Pendulum," 54-55, 89, 107
"Taking the Veil," 49-50, 54, 101, 108
"The Tiredness of Rosabel," 25-29, 101, 107
"The Flower," 58
"Two Tuppenny Ones, Please," 84
"Violet," 78, 79-80
"The Voyage," 24, 39, 40, 70, 86, 87, 88, 109
"The Wind Blows," 50, 53, 59, 96-98, 101, 109, 110, 118, 121-122
"The Woman at the Store," 71, 82-83
"The Wrong House," 35, 37-38, 85, 108
"The Young Girl," 47-49, 53, 82, 101

Marlow, Christopher, 19, 21

Maugham, Somerset, 4, 17

Maupassant, Guy de, 19, 31

Melville Herman, 31, 33

Moore, George, 17-18, 19

Morrell, Lady Ottaline, 23

Murry, John Middleton, 1, 2, 5, 6, 8-9, 14, 15, 20, 23, 33, 35

Murry, Richard, 2

Poe, Edgar Allan, 29, 31, 33

Proust, Marcel, 19, 20

Richardson, Dorothy, 17

Schiff, Sidney, 8, 13, 20

Shakespeare, William, 21

Shaw, George Bernard, 5

Stein, Gertrude, 17-18

Stendhal, 19, 20

Tolstory, Leo, 19, 21

Wells, H. G., 16

Welty, Eudora, 31

Wharton, Edith, 17-18

Woolf, Virginia, 17-18

Young, Brett, 5, 12